FORGHIERI ON FERRARI

1947 TO THE PRESENT

FORGHIERI 1947 TO THE PRESENT ON FERRARI

Giorgio Nada Editore Srl

Editorial manager
Leonardo Acerbi

Editorial
Giorgio Nada Editore

Graphic design
Yoshihito Furuya

Cover
Yoshihito Furuya

Layout
Sansai Zappini

© 2013 Giorgio Nada Editore, Vimodrone (Milano)

Giorgio Nada Editore
Via Claudio Treves, 15/17
I – 20090 VIMODRONE MI
Tel. +39 02 27301126
Fax +39 02 27301454
E-mail: info@giorgionadaeditore.it
http://www.giorgionadaeditore.it

Allo stesso indirizzo può essere richiesto il catalogo di tutte le opere pubblicate dalla Casa Editrice.

The catalogue of Giorgio Nada Editore publications is available on request at the above address.

Distribution:
Giunti Editore Spa
via Bolognese 165
I – 50139 FIRENZE
www.giunti.it

Forghieri on Ferrari
ISBN: 978-88-7911-565-0

Photographs
Giorgio Nada Editore archive
Adriano Cimarosti collection
Happy Motoring collection
Famiglia Musso collection
Actualfoto Bologna
Agenzia Terreni
Alfa Romeo Automobilismo Storico - Centro Documentazione (Arese, Milan)
Franco Bossi
Ercole Colombo
Mauro Forghieri
Giorgio Proserpio
Rosenthal ML
Franco Varisco
Ugo Vicenzi
Aldo Zana

The publisher would like to thank Enrico Mapelli for the consultancy work he has provided

MISTO
Carta da fonti gestite in maniera responsabile
FSC® C023532

Mauro Forghieri and Daniele Buzzonetti

FORGHIERI ON FERRARI

1947 TO THE PRESENT

technical drawings by Giorgio Piola

GIORGIO NADA EDITORE

SUMMARY

Preface by Gian Paolo Dallara   **7**

1947-1951   **10**
Maranello's first steps. At the origins of a legend   13
A family of great personality: portrait of Reclus Forghieri   *16*

1952-1959   **30**
From Ascari to Hawthorn. The first decade of F1 success   33
A conversation with Romolo Tavoni: Ferrari's early years   *40*
Now, top among the sports racers. The lessons of Lampredi and Fraschetti   51

1960-1969   **58**
The Forghieri era begins. From his debut in Formula 1 to his first world championship   61
Spring 1962: the move to Great Britain   *70*
A V12 behind the driver. The golden years of sports car racing   87
The Way We Were: Ferrari's away races of the Sixties and Seventies   *100*
From the departure of Surtees to the arrival of Ickx. The difficult 1966-1969 seasons   111
Black day at Monte Carlo   *124*
On road and track, the F2 Dino engine   132

1970-1973   **136**
The slow return to the top. The 1969-1973 F1 seasons   139
The curious tale of the Ferrari B3 Snowplough   *152*
Last world championship before the goodbye. Epilogue of the Prancing Horse in sports car racing   157

1974-1979   **164**
Seasons of Glory. Happy days: world championships with Lauda and Scheckter   167

1980-1983   **194**
The Turbo Arrives. Among triumphs and defeats   197

1984-1987   **218**
Ferrari Epilogue. My last Formula 1 seasons   221
Beyond Formula 1. Ferrari Engineering   229

1988-2011   **234**
From Lamborghini to Oral Engineering. After Ferrari   237

F1 1986-2011   **244**
From Prost to Alonso via Schumacher. The 1986 – 2011 F1 seasons   247
The 22 months of Cesare Fiorio at Ferrari: jealousy and spite   *262*

Preface

Engineer Gian Paolo Dallara is not famous just because in 1972 he created a "factory" for the construction of racing cars and is currently the world's number one in his field, with 13 500 Miles of Indianapolis victories to its credit. Dallara Automobili, which has its headquarters at Varano Melegari, Italy, not far from Parma, was developed in line with the most advanced technology in the use of new materials and aerodynamic studies through the establishment of exceptionally modern wind tunnels. Characteristics that have enabled Dallara to collaborate with many manufacturers in the design of both racing and road cars, among them the Audis that won the 24 Hours of Le Mans 10 times, the Bugatti Veyron and, before them, the Lancia Beta Montecarlo, winners of the World Endurance Championship. But in the '60s, the engineer from Parma worked for De Tomaso, Lamborghini – he designed the renowned Miura together with Marcello Gandini, who defined the style – and Maserati. After graduating from the Milan Polytechnic, he joined Ferrari at the end of 1959. He was just preceded there by engineer Mauro Forghieri, and it was probably no coincidence that the Commendatore gave the two youngsters their start under the same roof as they subsequently became the best of their and other generations in the car field.

Starting with those first recollections, Gian Paolo Dallara drew this profile of his colleague:

"Mauro Forghieri was an almost unique designer in a period that was already on the way to specialisation. He successfully became directly involved in dozens of different projects: engines, gearboxes, chassis, suspension… An array of activities nobody could progress today. He was a real orchestral conductor, able to create an engine from start to finish, but to become involved at the same time with the whole car. Now, there are only "soloists", perhaps excellent at what they do but they have to integrate with each other. Mauro's was an unrepeatable career, partly because he didn't have a large staff under him, just a number of talented collaborators who were certainly carefully selected, and they had to develop his ideas. It was an excellent team system that worked well, because it was fed by Mauro's ideas and he was able to go to the drawing board and conduct detailed examinations of his intuitions. And that is not a common gift. For example, engineer Carlo Chiti, the technical director in our time at Ferrari, had an optimum culture but he just coordinated. I never saw him with a pencil in hand.

"Mauro sometimes surprised me with projects I didn't always agree with, yet in the end he was right. Among them was the transverse gearbox; why add an extra drive gear to the transmission, I asked? I didn't think it would work, yet that gearbox turned out to be more compact, enabled the centre of gravity to be lowered and achieved reasonable angles for the drive shafts. A real success. Like many other projects of his, because don't forget he won in F1 and F2, with sports racing cars and even in the European Mountainclimb Championship, clashing, perhaps, with giants like Ford".

Engineer Dallara stayed at Ferrari for 18 months, leaving just before the "sacking" of the seven managers, who had suggested the promotion of Mauro Forghieri "in the field" to Ferrari.

"I never regretted it", continued engineer Dallara, "in part because at the time Mauro already had a complete vision of the racing car, which I never possessed. Perhaps because his father had been a collaborator of Ferrari's since the '30s and had passed onto his son a kind of technical legacy. I wouldn't know, but compared to him I was less mature, not like him able to propose ideas. At that time, I was involved more than anything else in calculations and corrections of the gearbox and transmission gears, but the designer was Walter Salvarani, a technician of great experience. Pushed by Chiti, I started to also study vehicle dynamics, paying particular attention to roll centres. But I was at the beginning, I can't take on merits I don't have. Then I received an offer from engineer Alfieri, who was technical director of Maserati at the time and was still involved with racing. But I never explained to Ferrari that I would be transferring to Maserati: to avoid any embarrassing situation, I said I was going to work for my father. But a few months later, Ferrari invited me to dinner to ask me to return. That was very satisfying to me. We met and spoke in a trattoria on the outskirts of Modena, but I explained that, at that point, I couldn't say to Alfieri that I was going back. After that, I kept track of Ferrari from a distance but with the friendship of Mauro, a man I have always admired.

"A man to whom many technicians should be grateful for having taken some of his innumerable ideas".

Gian Paolo Dallara

1947-1951

Maranello's first steps
At the origins of a legend

Enzo Ferrari was a notoriously impatient man. When he went after a result he did everything he could to try to achieve it. He defined himself as an "agitator of ideas and men". A perfect description by which to picture his character, but he should have added that in him everything was taken to excess: the untiring energy together with passion, courage, determination, love, hate, ambition... He had his way of fully involving his collaborators, but more than anything else he involved himself in projects that would have petrified anybody else. As one reviews his story that trait is easy to see, and it is a story in which I myself was a key player from 1960 until 1987.

During the post-war years, Ferrari was well-off but not rich. He was not an industrialist, who could re-ly on other activities that were simpler and made more money to eventually cover the risks triggered off by his passion for cars and for racing.

There was already a factory of reasonable size at Maranello, certainly well equipped, special-ised in the construction of oil pressure grind-ing machines. A profitable industrial activity, which was not immediately abandoned in fa-vour of cars. But he was a long way from se-curing enough money for a total commitment to racing and the construction of road cars.

Despite everything, despite the frightful war, Ferrari threw himself into increasingly risky oper-ations, from the construction of a 12-cylinder engine – an exceptional choice during that pe-riod – to racing the first cars he built. And at the same time, he tried to establish himself as a manufacturer of road cars, without the chance of making large investments and without a sales network. On top of that, there was the enormous difficulty of taking on the development of his first Grand Prix single-seaters. All in the same period starting from the summer of 1945, when Italy slowly began to find itself again.

Fortunately he was able to rely on the right men, whom he had known for some time: almost all of them had worked with him during the Al-fa Romeo period before the war. But he could not work with his favourite, Vittorio Jano, on his basic project as Jano was under contract to Lancia. So Ferrari opted for Gioachino Co-lombo, who was a Jano pupil. Colombo was

Monza, May 1938: Giuseppe Farina getting the feel of an Alfa Romeo 312 for the GP of Tripoli. As well as the mechanics, test driver Attilio Marinoni and Enzo Ferrari look on. The Commendatore had only just finished working with his Scuderia and had returned to Alfa Romeo as director of the racing department. The 312 was built to comply with new Grand Prix regulations: 3000 cc with supercharger or 4500 cc normally aspirated. Alfa chose the former, but the car's 350 hp power output was not enough to beat the opposition, especially the Mercedes-Benzes and Auto Unions. But in 1937 Ferrari had begun the construction of another single-seater, taking advantage of the structure of his Scuderia at Modena and with the support of Gioachino Colombo "on loan" from Alfa. The car was the Alfetta 158 1500. Below, left: the 158 during one of its first tests in June 1938 on the city circuit of Livorno, where it made its debut in the Coppa Ciano on 7 August and won, driven by Emilio Villoresi. Below, right: illustrations of the Auto Avio Costruzioni 815, the first car Ferrari ever built after the Commendatore left Alfa. In the drawing by Carozzeria Touring, the car was called a "Torpedino Super-leggero Tipo Brescia", the city from which the Mille Miglia started and where the car would make its debut in April 1940. Opposite page: a cutaway of the 12-cylinder engine designed by Gioachino Colombo for the first real Ferrari, the 1947 125 S.

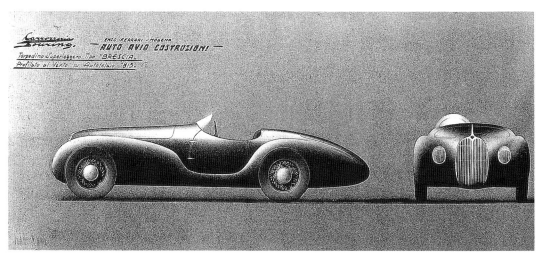

an expert technician of considerable talent who knew perfectly well how to interpret Ferrari's expectations. Engineer Giuseppe Busso from Alfa Romeo was also a member of that first nucleus, as was Luigi Bazzi, Ferrari's right hand man who had a profound mechanical knowledge, Federico Giberti, Aurelio Lampredi and also my father, Reclus Forghieri, who had great experience in their field of mechanical equipment. There were very few mechanics, just 13 of them, and they initially worked on the development of the first Ferrari, although there were many more employees in the grinding sector.

So the future constructor started in a cautious manner, but with a good base and the results of the demands he made of his collaborators were undoubtedly sound. Even more so if one evaluates the project's development in subsequent years. In fact, Gioachino Colombo did not create a racing car, rather a car that raced. The Ferrari 125 S was not an extreme car but an excellent base for racing and road car development. It made its debut as a two-seater sports racer with Franco Cortese on the city circuit at Piacenza on 11 May 1947 and won two weeks later in Rome; a feat repeated another six times and one that enabled Tazio Nuvolari to score his last two victories on a track at Forlì on 6 July and at Parma a week later.

They could not be called high level races, and on one occasion at the Circuit of Florence the 125 was beaten by the much more arti-san Stanguellini 1100. It seemed the Ferrari's roadholding was not up to the standard of the engine, and pictures from the period show the car's excessive tramping when cornering. But the most humiliating defeats came from the two victories of the new Maserati at Pescara and on its home ground in Modena! Ferrari was probably impatient, perhaps perplexed by the fairly long, 20 month gestation period of the project between the summer of 1945 and March 1947. That could seem a normal period of time, until one remembers that Scuderia Ferrari was able to create the complex Alfa 158 in just 12 months starting in May 1937 from a blank sheet of paper.

The coming and going of high level technicians

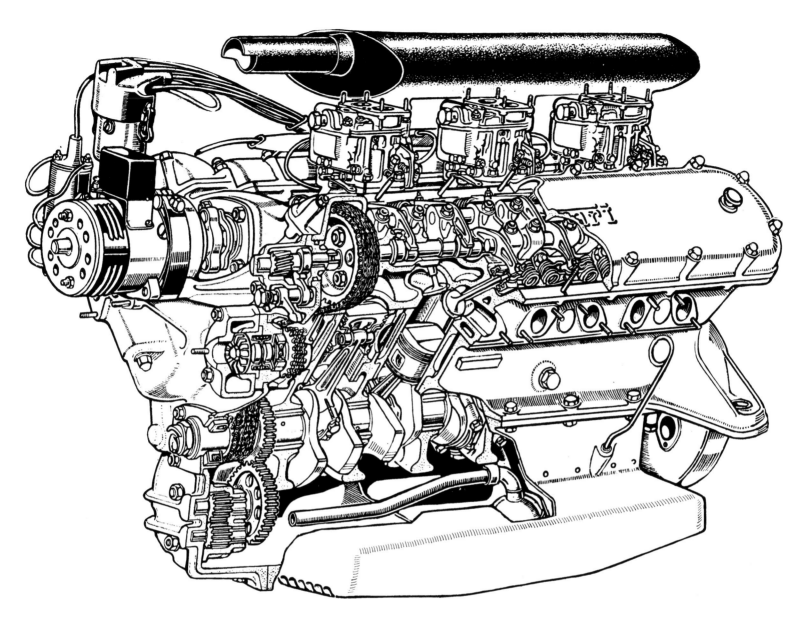

was also amazing, typical of Ferrari's most difficult period. Colombo designed the whole car but he returned to Alfa Romeo at the end of 1945, so engineer Busso became the head of development. Then Busso went back to Alfa in late 1947 and Colombo returned to Maranello as the number one. But another technician was already standing in the wings itching to go, one who would later be determinate for Ferrari. His name was Aurelio Lampredi, who came from the famous aircraft engine manufacturers Officine Reggiane. He joined Ferrari in 1946, but left a year later because he felt little "used" – then he returned again on 1 January 1948. Apart from anything else, the merit of employing two exceptional design engineers, Franco Rocchi and

Walter Salvarani, goes to Lampredi. They were the advanced guard of the so-called "second line", who knew how best to interpret the bosses ideas and also played the important role of ensuring the continuity of accumulated experience. Both were there during my period, Rocchi in the engine sector and Salvarani the gearbox and transmission section, although he was also a chassis expert.

The 1496.7 cc 60° V12 engine excelled during Ferrari's debut and to say the least it was a sensation for the period. It was a "supersquare" unit (bore and stroke 55x52.5 mm) so it was modern for those days when engines had a longer stroke. It astounded people with the number of revolutions it could achieve, which were 5,600

rpm for the 72 hp version and no less than 7,000 for the racing unit that generated over 100 hp. The engine was a major revolution, but its general characteristics were those of a classic power unit as described in technical books for engineers, even if the simplicity and equilibrated decisions of its creator stood out in the result. It only had one overhead camshaft per cylinder bank and the valve springs were the needle type, which Ferrari continued to use until 1959. In addition, it had no dry sump but a normal one with a pump for lubrication, like all the conventional cars. And the chassis was also rather traditional, with a rigid rear axle and semi-elliptical springs. There were a few touches of refinement: the complex of 1.5 mm steel tubes initially weighed

A family of great personality: portrait of Reclus Forghieri

The strong personality and temperament of engineer Mauro Forghieri were probably influenced by the unusual happenings associated with his grandfather Anselmo, and his father Reclus, the latter born on 4 July 1912. From the early 20th century, Mauro's grandfather was a politically committed socialist as well as a friend of Mussolini and Sandro Pertini. He fought in the Great War with the Italian assault regiment but in the early years of Fascism he was forced to take refuge in France due to the bold opinions he expressed in socialist-type newspapers. He was later joined by his son Reclus, who had distinguished himself as a young man in his opposition to Fascism, but he had also attended the renowned Fermo Corni Technical Industrial Institute to refine his natural aptitude for specialised design.

"My father was handsome", recalled Mauro Forghieri, "and had an athletic physique, which he developed at the Panaro Gymnasium in Modena. He lived on the French Riviera between Monaco and Nice, where his technical ability enabled him to work on high class cars in garages. But to live, he also occasionally posed as a model for artists. My grandfather and father then returned to Modena and I always heard it said that Mussolini had not forgotten his old friend and he intervened in his favour. Sandro Pertini was also a friend of my grandfather's, so much so that many letters the two had written to each other were kept at my home for a long time. Unfortunately, they were stolen later and that upset me a lot. "My father eventually married and started to work at Scuderia Ferrari as a technical toolmaker. An almost logical move, because my

family and Ferrari's knew each other, although not intimately, and my father's ability in mechanical work was well known. Between 1937 and 1938, he was a member of the team that created the Alfa Romeo 158, which was commissioned from Ferrari by the Milan manufacturer".

Having finished that job, Reclus Forghieri was employed directly by Alfa and the family moved to Milan. "We lived in Viale Zara and I went to the elementary school in that area but I continued my schooling at Pozzuoli, to which my father moved when he became workshop manager at Ansaldo".

But the war was on and it was destiny that the Forghieri family would move yet again. "During the bombing, we sheltered in the natural grottos around Pozzuoli and for me as a child, it was fun. Then we were 'dispersed' to Lurate Caccivio around Como, with relations. But only me and my mother Afra, because my father's work – he was militarised – was in Naples". Then, after 8 September it was impossible for a husband and wife to know each other's destiny. "I remember perfectly well my mother's attempt to return to Naples as she took me with her. The soldiers at the front convinced her to give up and so we went back to Modena, where one day at the end of spring 1945 we heard the doorbell of our house ring. It was so emotional: my father was on the doorstep with a really long beard and a bicycle on which he had tied his suitcase in some way or other".

During the same period, Enzo Ferrari was starting to build his first car and a door opened for Reclus at Maranello, where he re-

mained until 1973, beyond pensionable age. "My father was a real magician with manufacturing machines", recalls Mauro Forghieri, "and he soon became head of the mechanical workshop, where they made all the detailed components for the racing cars. Fascinating work, but I didn't know much about it as a boy. My father was not an introvert, but outside his work he had hobbies that absorbed him completely: hunting, fishing, ski-ing and rides in the mountains on his motorcycle. He also tried to teach me to fish in the streams of the Apennines, but that was not for me. He had a sort of German approach with me, without much affection, unlike my mother. But my father was really coherent about his work, to an extent that perhaps he didn't have in his private life. But he gave me a mental outlook based more than anything else on seriousness and determination, which was fundamental to my growing up".

A father who contributed substantially to cars that won world championships. It seems obvious that his son would fall in love with racing. "That's only partially true, because my enthusiasm grew by degrees. My father followed racing but not in a visceral way. Only the Mille Miglia, which ran past our house, made him enthusiastic. Sometimes, we would go and see the cars passing through Ravenna at night and then see them again at Bologna on their way back from Rome. When I was 14 or 15 I gate crashed the social lunches of the Scuderia sometimes, which had a much simpler relationship with outsiders at the time. I remember the driver Clemente Biondetti, who was the number one to me because he had

won the Mille Miglia four times. Formula 1 was more distant to me then, rather isolated and I didn't know much about it".

Mauro Forghieri graduated in 1959 and it seemed inevitable that his father would push him towards Ferrari. "But that's really not what happened. My father and I spoke about it, but I ended up there by chance. I had sent out other job applications and I noted that salaries at Maranello were 25%-30% lower. Then Ferrari, who knew me from the time when I did an internship in the factory in 1957, insisted and I put to one side my dream of working for a company specialised in aircraft turbines. So I came to understand just how important the work of my father and his colleagues was; it was of an equally high level. In racing, it is often hard work to carry out a project and to

be able to count on a department that resolves problems for you even at the last minute, due to the excellence of those who work there; it's an enormous help. And it's not that my father did me a favour: at work, the relationship was always distinct. So much so that sometimes he complained to me personally if a project seemed excessively complicated or was not explained clearly. But that was rare, because men of that generation were real creators in the art of mechanics".

The Ferrari racing department at Maranello: the picture was taken in the summer of 1949 and shows well the different state of mind of the two technicians, Gioachino Colombo and Aurelio Lampredi, who worked together at the time in a comparison that was certainly favoured by Enzo Ferrari. Colombo thoughtfully follows work on a 125 F2, while Lampredi, in a white shirt and light coloured trousers, brought a smile to the lips of test and racing driver Felice Bonetto during an apparently calm conversation in which Enzo Ferrari is also taking part. At that time, the difficulty of developing the 125 C with single and double stage superchargers was coming to the surface, both of them designed by Colombo. Lampredi was a firm believer in normally aspirated engines and this was just before his promotion to number one in the project that would lead to the F1 car for the 1950 season. In 1949, the greatest success came from F2, the rules of which catered for cars with aspirated 2000 cc aspirated power units. The 166 F2 was suggested by the Commendatore, who defined it as a "technical immorality": he meant the use of a V12 aspirated engine in a 125 C Grand Prix chassis. From it came a light and sufficiently powerful car of 160 hp that achieved great success after the move from a rear axle with independent suspension and oscillating half axles to the more traditional De Dion.

Pescara, 12 August 1947: start of the sports car race. Franco Cortese's Ferrari 159 S (21) recorded the fastest time in practice. The car is the same two-seater that made its debut at Piacenza in May, but with an uprated 1902.8 cc, 125 hp engine (below) that revved to 7000 rpm. The opposition was not especially strong, so that the third fastest time went to the Milanese driver Beltrachini in the Auto Avio Costruzioni (top left, car right) built by Ferrari seven years earlier. Cortese had no problem in the 20 lap race on the difficult 25.8 kilometre circuit, even though a pit stop of over 20 minutes with an oil radiator problem meant the outright win slipped through his fingers and he was beaten by the "little" Stanguellini 1100 driven by Auricchio. Below: summer, 1947 and the first Ferrari in history leaves the inner courtyard of the Maranello plant for a road test. Nando Righetti is at the wheel and the set features of Enzo Ferrari reflect the importance of the moment. The car is the 159 S, which had already been modified beyond the debut version. In its 125 S guise, the car made its first run on 14 March without a body and with the Commendatore driving. Also in the picture is Adelmo Marchetti (front, right), one of the original 13.

56 kg, but Ferrari insisted that they should not exceed 50 kg and still have with the same resistance qualities: after having given the task to Gilco of Milan, the weight came down to 44 kg. It should not seem strange that a Ferrari chassis was entrusted to an outside company. At Maranello, studies in that area were still limited and the technicians available to Ferrari were excellent, but mainly in the mechanical area. It was no coincidence that Gilco, founded by Gilberto Colombo – no relation to the designer of the 125 – had a privileged consultancy relationship with Maranello, participating in the various projects. That continued until more or less the end of the '50s, when Alberto Massimino left Maserati so that Ferrari was then able to work

Brescia, the eve of the Mille Miglia, 2 May 1948: an extremely elegant Franco Cortese next to a Ferrari 166 S he was to drive in the race. It was chassis 02 – in practice that of the first Ferrari – modified in 1947 and updated with the 1995 cc engine that put out 140 hp the following year. Cortese started from Brescia at 4.22 am and was third at Rome after 5 hours 53 minutes, but already 13 minutes behind Tazio Nuvolari, who was driving the same kind of car but with motorcycle-type mudguards. Cortese retired on his way back to Brescia.

There were five cars built by the young Maranello company in that Mille Miglia, but not all of them were works entries. Below: a poster for The Primavera Romana del Motore (Roman racing car spring), an event that included three days of races on the Caracalla road circuit. Franco Cortese drove the 125 S to Ferrari's first motor racing victory in the event of 25 May 1947.

with a technician who had more advanced ideas in the chassis and suspension areas.

Someone once wrote that the 125's engine was considerably superior to the rest of the car. That was correct, at least in part, but it is untrue the general technical decisions were dictated by the impossibility of taking more refined paths. The car's technical staff had achieved great success with the celebrated Alfa Romeo Alfetta 1500 Grand Prix with which the Milan constructor won the 1950 and 1951 Formula 1 World Championships.

And it should not be forgotten that we are talking about the years not long after the Second World War; the level of the 125's competitiveness was sufficient for that period.

Importantly, the entire project had the great advantage of being used for road cars without requiring any change, in line with Ferrari's original plan. For quite a few years, these were extremely small production runs, but the cars built in subsequent years were close relations of the first 125, even though many of their details had been improved and the engine had been taken to 1902 cc immediately after the Piacenza debut, later 1995 cc for the 166 and then 2341 cc for the 195. But it was clear that the successes of the 125 and 125 SC were not enough. Documentation tells us that when he first started working at Ferrari, Gioachino Colombo was given the responsibility of transforming the 1.5-litre V12 engine into a Grand Prix unit, which was finished

During his long career, Tazio Nuvolari certainly won many of the top motor races, but his 1948 Mille Miglia feat is definitely among his most memorable. To begin with, Nuvolari was not scheduled to compete in the race: he was not well and, due to lung problems, he was in a convalescing in a retreat on Lake Garda.
But on the Friday before the race, there was no way he could resist the temptation of seeing his old friends again, so he went to the Piazza della Vittoria, Brescia, where scrutineering was taking place. He had not practiced even a metre of the route, yet the Alfa Romeo managers and Enzo Ferrari immediately courted him so that he would drive one of their cars. Ferrari (below, with Tazio Nuvolari) was the one who convinced the Flying Mantuan to drive the Prince Igor Troubetzkoy 166 SC with the support of 28 year-old Sergio Scapinelli, a talented engine specialist who worked on Maranello's client cars. The picture on page 20 has great impact and was taken just before Nuvolari started at 4.33 am: the driver seems calm and concentrating on his preparation, while the ecstatic spectators try to interpret even his smallest movement. For about 10 hours after that, everyone was glued to the radio, entranced by the story of the 56 year-old champion's famous drive until his final surrender at Reggio Emilia, where Enzo Ferrari was waiting for him to refuel. Tazio had a 20 minute lead on Clemente Biondetti, but a broken spring bolt took the satisfaction of a third victory in the event away from him.

in 1947 by engineer Busso. A courageous move by Ferrari, because at the time the regulations allowed cars to compete that had either a 1.5-litre supercharged engine or a 4.5-litre normally aspirated unit and the sport was dominated by the Alfa Romeo 158s and the Maserati 4CLTs, built specifically for racing.

After that, many asked themselves whether or not it was logical to combine the 12-cylinder engine with the Roots supercharger, obviously considering the lack of the operation's final success. In reality, the project did not work perfectly in technical terms, because it seemed clear that Maranello was following the example of the period's high-revving aircraft engines: the 1949 two-stage Ferrari V12 produced a good 8000

rpm. But it was not a simple path to take, especially as it was extremely expensive for a newly established company because to develop the supercharger it would have been necessary to make many prototypes and test them. Some people were astounded at the time by this trip-up of Ferrari's, remembering that they were the men who designed the Alfa Romeo 158 engine. But they had created it, not developed it: that was done by Alfa Romeo itself and it took some time. It was a particularly expensive task, which neither Scuderia Ferrari before the war nor the post-war Ferrari would have been able to shoulder. So it was a risk, one of the very few Ferrari ever took – he was an extremely astute man and manager – at least at that level.

The first real Grand Prix single-seater Ferrari was, therefore, the 125 C with the single stage supercharger, which made its debut on 5 September 1948 in the Grand Prix of Italy, which took place in Turin on the city circuit in the Parco del Valentino. The 1.5-litre engine was said to generate 230 hp and it still had just one overhead camshaft per cylinder bank. A limited power output even for that period, but it was clearly a project under development. The kerb weight was declared at 700 kg and that was fairly high. Colombo's comments emphasised the weakness of the transmission and the limited road-holding. Yet even though Alfa Romeo were on another planet, Enzo Ferrari did not react badly to Raymond Sommer's third place in its first race

as he had scored the same result in practice. So the development of the 125 C went ahead, but Ferrari was long sighted and knew he needed an intermediate car that would not cost much to ready and would allow him to soon compete in racing. It was a question of image, but also one of convincing customers as well of start money in the case of works cars. It was Ferrari himself who suggested what he called "technical immorality", a concept he also expressed in later years. In 1949, this "immorality" was based on the use of a 12-cylinder, 2-litre 160 hp aspirated engine installed in the 125 C. Setting the car up didn't seem easy because after much testing, the refined rear end with independent wheels and oscillating half-axles were replaced by the more traditional De Dion rear axle. A step backwards that would not be the only one taken in Ferrari's first 10 or 12 years and which is partly explained by the needs of private entrants, who were more attracted to the "predictable" roadholding of the De Dion axle.

The new 125 two stage Grand Prix car appeared in 1949, a revolution compared to the debut car. Not only did the 1.5-litre engine have a pair of Roots superchargers, but the valve gear had twin overhead camshafts per cylinder bank. That was a real racing engine, theoretically capable of competing in a sector of the sport that would be called Formula 1 the following year.

It was a gamble for Ferrari: would the company have the strength to develop such an ambitious

From the beginning of the company's activities until 1957, Ferrari's chassis were not built at Maranello. That work was done by Gilco of Milan and the picture above shows the welding of a tubed chassis for a Formula 1 single seater. After the war, there was an increasing use of trellis structures in place of the traditional longitudinal members, and it was not easy to find experts in that area. That is why Ferrari preferred to circumvent the obstacle by giving the work to young Gilberto Colombo, who had expanded the business established by his father as a result of his engineering studies and his collaboration with Mario Speluzzi, a technician and lecturer at the Milan Polytechnic. Above: the 12-cylinder Ferrari engine of Clemente Biondetti's 166 S, winner of the 1948 Mille Miglia.

Brescia, the eve of the 1948 Mille Miglia: the Besana brothers, Soave (at the wheel) and Gabriele in their Ferrari 166 SC in which they started at 4.34 am, immediately after Tazio Nuvolari. Perfect examples of gentlemen drivers, they were sixth overall at the Rome control, although 21 minutes behind leader Nuvolari, while the eventual winner Clemente Biondetti in a 166 S with the same power output, was a minute behind the brothers. But the Besanas had to retire right after Rome.

It is strange to note that all the early Ferrari clients, who were fundamental to the company's growth, were noblemen; the Besanas were counts, as was Bruno Sterzi of Novara with whom they founded the Gruppo Inter team. There were other aristocratic customers including Prince Igor Troubetzkoy, who was born in Paris in 1912 and a descendent of the founders of the small realm of Belorussia. A fine sportsman and handsome with it, he married American millionairess Barbara Hutton in 1947 and after his motor racing debut, he often entered simply as Prince Igor. As a result of the determined contribution of Clemente Biondetti, he and Troubetzkoy won the 1948 Giro di Sicilia.

car with constant financial anxiety and the social difficulty of that period? A good basis was there: the weight of this single-seater was under 600 kg, not much at all. At least 100 kg less than the Alfa 158, which put out 350 hp in 1950 (the Milan constructor did not compete in 1949), while the Ferrari could produce a maximum of 320 hp at no fewer than 8000 rpm at the end of 1949. And with a generation of power the drivers always said was "too brusque".

In the initial development phase there were many overheating problems typical of supercharged engines. Mid-season, the two stage seemed ready and in September it won the Grand Prix of Italy at Monza, although the entry was not the most competitive. The pictures taken during pre-race testing in late August showing Ferrari especially taciturn speak for themselves: the decision had been taken. The car was not competitive against the Alfa Romeo of the previous year so it would be abandoned, apart from a few appearances in early 1950 while waiting for the new arrival.

Giving an opinion with the benefit of hindsight, that seemed to be a sensible decision. Ferrari had lost his gamble with the complicated world of supercharged engines, but he had had the courage to stop in time and radically change direction.

The practical consequence of that decision was to assign Colombo to car production: another rational move, because he felt the need of an ex-

Left: two pictures, two races fundamental to the history of Ferrari. To emphasise that statement, we reproduce here the words of Enzo Ferrari in his book 'Piloti, che Gente': "I remember the emotion his (Raymond Sommer, in the photo above, Ed) victory made me feel at the Grand Prix of Turin on 12 October 1947, an encouraging result as a result of which I found myself a victorious constructor in that Parco del Valentino where, with my father and dead brother, in 1919 I had cried, was unemployed and without a penny. The following year on the same track I entered three cars for the 19th

Grand Prix of Italy, driven by Sommer (photo below, front row, right in the 125 C single stage, Ed) Farina and Bira. That day also generated deep emotion within me: it was Ferrari's first real Grand Prix, the first time we took on the manufacturers: Alfa, Maserati, Talbot. Wimille won in the Alfa Romeo and Villoresi came second with the Maserati, but Sommer's third place was an equally important result for me, because it convinced me that we were on the right road".

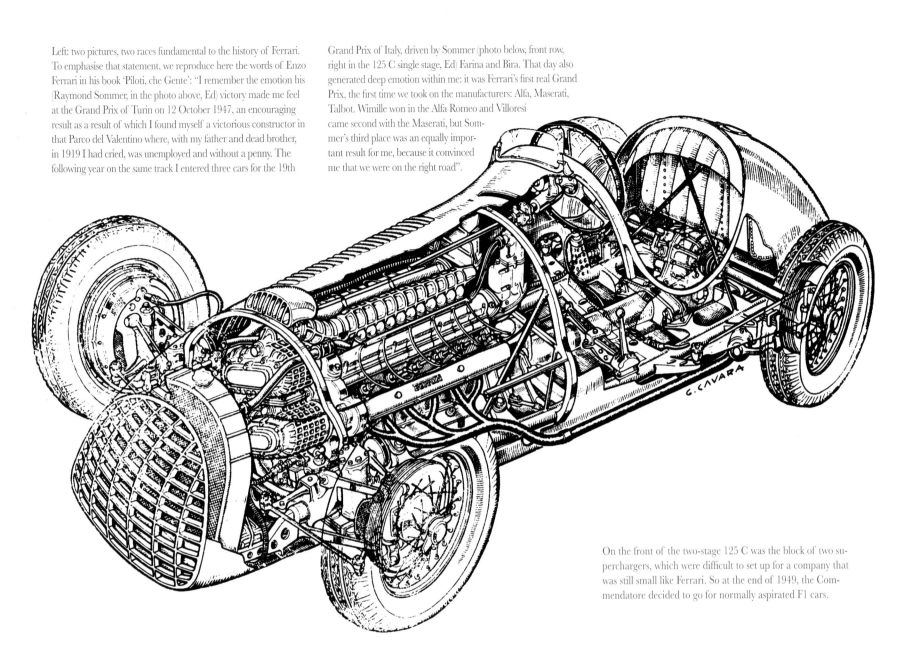

On the front of the two-stage 125 C was the block of two superchargers, which were difficult to set up for a company that was still small like Ferrari. So at the end of 1949, the Commendatore decided to go for normally aspirated F1 cars.

perienced man to organise that sector. Even if slowly, the number of road cars built increased: 21 in 1949 – but this included the two-seater sports racers – and 26 in 1950. With that growth, another happy intuition of Enzo Ferrari's counted for quite a lot: the installation of an internal foundry at Maranello, supported especially by Federico Giberti, technician and long-time collaborator of the Commendatore going right back to the Scuderia days. The foundry department has always distinguished itself for its perfection of execution and over the years enabled Ferrari to quickly vary its technical decisions without depending on suppliers.

At the end of 1949, the Grand Prix single-seaters were handed over to the then 32 year-old Au-

relio Lampredi, who certainly didn't have to put much effort into convincing Ferrari of the need to go for the simpler, less expensive normally aspirated engine for F1 in 1950. It's also possible that the two technicians were pitted against each other to draw the best out of their projects – in line with a policy that would be seen more than once at Maranello. But it is evident that Ferrari did not want to take the complicated path any more to the point that the new F1 V12 engine – initially a 3.3-litre, although the regulations permitted up to 4.5-litres – was nothing other than an evolution of the original engine that first appeared in 1947. Prolific, fast, technically ready, in early 1950 Lampredi went back to the design of the V12 with the intention of achiev-

ing a much higher cubic capacity compared to the Colombo unit, coming close to 5000 rpm, but the original characteristics of the unit were unchanged. A notable example of validity and longevity, considering the long list of motor racing and commercial successes it achieved, an engine that was always developed and never revolutionised, until the '60s.

The V12 F1 still had a single overhead camshaft for each cylinder bank, but it also incorporated a number of interesting, well designed innovations. For example, the cylinders screwed into the head, a technique that eliminated the problem associated with the seal between the head and the block, which was always a possible cause of breakdowns. It was a fundamental

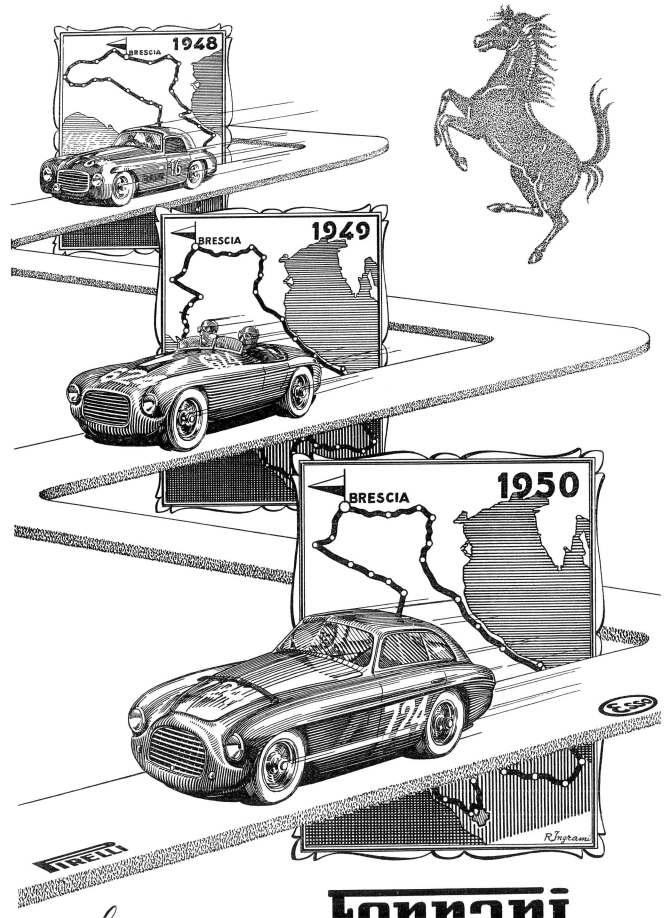

un solo nome: MODENA **Ferrari** ITALIA

Monza, 11 September 1949, the Grand Prix of Italy: Alberto Ascari crosses the finish line to victory in a two-stage Ferrari 125 C F1 car. The Milanese driver scored a significant win, 25 years after his father's success at the same circuit in an Alfa Romeo P2. Alberto's day was a triumph cheered by the spectators until they were hoarse, but for Maranello it was only a partial joy because Ferrari was becoming convinced of the difficulty of developing the car, which had emerged during pre-season testing and especially the pre-Monza trials on 26 August. But for Gioachino Colombo, who had developed all the early years' Ferraris and was the man behind the two-stage, that Grand Prix of Europe was his last time in the Ferrari pits.

Left: it had always been said that Ferrari never descended to advertising its products and Henry Ford made his famous comment saying Maranello had guaranteed publicity in the daily newspapers every Monday morning.

But that's not true about Ferrari's early period when advertising, especially in the specialised press, was rather frequent. For instance, to promote its three consecutive victories in the 1948/9/50 Mille Miglias, this page was designed by Renato Ingrami, an artist from Serramazzoni, a few kilometers from the Ferrari factory.

engine for Maranello, the technical philosophy of which – at least until the early '70s – was always maximum financial exploitation of projects. It was no coincidence that I started from the old 3-litre F1 engines used from 1966 and also the 5-litres of the 1970 512 S, at least for casting the block. They were heavy but reliable power units.

Ferrari had two top drivers for the 1950 season, Alberto Ascari and Luigi Villoresi. Commentators speak of the "excellent technical recovery by Maranello" and, in fact, the revolution happened fast. Even if it was only from the GP of Italy on 3 September that Ferrari was able to field the new 375 F1 cars with 4.5-litre engines.

The "intermediate" cars' 3.3-litre units put out

300 hp, but the 4.1-litre took that to 335 hp, 15 hp more than the best of the previous two-stage 125s. When that rose to 350 hp with the 4.5-litre, Ferrari was able to challenge Alfa Romeo and its 8-cylinder in-line engine, which had a superior power output of 380 hp, but the 375's was highly elastic; it could be exploited better by the drivers under acceleration due to its torque at low revs. At the time, Lampredi often went to the circuits with the team, even if that official responsibility belonged to Girolamo Ferrari Amorotti, a clever technician who gained his experience at Alfa Romeo before the war.

'Mino' Amorotti was an unusual man, fundamentally a rich country gentleman who was in love with motor racing. A position that allowed

him a certain intimacy with Enzo Ferrari, partly because it seemed there was no financial arrangement between them. Yet throughout the Fifties, Amorotti worked with the team with intelligence and diplomacy, always in favour of détente in the less than rare moments of difficulty.

The real improvement in quality came during the 1951 season. Lampredi had been able to take the power output of the V12 F1 to 380 hp, a good result and one that amazed Ferrari. Alfa had achieved 425 hp, but the engine the Commendatore wanted had the advantage of consuming less fuel than the Milanese car, which did less than a kilometer to a litre of a special fuel cocktail. So it had two fuel tanks with a total capacity of 225 litres against the 195 litres of the Ferrari.

And with Grands Prix 500 km long the fuel situation counted, as Ferrari had worked out when he opted for an aspirated engine. After the historic victory of Froilàn Gonzàlez in the British GP on 14 July, Ferrari repeated that success in the GPs of Germany and Italy: it was definitive confirmation of the Prancing Horse's growth.

So the battle between the two companies was based more than anything else on engines. They were just about the same as far as their chassis technology went, but without anything special. Their chassis simply expressed the best of what had been seen before the war: quadrilateral front suspension with a lower transverse spring, a De Dion axle rear end and upper leaf spring.

Brescia, 23 April 1950: the start of the 17th Mille Miglia, for which two Ferrari 275 S were entered, number 728 for Alberto Ascari-Senezio Nicolini (behind them is the Biondetti-Bronzoni Jaguar XK 120) and 731 for Luigi Villoresi-Pasquale Cassani, both of which retired. They were powered by the new 3322 cc engine, which was an important stage in the V12's evolution updated by Aurelio Lampredi on his way to the prophetic 4.5-litre permitted by the regulations. Having achieved that objective, the first historic victory in a world championship Grand Prix was scored by Gonzàlez (right, above) opposite locking the 375 during the GP of Great Britain at Silverstone and (below, right) crossing the finish line to win. It was 14 July 1951.

1952-1959

From Ascari to Hawthorn
The first decade of F1 success

During my long career at Ferrari from 1960 to 1987, I rarely heard comments on the period before I joined. There was not much talk, people looked ahead and the first person to do so was Enzo Ferrari. So I never fully understood the decision to unofficially enter four 375s in the 1952 500 Miles of Indianapolis, one of them for Alberto Ascari. It was an initiative that has remained part of history, but it was also a gamble for a very small company with so many other commitments.

Let's be clear about it, Ferrari was fully aware of the Indianapolis legend, perhaps also because of his understandable provincialism. But I'm certain he knew perfectly well that a specially designed car would be needed for that race, the road Lotus took about 10 years later. It seemed the Commendatore was extremely doubtful about competing at Indy, but wanted to please Luigi Chinetti, the new Ferrari importer in the United States, yet he knew that not doing well would go down badly with his potential clients.

Certainly, there were also financial reasons: the prize money was big and in Ascari's case the costs would be covered by a piston manufacturer. It is also known that Alice Caracciola, wife of the famous German driver Rudolf, and various friends in the U.S. had put Maranello in touch with the race organisers some time earlier, as they wanted a European attraction. All interesting reasons, yet it was difficult to believe Ferrari expect a positive result. Alberto Ascari was more optimistic, and in the various interviews he gave before leaving for the United States a month before the race, he compared Indy with Monza where, even with corners, the F1 cars lapped at an average of 185 kph. A European driver's way of reasoning by one who did not know much about such a completely different kind of racing. Ferrari harboured a few doubts, given that the cars he would enter were all the previous year's 375 F1 derivatives with 4493 cc V12s that put out 400 hp. But he had their chassis made more robust to stand the stress of the long, banked corners. And there was no problem from that point of view, but other difficulties emerged, like not

Previous page: with Alberto Ascari committed to Indianapolis, the GP of Switzerland on 18 May 1952 was monopolised by the Ferrari 500 F2s of Giuseppe Farina and Piero Taruffi (numbers 28 and 30), on the front row together with Robert Manzon (Gordini). Taruffi won on the difficult Bremgarten circuit after Farina retired with an ignition problem.

Left, above: the Ferrari 500 F2 made its debut at Modena on 23 September 1951, when Alberto Ascari is shown taking a corner opposite the Via Emilia entrance. The car dominated the GP at the 2,306 meter permanent Autodrome, which was opened the previous year. It was a victory that began one of the longest periods of success by the same car and driver in the history of motor racing: they stayed at the top until the end of 1953. At Modena, Ascari had no difficulty in beating Froilán González, who was driving a Ferrari 166 F2 entered by Scuderia Marzotto, although Luigi Villoresi in another works 500 was forced to retire on the 28th lap with engine problems, a rare occurrence in the long, competitive life of that model. The 12-cylinder González 166, derived from the 1948/9 version, had previously dominated the works and private entry categories. It was an excellent win that was also a good pay day for the newborn Prancing Horse, which carefully evaluated the many international F2 races in relation to their start and prize money. The Commendatore was by no means unprepared when he had to replace the 166, but technician Aurelio Lampredi had taken a completely new direction with the 500, based on lightness, practicability and economy. The 12-cylinder remained as the basis of Ferrari production, but Maranello's first 4-cylinder 2000 cc engine in the 500 enabled the company to go from the 200 kg of the 166 to 158 kg with a reduction of the car's mechanics that came close to 70%.

Left, below: the Ferrari 375 Special on the track at Indianapolis in readiness for the 500 Miles of 30 May 1952, driven by Alberto Ascari: note the original track's brick surface from the famous Brickyard days, which were retained as the start line. The car had been derived from the F1 375, its engine increased to an output of 400 hp and its chassis made more robust. Three of these cars first appeared at the GP of Turin on 6 April – a city circuit totally different from the Indianapolis track.

enough speed and little traction when exiting Indy's turns. So the race had been underestimated and the whole affair could have turned into a disaster, because that far away from home technical help was difficult to come by. Romolo Tavoni would later become the team's motor sport director and was Enzo Ferrari's personal secretary at the time: he recalls the Commendatore being very tense before hearing the result of qualifying on the phone. Ferrari didn't let out a sigh of relief until he found out Ascari was on the seventh row of the grid with the 29th fastest time. During the race, the future world champion managed to overtake a number of cars before having to stop with a broken right rear wheel flange joint. All in all an honourable race,

Indianapolis, 30 May 1952: having started from the 7th row and after overtaking a number of cars, Ascari was eighth after 41 laps and 37 minutes of the race. But the flange joint that held the Ferrari 375 Special's rear right wheel spokes together broke. Then came the inevitable retirement, but Maranello had salvaged its honour. Left: Ascari with technician Aurelio Lampredi and mechanic Stefano Meazza.

because severe damage to Maranello's image had been avoided. The fact is that after 1952 Ferrari returned to the subject of competing at Indy from time to time and did not hide the fact that he was tempted by that dream. But he always added that he would only go to Indy with a car especially designed and developed for the race: however, there were other priorities and he never made such a serious attempt again.

In 1952, Enzo Ferrari and Alberto Ascari had far different reasons for consoling themselves. After the great success of the F1 with its 12-cylinder engine, designer Aurelio Lampredi certainly enjoyed the full confidence of the boss and he was in the right frame of mind to create the car that dominated the world championships of 1952/3 driven by Ascari. After its first two years, the Formula 1 World Championship experienced a crisis, because supercharged cars had become extremely expensive, forcing Alfa Romeo to retire from racing. So the Federation decided to allow only F2 cars with 2000 cc aspirated engines to compete for the world title and Ferrari quickly took advantage of the new technical regulations. It was a move that was fundamental in building the Ferrari legend, which has continued to this very day.

Ascari was at the peak of his form, achieved Nuvolari-style popularity at the height of his career and he drove an excellent car. The 500 F2 was of traditional conception, but it was effective and really robust. The 1985 cc 4-cyl-

inder engine only had two valves per cylinder, yet it produced high power and revolutions for the period: 170 hp at 7200 rpm during the first year and 185 hp at 7500 rpm in 1953. In the second case the horse power per litre was over 93, yet the drivers always praised the engine's excellent torque; it was so good that modifications to the gear ratios were unnecessary. The 'box was at the rear en bloc with the differential, a layout that certainly influenced the good weight distribution of the car and, therefore, its handling qualities.

At the rear was a De Dion axle with a transverse lower spring, a typical Ferrari set-up both before and in later years and the reason for the many tests of coil springs, the subsequent return of

the leaf spring and, finally, springs for the last front engined car in 1959 with the debut of independent wheels. Uncertainty mainly came from the fuel tank being in the back: the 500 F2's was in riveted aluminium and had a 150 litre capacity. A weight that had to be supported by the lower transverse steel spring, similar to the one at the front end. It was not easy to achieve because of the difficulty in finding refined metals and that the technology was still at the experimental stage. What happened was that, as the full tank emptied, the car was subjected to a succession of modifications, but the fact that the spring gave under the weight, reducing its elasticity, was well thought out. In a rather empirical but practical way, excessive variation of

At 5,500 metres long, the Syracuse circuit hosted F1 races until 1967. It had purpose-built pits and walls at the sides of the track, but part of it was the S 124 public road and another a secondary provincial road. Quick and demanding, to Ferrari it was a point of reference on the eve of the F1 World Championship. This picture, taken on 16 March during the 1952 race, shows Ascari driving the Ferrari 500 F2 to victory, ahead of his team mates Piero Taruffi and Giuseppe Farina plus a private 500 driven by Swiss Rudi Fischer. Enzo Ferrari got it right in anticipating the opposition when the F2 500 was being designed and developed: it was a doubly happy choice, because the Federation had decided to run the 1952/3 world championship for F2 single-seaters instead of the dormant F1s. Even better, in 1952 alone Ferrari had built 10 500s, four of which were sold to privateers. Officially, Maranello competed in 18 events, won seven world championship GPs and 10 other international races with the cars. Note the slightly modified lines of the version raced at Syracuse compared to the 500 F2 that made its Modena debut six months earlier: technically, only details were changed because the Scuderia got the car was right first time.

Examined in detail, one of the Ferrari 500 F2's major strengths is immediately evident: the correct centring of the mass, obtained by moving the 4-cylinder engine back towards the cockpit and placing the gearbox – four speeds, en bloc with the differential – just behind the driver's seat and, therefore, inside the rear axle, a De Dion with the lower transverse spring, as can be seen from the detail (top, right). The front end with independent wheels had dou-ble quadrilaterals and a lower spring, which was also transverse. It was a more conventional layout, not a revolutionary one, partially taken from previous Ferrari single-seaters, but it was much refined in its key details, the work of those formidable designers who brought together the ideas of the technical director to perfection and have always been at the heart of Ferrari's success.

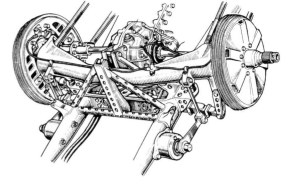

G.CAVARA

the set-up between the front and rear ends was avoided at that discharge point.

In the two years after winning the double world championship with Alberto Ascari, Ferrari went through a period of crisis. It was not that, with the new 1954 regulations aspirated engines of up to 2500 cc, high level opposition appeared like the Mercedes-Benz W196 and the Maserati 250F, and that Ferrari's top drivers, Ascari and Gigi Villoresi, had accepted the inviting offer of Lancia, which was about to make its F1 debut. Ferrari continued to fight on all fronts in its attempts at winning, but success in the world championship was not matched by the necessary investment.

That is why it wasn't possible to design and de-velop really new cars, because the ones they raced were always evolutions of the 500 F2. The first single-seater derived from the extreme evolution of the F2 was the 553: it had a 4-cylinder (100x79.5 mm) engine that produced 260 hp at 7200 rpm, lateral fuel tanks and was the famous Squalo that became the 555 Supersqualo in 1955. Between 1954 and 1955 Ferrari also entered the 626 F1, based on a more traditional F2 car: that had a 4-cylinder unit (94x90 mm) that put out 250 hp at 7200 rpm.

Those cars had rather traditional chassis. The rear suspension was the much tried and tested De Dion axle and that ensured a certain efficiency, but it was essential to profoundly update the front suspension, which still had the obsolete transverse lower spring. From 1948, technician Valerio Colotti became involved in Ferrari's kinematic mechanisms, but he moved to Maserati in the summer of '53 and was sorely missed. So much so that the important project of a new front suspension with the more effective coil springs for the 553 was handed over to Alberto Massimino, who had worked with Ferrari before the war. He returned to the fold in 1954, but as a design consultant. As technical director, Aurelio Lampredi barely tolerated this outside interference, but it was typical of Enzo Ferrari's management system. On the other hand, the Squalo 553 turned out to be effective but difficult, so much so that it could only be driven on the limit by top class drivers because

of its weight distribution. It had a low moment of inertia with minimum variations due to the mass being concentrated within its wheelbase. Mike Hawthorn drove the Squalo to victory in the 1954 GP of Spain, the first after its update. And luck played its part in the more driveable 625 winning two Grands Prix, one driven by Froilán González at Silverstone in 1954 and the other by Maurice Trintignant at Monaco in 1955.

Among the doubts and attempts to devise really new projects – the financial side was certainly a major drawback – the 625 was modified in mid-1954 and was given a hybrid engine half way between that of the 553 and the 625 – and the cocktail worked.

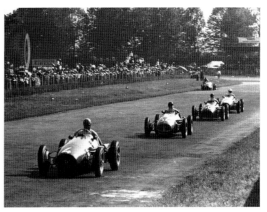

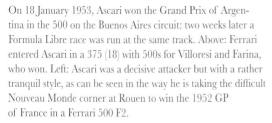

On 18 January 1953, Ascari won the Grand Prix of Argentina in the 500 on the Buenos Aires circuit: two weeks later a Formula Libre race was run at the same track. Above: Ferrari entered Ascari in a 375 (18) with 500s for Villoresi and Farina, who won. Left: Ascari was a decisive attacker but with a rather tranquil style, as can be seen in the way he is taking the difficult Nouveau Monde corner at Rouen to win the 1952 GP of France in a Ferrari 500 F2.

World champion in 1952/3, during the same period Ascari won 11 rounds of the title chase driving the Ferrari 500 F2, but he only came fourth in the 1953 GP of France (above) on the fast Reims circuit. The race was made famous by the duel between Hawthorn (Ferrari 500 F2) and Juan Manuel Fangio (Maserati A6GCM): the Englishman won at an average of 183 kph. Below: another famous GP of Monza on 13 September 1953, when the Ferrari 500 F2s of Ascari and Farina closed in on Onofre Marimòn's lapped Maserati A6GCM and that of Fangio. The battle ended at the last corner of the last lap with victory for Fangio.

Meanwhile, Lampredi also tried the twin cylinder 2500 cc path, the strangest engine ever built by Ferrari. In choosing that direction he was undoubtedly influenced by the theories that conditioned power units for the 500 Miles of Indianapolis, almost all of them Offenhauser 4500 cc 4-cylinders. The reduced number of cylinders favoured torque and, therefore, pick-up at low revs, necessary at the time because F1 gearboxes did not have a great selection of speeds. Theoretically, the 2-cylinder Ferrari with a bore and stroke of 118x114 mm would have been useful on tortuous circuits like Monte Carlo, but the difficulty of balancing a 2-cylinder engine was not taken into account. The mechanics told me later that the unit vibrated so much during

the early tests that it tore off the test bench fixing iron beam. Small and compact, it also had a strange shape, so much so that the mechanics jokingly named it 'scranein da giarden' or garden bench.

Some have said Ferrari was not in agreement with that project, but he must have approved it because nothing was done at Maranello without his blessing. Anyway, in July 1955 Lampredi left and joined Fiat. A sudden departure that resulted in Ferrari being without a technical office director for at least six months. But in this case, too, the Commendatore had worked out everything: he knew he could count on external collaborators who had been working for the company for some time: they included Alberto

Massimino of whom we have already spoken, and Vittorio Bellantani, who was also with Ferrari before the war, mainly in production. Both had previously worked with Lampredi and subsequently in January 1956 with the new boss, engineer Andrea Fraschetti, as well as with Vittorio Jano. A general situation that was not so clear and one which only a man like the Commendatore could manage.

But as early as two years before that, Enzo Ferrari probably had a winning F1 car close at hand. It would have been sufficient to 'steal' the great technician Vittorio Jano from Lancia, which he had already done successfully during his Alfa Romeo days in the mid-Twenties. But Ferrari knew he did not have the means that

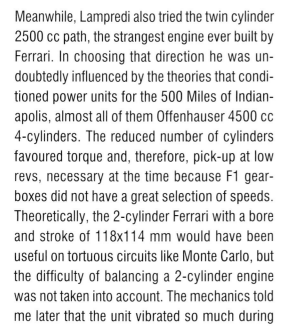

A conversation with Romolo Tavoni:
Ferrari's early years

Born in 1926, accountant Romolo Tavoni is the keeper of Ferrari history for the period 1949 to the end of 1961. From Casinalbo, just a few kilometres from Maranello in Italy's Reggio Emilia, he has always been close to the Commendatore, initially as his secretary. In 1957 he was promoted to become an executive – the youngest in the province – and was appointed director of the racing department. Under him, Ferrari won the 1958 and 1961 Formula 1 World Championships, but in October of that last year he was forced to leave Maranello together with seven other top managers. It was that famous case that began with a letter of complaint sent by the group of eight to Enzo Ferrari and caused by the interference of the Commendatore's wife, Laura, during the week and even at the circuits. It was substantiated, annoying, but not determinate. Ferrari considered their gesture as a sign of immaturity, not coherent with an executive's the position of responsibility and fired them all. Even today Tavoni says Ferrari would not have acted differently, although he does emphasise that "leaving Maranello was very painful for me".

This attitude and his clear recollections and ability to judge, make Tavoni a valuable witness to the period.

"I joined Ferrari on 16 January 1950 as the Commendatore's personal secretary. I had graduated in accountancy, but I had limited working experience and was still only 23 years-old. I immediately realised that my work would be extremely interesting but it needed continuous attention, because Ferrari was extremely limited with information and his re-

quests; you had to interpret him and make sure you didn't make mistakes. For example, after less than a month Ascari and Villoresi, the team's two top drivers, called from Milan and said they would visit Maranello the next day. 'You meet them' said Ferrari after I had spoken to him. 'If they arrive at 10 I will not receive them until after 11; meanwhile, take them on a tour of the Scuderia and make them tell you – but separately – something about what they want. And avoid them going to Maranello, because I want to go there with them later…'. They were two famous drivers and becoming part of such a special world was something of great fascination to me.

"I knew I was working for a ruthless man in terms of his needs, but he could be like that because he was even more demanding of himself. The company was still small and Ferrari liked to involve everyone in his personal problems – and he had a lot of them.

He 'spoke' on Tuesdays at Maranello, which I also travelled to as my office was at the Scuderia in Modena, the upper floor of which was occupied by the Ferrari family. The boss was always intriguing at these meetings, because he knew how to motivate and involve people. He gave you a sense of belonging. Today, people study human resources management. He understood perfectly how it was done when all his closest collaborators were sitting around the table. I sat on his left and I took the minutes, then there was Luigi Bassi and Federico Giberti, long established Ferrari technicians, engineer Lampredi and various heads of section, like the foundry, the workshop, administration and sales. They were all managers. There were no executives. The only executive was Ferrari, owner and boss. He hid nothing about the factory from us and it wasn't even necessary to ask everyone for secrecy: if someone gossiped outside, he would be fired on the spot. For example, nobody ever mentioned that for a long time Ferrari was undecided as to whether he should stop the construction of oil pressure grinders – the reason for which the Maranello factory was established in 1942 – to produce cars alone. It was obvious that car production was the dream of his life, but machine tools made a profit, while there was no certainty that cars and racing could bring in money. Anyway, grinders kept 60 people in work against maybe not even 20 in the car sector. The Commendatore was tortured by the horror of losing everything and by the eventual necessity of sending the men he had transformed into factory workers back to the land.

Left: motor sport director Tavoni congratulating Richie Ginther after the 1961 GP of Monaco, in which the American came second to an outstanding Stirling Moss, who won in a Lotus-Climax. Behind Ginther is the well-known journalist Denis Jenkinson and next to him Franco Gozzi. Right: Eugenio Dragoni and Mauro Forghieri in the pits.

"Just three years later, after the first car (the 125 S in the spring of 1947, Ed) made its debut and I called Giberti, who was a sort of director of the factory, and asked him to find a buyer for the whole grinding department, which was sold to OMA of Bologna.

"But too few cars were built each year to keep a factory with just about 100 employees going: just four in 1948 and 26 in 1950. When Ferrari won its first world championship with Ascari in 1952, there was a push inside the plant to bring the number of cars commissioned to 10, which included the road cars. Even if this evidently meant increasing the work carried out on simple stands: there was no assembly line and one wasn't installed until 1954/5. Its arrival was something that filled the workers with pride, because they believed the factory had come closer to mass production. However, to build 10 cars at a time, needed time. 'But Commendatore, with five orders the suppliers don't do discounts', his collaborators objected. But Ferrari did not hide the reality: "Well, I have the capital for five cars, not for 10". And he sometimes added, 'I have opened lines of credit with three banks, but if their managers start talking together and reveal how much they have advanced me, the morning afterwards I won't have a company'. He had a simple means of keeping his eye on expenditure: the little book of the accountant Carlo Benzi, the man who looked after the factory's accounts from 1946 until 1988 and then Enzo Ferrari's personal ones". They spoke almost daily: 'Yes, OK Commendatore, we are covered. No, with that amount for that bank we're not…'. It's obvious that Ferrari had to

have enormous strength to solve such problems every day. Because then there was motor racing, the part of his job he loved most, and that he always dealt with personally. Racing helped to increase the prestige of the brand, so part of what he made he reinvested under the heading 'experience'. He had a simple but effective system to avoid a financial crisis at the Scuderia, a situation in which many of his adversaries had found themselves. Apart from technical sponsorship, at the time the team kept itself going with money offered by the race organisers. Ferrari always did the negotiating and it was always through a deluge of correspondence or, in the final stages, telegrams. He dictated in French, a language he spoke very well, and I took notes. He ignored the English language, but we had an excellent interpreter in Clara Gavioli. 'But all things considered, the numbers are the same, even in England…' he liked to say, but he always wanted to be paid in Italian lire and he made that clear in the agreement.

"The amounts were always the same: 1,500,000 lire per car per race in England and 1,250,000 in the rest of Europe. And often three or even four cars were involved. Negotiations were even more direct over races in Italy and he could make good money: with his friend Caflish, vice-president of the AC of Naples, it got up to 2,000,000 a car for a GP at the Posillipo circuit and slightly higher amounts for the GP of Syracuse. And that's without counting possible prize money, which varied a lot from race to race. Of all that money, contractually 50% went to the driver and the other 50% was divided in three parts by

Ferrari: they were travelling expenses, technical repairs of the cars after the race and experience for the development of the cars. He was very careful: so even if he had financial problems because he had to invest in production, the Scuderia was never hit by a crisis. With sports car races, the amounts and divisions were the same and if the drivers were two per car, they split the money. But nobody ever complained, because they earned well for the period: a top driver like Ascari could count on a safe one million lire per race apart from prize money.

The leading drivers also split the money Ferrari negotiated with suppliers: fuel, oil, tyres, spark plugs, dampers, brakes… As always, negotiations were carried out exclusively by Ferrari and, even if they did not involve large amounts, the method of persuasion never changed: 'If they don't agree, write that we are sorry but we must change supplier…'.

enabled Lancia and Jano to create the sensational D50 with its semi-load carrying V8 engine and gearbox en bloc with the differential, the car that turned out to be the financial ruin of the Turin manufacturer.

So much so that Lancia had to retire in mid-1955 and Ferrari was given their six V8 D50s, complete with spare parts, on a silver platter. To say nothing of a special contribution of 50 million lire by Fiat, which always had a high opinion of the Scuderia. No less important to Ferrari's immediate future was the certainty of being able to count once more on the technical brilliance of Vittorio Jano, who was back as a special consultant to the Commendatore. But he had to stay in the background a little, because

his Lancia contract stipulated that he could not work for another constructor for four years. Ferrari wanted to run the D50s immediately, but the impossibility of using special Pirelli tyres forced him to postpone the debut until 1956, because Maranello had a contract with Englebert: but in a test session at Monza, their tyres proved completely unsuited to the Lancias.

Renamed Ferrari, the Lancia D50 won the Modena 'derby', because Mercedes-Benz retired at the end of 1955 and that meant a straight fight between the Scuderia and Maserati, with the 1956 world championship going to Juan Manuel Fangio in the V8. The following year, it was confirmed that the Lancia D50 was based on a refined project but it was difficult to man-

The debut of the Mercedes-Benz in F1 and the World Sports Car Championship proved to be serious opposition for Ferrari in 1954 and 1955, a difficult period for the Scuderia both financially and technically. But there was some success: above, González and Hawthorn, their 625s line astern in the pits during practice for the 1954 GP of Great Britain. The Argentinean won and Hawthorn came second in the race. Above, right: the second world championship GP victory of the season came when Hawthorn won the GP of Spain in his works 625 Squalo with its lateral fuel tanks.

At the end of 1953, Ascari had become world champion in a Ferrari for a second time, yet the association between the Scuderia and the driver ended in divorce. Alberto signed for Lancia (above, left the original first of a four-page contract between Lancia and the Milanese driver) and Villoresi did likewise.
The human aspect of the Ferrari-Ascari relationship did not change, but the Commendatore would not have been able to afford Ascari at the same money as Lancia were paying him: 25 million lire, increasing to 30 million. Above, right: Maurice Trintignant winning the 1955 GP of Monaco in the 625, Ferrari's only F1 victory that season.

age. Many of the updates of the 801, as the car was subsequently called, even turned out to be counterproductive and were of no use in trying to beat the opposition; in fact they gave the impression that Ferrari had lost its way somewhat. It must be emphasised that Maranello's season was influenced by the tragic death of Eugenio Castellotti at the Modena Aerautodrome in March and the fatal accident of De Portago-Nelson in the Mille Miglia, in which 10 spectators were killed. Ferrari was taken to court over that disaster and, even though acquitted, he was probably unable to manage men and events with his usual lucidity.
From the technical point of view, the engine was given more power – in secret, as usual –

by Vittorio Jano, while the chassis was revised and then revised again in numerous detailed areas, especially the back axle. But the oscillating drive shafts at the rear and the wishbones with coil springs at the front – an alternative to the system taken from the 'old' Supersqualo, as I heard it – did not turn out to be enough to compete with the updated Maserati or the new Vanwall. The British car had a front engine, but it already had an English school chassis designed by Mike Costin and the future Lotus genius, Colin Chapman, as well as a light, much refined 4-cylinder engine.
In reality, Ferrari had been developing its future 'weapons' from early 1957: the 1958 regulations laid down the use of 'AvGas' at no more

Turin, Tuesday 26 July 1955: the six Lancia D50s plus a considerable amount of spare parts and six complete engines being loaded for their journey from Turin to Maranello after the their creator retired from racing. The gift was helped along by the executives of the AC of Italy as well as Fiat, who pushed to support Ferrari and had made a contribution of 50 million lire.

Above, left: Luigi Musso practicing for the 1956 Monaco GP in a 'classic' version of the Ferrari D50 that was driven in the race by Eugenio Castellotti.

Right: Juan Manuel Fangio, Peter Collins, Alfonso De Portago and Luigi Musso, but the car was also driven by Eugenio Castellotti and, occasionally, by Olivier Gendebien.

The Lancia D50 that became a Ferrari the following year was the result of an expensive project with avant garde aspects to it, like its weight distribution, V8 engine with semi-load carrying capability and lateral fuel tanks – supported by small tension links – that played an aerodynamic role. Yet that 'agitator of men' Enzo Ferrari was not happy about running the

D50 in its original form even if, to tell the truth, the Vittorio Jano project had more interesting technical content than the 1955 Maranello car. Thinking that the problem was the less powerful 4-cylinder (it seems the F1 in-line 6-cylinder was only at the design stage), Ferrari also had the Lancia V8 installed in a 555 Squalo chassis, which then became the Supersqualo (below with Mike Hawthorn at the wheel) but at the 1956 GP of Argentina the result was disappointing. With Jano's support, many modifications were made to the original D50, but they were not always definitive: a more powerful engine, a bigger fuel tank in the tail to lighten the laterals, independent rear suspension — only seen in practice — in place of

the De Dion axle, already updated with Houdaille dampers, the telescopic units having been dropped. In engineer Forghieri's opinion, the increased rear fuel tank size was a serious mistake, while the independent rear end would have been worth more extensive development and testing.

Right: the start of the 1956 GP of Germany at the Nürburgring, where the Collins and Fangio D50s lead, followed by Stirling Moss in a Maserati 250F and Castellotti in another D50.

than 130 octane and no longer the highly specialised mixtures that seemed to have made Maranello suffer, precisely the contrary to Maserati and Vanwall. So in 1957 the famous Dino V6 made its debut, the first version in F2 1500 cc form and then F1 2500 cc, an engine named after Enzo Ferrari's son, who died in June 1956 and who laid down its general lines. According to engineer Carlo Chiti, who was replaced by Andrea Fraschetti, later to die while testing, the attribution of the V6 seemed clear. He wrote, "The engine was conceived by Vittorio Jano in his Turin apartment, because he was unable to work officially for another constructor for four years after he left Lancia in 1955". So it was another masterpiece by the Piedmont technician, who was 66 years-old in 1957.

The new V6 for the last front engined Ferrari was certainly not short of horse power: the initial 1489 cc F2 version put out 180 hp at 9000 rpm, 280 hp at 8300 rpm as a 1958 2417 cc F1 unit and 290-295 hp during the 1959/60 season.

The single-seaters used in F2 and F1 between 1958 and 1960 were called the 156 and 246. They were extremely important cars in the Scuderia's history, as the team had not begun to design a new car from a blank sheet of paper since 1951/2. And that shows the technical but especially the financial difficulties that Enzo Ferrari had to face in his first decade. There is a photograph that perfectly illustrates all the anxiety and grit of the Commendatore in that

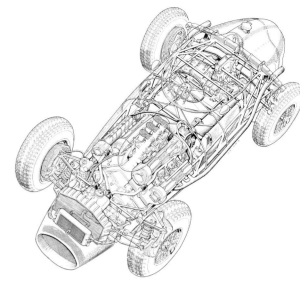

Peter Collins won the 1958 GP of Great Britain at Silverstone in the new Ferrari-Dino 246 (above left). Two weeks later, he competed in the GP of Germany in the same car (below, left) and was killed at the Pflanzgarten corner as he was trying to hold on to the Tony Brooks Vanwall. Luigi Musso died at Reims on 6 July: it was a terrible season that ended in world championship success for Mike Hawthorn (below) and Ferrari; but immediately afterwards the British driver retired from motor racing. Above: a cutaway of the Ferrari 246 and its V6 Dino engine, a traditional layout revised with modern ideas. Right, above: GP of Italy at Monza: Mike Hawthorn (Ferrari-Dino 246 no. 14) leads the Stuart Lewis-Evans Vanwall (30). Right, below: Hawthorn leaving the pits at the same event.

period: it was taken as he watched the 156 F2's first test from the San Venanzio corner above Maranello.

The 156 and the 246 were, naturally, front engined and rather conventional, designed when engineer Andrea Fraschetti ran the technical office and Alberto Massimino was a consultant, but the improvement in driveability was considerable. For the first time – apart from the 801 compromise – the trellis chassis was made of small diameter tubes, with a low centre of gravity and good mass distribution. The car's star feature was its weight, at least 100 kg less than previous Maranello single-seaters. With a weight of 560 kg and a power output of 280 hp, the 246 F1 was decidedly com-

petitive and the drivers especially appreciated its driving 'sincerity', which was notable for that level of a not very simple front engined open wheelers of the period.

The car still had drum brakes, even if perfected, because the Dunlop disc system was not brought in until Monza 1958. A delay for which Ferrari was accused of not wanting to accept technical progress at the time, yet he was close to making the important decision of using rear engines for his F1 cars. But there is an explanation for the brake situation: the Commendatore could not go with discs because he had a previously agreed commercial commitment to use drum brakes and he would have been forced to pay a penalty if he had not respected it.

He had signed a contract to use the optimum Alfin patent, which was based on the casting of an iron ring in the aluminium drum. After that came Ferrari's debut with disc brakes, the system having first been fitted to driver Peter Collins' personal 250 GT sports coupé in July 1958 at the driver's request by a British firm! But the arrival of two English technicians at Maranello to check the innovation before Monza suggested an expedient to get around a thorny problem. All went well and the system worked fine: Mike Hawthorn took second at Monza and went on to the season's end GP of Casablanca to win the world title and confirm the validity of the 246, even if Vanwall did win the constructors' championship.

The 246's Dino V6, which was now putting out 290/295 hp at 8500 rpm, made a good start to the 1959 season, although significant innovations had been brought in, like a rear end designed by Carlo Chiti with independent wheels at last, and the adoption of coil springs instead of the upper transverse semi-elliptic, but the 1959 car was still plagued by set-up problems compared to the much lighter British rear-engined single-seaters.
In 1960, the 246 reached full technical maturity and was said by the drivers to be the best front-engined car ever built – but a revolution was just around the corner.

With the 1959 season on the horizon, the Ferrari 246 Dino underwent long development sessions at Monza (above, being driven by tester Martino Severi) and the Modena track. The rear engine was still some way off and Ferrari was pushing hard to make its last front-engined single-seater competitive: new features included the adoption of the Tipo 2474 cc 256 V6 that put out 290 hp – instead of the Dino's 250 hp – with single overhead camshaft valve gear to improve torque, moving back the engine and lateral fuel tanks to improve weight distribution, bringing in independent rear suspension with coil springs and other initiatives. But it was a lost battle and the encirclement of the little Coopers at Monte Carlo in 1959 (right) seems to say it all: note Phil Hill in the Ferrari 246 (48) hemmed in by the Cooper T51-Climax of Stirling Moss and followed by its sister car driven by Bruce McLaren; and Tony Brooks' 246 (50) is being attacked by both Jo Bonnier in the BRM P25 (18) and Harry Schell (16).

Now, top among the sports racers
The lessons of Lampredi and Fraschetti

The 4-cylinder engine project for the 500 F2 was extremely important. With that brand new engine a new school of thought was opened up at Maranello at the end of 1951, until which time technology had been all about the V12. And it was a great new school for both Formula 1 and two-seater sports racers, although Ferrari was unable to re-emerge after the 1952/3 world championships. Sports cars were fundamental to the factory's financial success. Previously, Ferrari had shot to the top more or less right away due to the robust V12, which was powerful enough to reach a markedly higher cubic capacity than the initial 1496 cc. One of the many examples of that was Ferrari's complete domination of the Mille Miglia from 1948

until 1953 with identical or at least similar road cars. The combination of racing road cars was one of the pillars on which Ferrari had been built, so much so that Fiat boss Gianni Agnelli allowed himself to be tempted to buy a 166 MM Spider, which he used as a tourer even if it had no hood at all.

When the opposition became more of a threat – Jaguar, Maserati, Mercedes-Benz, Lancia, Aston Martin and also Porsche, at least on slow tracks – Ferrari went for the most obvious improvement: it increased cubic capacity to produce more power thanks to engineer Lampredi, who until 1950 had developed the "big" Formula 1 engines that were then used for sports car racing. That's how the 4102 cc,

4522 cc and lastly the 4954 cc V12s came about: engines that were really quite simple, because they had the traditional single overhead camshaft per cylinder bank, but generated a substantial power output of up to 340 hp by 1954. There was the weight handicap – the 375 MM weighed over 1,000 kg – that made them difficult to drive for both privateers and professionals on slower circuits. The big V12s were created for the classic races of the period, like the Mille Miglia, Carrera Panamericana, 24 Hours of Spa and the Le Mans, all of which had long straights.

To obviate the problem of these fascinating cars that were not easy to handle, the prolific Lampredi went to work again. Starting from

Previous page: scrutineering at the 1952 Mille Miglia in Piazza della Vittoria, Brescia. Ferrari had only been established five years, yet 26 Maranello sports racers were entered for the event by privateers and the works. The factory 250 S driven by future winners Bracco-Rolfo is number 611, the Taruffi-Vandelli 340 America 614. Page 51: Franco Cortese's Ferrari 500 Mondial at scrutineering for the 1954 Mille Miglia. Page 52: The Mille Miglia again, but this time the 1953 race: above, the man who won the 1950 Brescia-Rome-Brescia marathon wearing a double breasted suit, Giannino Marzotto, with Marco Crosara, trying to make their way through a packed Piazza della Vittoria in their 340 MM (547). Enzo Ferrari was also there, courtesy of the mechanic's badge on his lapel. Below, left: the 1953 1000 Km of the Nürburgring: Alberto Ascari in the winning 340 MM, which he shared with Giuseppe Farina. Page 53: above, the González-Trintignant 375 Plus before the start of the 1954 24 Hours of Le Mans, which they won. Below, Paolo Marzotto in a Mondial crossing the 1954 Mille Miglia finish line to take second place.

the 500 F2's 4-cylinder, the Tuscan technician created a series of engines to install in more modern sports cars, taking account of the period and the minimal weight. But the turnaround also happened due to a number of financial reasons: the Ferrari of the period was already famous, but its balance sheet was regularly in a precarious state, as well as strongly conditioned by two-seater sports car production in which Maranello did a considerable amount of business. These were cars much coveted by the private teams and were simple 2000 cc and 3000 cc 4-cylinders that had various advantages, among them economy of construction and racing. Riding on the coat tails of the works cars' success, in 1954/5 30

750 Monzas were sold, an impressive number if one considers Ferrari also built 58 and 61 road cars respectively during the same period. When choosing to go the 4-cylinder route, power also counted because the 'docile' V12s, with their block designed by Gioachino Colombo, had not been developed to make sports racers competitive with a cubic capacity of around three litres. As we shall see, there is no way one should talk of them being on their way out, but the mid-Fifties was the time of the 2999 cc 4-cylinder 750 Monza, later taken to 3431 cc, which generated 260 hp and 280 hp respectively. The unitary cubic capacity of the latter was really impressive at 857 cc per cylinder, its fuel consumption was lower than

the big V12s and its weight did not exceed 750 kg. So the professional drivers could get the best out of the car, which was not exactly docile! On the other hand, a 2-litre 500 Mondial was produced for gentlemen drivers and was more or less identical to the 500 F2, but with its power cut to 155 hp. The evolution of the car appeared in 1956 and that was the famous Testa Rossa – a name that became a Ferrari classic – and its horse power went up to 180 despite the fact that the car came out five years earlier as a single-seater that Ascari drove to two world championships.

Yet it is natural to think that Ferrari generally wasn't happy about two-seater sports racers being powered by 'his' V12. He was never se-

cretive about liking endurance races even more than F1 GPs, specifically because of the direct parentage between racing and road cars – and what an effort it was in 1974 to convince him to leave the sports racing sector and concentrate on his F1 commitment! Right from the start, it was clear that the technical coherence between the sports racing and road cars was at the basis of Ferrari's plans. That's why he was pleased when the International Federation limited the cubic capacity of the endurance cars due to compete in the 1958 World Sports Car Championship to 3000 cc. Apart from 1955, when the Mercedes-Benz beat the Ferraris by one single point, Ferrari dominated the championship from 1953 until 1957.

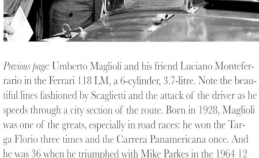

Previous page: Umberto Maglioli and his friend Luciano Monteferrario in the Ferrari 118 LM, a 6-cylinder, 3.7-litre. Note the beautiful lines fashioned by Scaglietti and the attack of the driver as he speeds through a city section of the route. Born in 1928, Maglioli was one of the greats, especially in road races: he won the Targa Florio three times and the Carrera Panamericana once. And he was 36 when he triumphed with Mike Parkes in the 1964 12 Hours of Sebring in a Ferrari 275 P.

Above: Maglioli next to his Ferrari 375 Plus, joking with a boy asking for his autograph before the start of the 1954 Mille Miglia.

Right: the 1957 Mille Miglia, with De Portago-Nelson easing their Ferrari 315 S down the starting ramp: not much more than 10 hours later, they would be the involuntary prime movers of the Guidizzolo accident in which the crew and 10 spectators died.

Below: among the Ferraris in procession is Eugenio Castellotti's 290 MM (548), in which he won the 1956 Mille Miglia. With Juan Manuel Fangio a month later, he came second in the 1000 Km of the Nürburgring. Above, right: practicing with the spare 860.

An enormous undertaking with a major impact on Formula 1, which partially due to the race dates, was not continued fully until after the 24 Hours of Le Mans in June. But the commercial reasons were indisputable because – and this shouldn't be forgotten – Ferrari started as a company to produce and sell racing cars. A commitment that only came to an end, at least at top level, many years later with the 1970/1 512 S.

From 1955, Ferrari had convinced himself that a sports coupé with a V12 engine of no more than 3-litres was the most logical future development of the Gioachino Colombo engine continued: the result was the famous 2953 cc V12 (bore and stroke 73x58.8 mm). To say the least, it was an engine that was eternal, robust, indestructible and powerful, its 1955 basic version putting out 240 hp and reaching 310 hp when it was installed in the GTO in 1962 and the 1963 250 Le Mans. It was an engine that gave personality and soul to Ferrari, the one that enabled it to expand its production of road cars to exceed 300 units a year by 1960. The term 3000-12-cylinder became popular, associated with both the road-going sports coupés and the racers that won the World Sport Car Championships.

The successes of 1958 and 1960 – in 1959 Stirling Moss won rather than Aston Martin – were scored by the 250 Testa Rossa, unveiled

in 1957 when Andrea Fraschetti, who joined Ferrari in 1955 after Lampredi left, was technical director. A traditional car, 22 Testa Rossas were sold to clients with its front engine but it was clear it was a modern design, taking weight distribution and chassis rigidity and its compactness into account. It was developed and tested on road and track by engineer Giotto Bizzarrini, who worked at Ferrari until the autumn of 1961.

Ferrari found its first modern turnaround with engineer Fraschetti. That became clear to me personally because in 1956, when I was still an engineering student, I spent a number of months at Ferrari in internship and it was Fraschetti who started me off on the study of

chassis rigidity. A concept that frightened me at first, because I knew nothing about it. But the Tuscan engineer was an extremely well-mannered and cultured gentleman, who was not only young but very clever: he reassured me and gave me the analysis of a tube-type chassis. It was a really new project, even if I personally only worked on a few details and did not have the overall view of things.

Fraschetti explained how important the study of a rigid chassis was to the exploitation of a car's power and roadholding. He added that in that period at Ferrari they chose the path of non-excessive rigidity, because they only built cars with front engines. With that architecture, the weight was mainly concentrated

Previous page, above: Brescia, 12 May 1957, 5.35 am: Piero Taruffi is about to start the last Mille Miglia in a formidable Ferrari 315 S. He is ready to be flagged off by his wife Isabella, on whose right is the Mayor of Brescia Bruno Boni . Below, right: in the early afternoon, Isabella was able to congratulate her husband after his sensational performance. Her look of affection mixed with tension reflects the hope that Piero will keep his word and retire from racing now that he has won. At 52 years-old and after an extraordinary, eclectic career, Taruffi did as his wife wanted.

This page, right: a fascinating cut-away of the 1957 two-seater 8-series, the most evolved Ferrari sports racer of the period. It was the only car with twin overhead camshafts per V12 cylinder bank, with a cubic capacity of 3490 cc, 3783 cc (315 S) and 4023 cc and a power output ranging from 330 hp to 390 hp. In 1955, Ferrari also installed a V6 in-line engine in its sports cars, a layout that was unique for the cars from Maranello of which the Commendatore was not at all fond. It was done by adding two more cylinders to the type 625 4-cylinder unit, so that the bore and stroke stayed at 94x90 mm. The 118 LM was installed in the 376 S (3747 cc) but the 121 LM was used for the 446 S (4412 cc, 330 hp). Driven by Eugenio Castellotti, the 446 S set the lap record at the 1955 24 Hours of Le Mans at 291 kph, 10 kph faster than its rival Jaguar. Below: the Musso-Gendebien Ferrari 250 Testa Rossa winning the 1958 Targa Florio. The car had a chassis similar to that of the S-series, but was powered by the simpler 2953 cc V12 with only one overhead camshaft per cylinder bank.

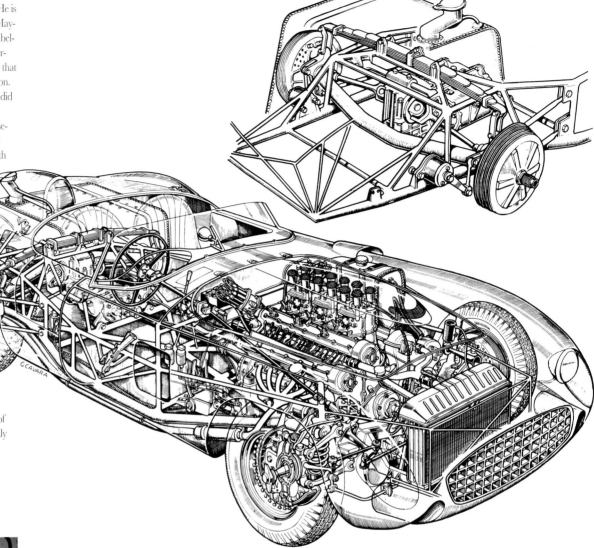

on the front axle, while under acceleration part of the load was transferred to the rear and the problem tended to cancel itself out, also contributing to driveability. Naturally with a limit, because a rigid chassis would also have been preferable in the Fifties. But we must emphasise that it was only with the subsequent front-mid engined cars of the Sixties that designers were able to go for absolute rigidity.

Regardless, Fraschetti had worked out that Ferraris had limits as far as their chassis were concerned and his contribution was extremely important. He was a wind of change, especially in the technical office. He had a more modern way of reasoning compared to the set Maranello process, where no tests were planned per degrees in succession – quite honestly, also due to the shortcomings of financial availability – multiplying the results to try to arrive at realistic conclusions.

Fraschetti was a man with a strong personality and was part of that generation of engineers who also tested the cars on both the road and track. Unfortunately, he overturned an F2 single-seater he had designed himself when cornering at the Modena Autodrome on 29 August 1957 and was killed.

1960-1969

The Forghieri era begins
From his debut in Formula 1 to his first world championship

It was probably written that I was to work at Ferrari: but it was not so clear that I was to stay there 27 years.

My father worked at Ferrari from the Thirties. The Commendatore knew him and, in particular, was a friend of my aunt. Modena was a small town where everybody knew everyone else. Even before the Second World War, the future constructor was a well-known personality in the town and they called him *"Al matt Ferrari"* (mad Ferrari) in a friendly way.

And when Modena entered the world of motor racing – the Mille Miglia, the local Autodrome – I went to see them with my father, so Ferrari began to get to know me and ask me a few questions, especially when I started to study en-

gineering at Bologna after graduating from the Alessandro Tassoni High School of Science. I think he asked me things to please my father more than anything else. My answers were invariably about aircraft engines, which were my passion. Then in 1957, half-way through my university studies, I was taken on by Ferrari for a period as an intern, or 'stage' in Italian. I was given a table in the factory's library, where there was also the 'museum of horrors' (mechanical components that broke during races, Ed). Engineer Andrea Fraschetti kept an eye on me and taught me calculus relative to the construction of tubed chassis. This concerned a real project, not just a study that was an end in itself. But I only worked on a few details and did not have

a general overview of the project: and I never knew for which car the work was being done. I carried out an enormous number of calculi to see whether or not the rigidity was right.

Once in a while Ferrari came into the library, either with Fraschetti or on his own. He looked at what I was doing and we would exchange a few words. "What are you doing", he would ask. "I'm checking this ..." and I would explain a few details. "Are they really useful?", he would ask. "Commendatore", I would reply, "these are very important studies, please believe me: they concern avant garde theories which affirm...". He did not reply, but seemed to try and understand what kind of person I was and my remarks stayed with him, so much so that a couple of

years later he made some enquiries about me. *"Ma to' fiol al s'e laureè"* (Has your son graduated yet?)", Enzo Ferrari asked my father in Modenese dialect, the 'official' language of the factory: but the conversation went no further at the time.

I graduated from university in February 1959 with a thesis on 'A medium car for the European market', a project for which I was inspired by the Panhard Dyna 850, which I thought was very modern. In the meantime, I taught in a school for technical experts in Reggio Emilia, as I wanted to move to the United States to pursue my dream of working on turbo-jet engines. They were delightful, unforgettable days at Reggio; the students wanted to learn, they reacted, I

had an excellent rapport with them and we lived in a fantastic period for all of Italy. I didn't earn much, but at least my father didn't have to maintain me anymore.

Towards the end of 1959, Enzo Ferrari returned to the subject: *"Ma to fiol c'sa fall?"* (What's your son doing?) he asked my father. *"L'aspeta d'andèr in America per i motor di aeroplan"* (He's waiting to go to America to work on aircraft engines) he replied. *"Ma degh bein cal vegn da mi, clè mei cal perda brisa dal temp, almein al farà esperienza"* (Tell him to come and see me. It's better not to waste time; at least he'll gain experience).

Obviously, I went to Maranello right away, if for no other reason than to thank him, but the Com-

Previous page: the width of the Monza track enabled the drivers on the front row of the grid to attack immediately. Here, it is 4 September 1966 and Ferrari entered the updated 312s with a 3-valve per cylinder engine: the fastest to get away was Ludovico Scarfiotti (6) followed by Lorenzo Bandini (2) and Mike Parkes (4), with Jim Clark's Lotus-BRM on the extreme left. Scarfiotti won ahead of Parkes in a real Ferrari-fest. Page 60 The 1961 GP of Belgium was dominated by the new Ferrari 156; at first, Olivier Gendebien did well, followed by Phil Hill, Wolfgang von Trips and Richie Ginther. But Hill eventually won at an average of over 206 kph, just seven tenths of a second ahead of von Trips. Pag. 61 Enzo Ferrari in the Monza pits talking to Romolo Tavoni (behind the pit wall), with Eugenio Dragoni and some distance away and a young engineer named Mauro Forghieri.

Above: GP of Italy, 4 September 1960, Wolfgang von Trips on one of Monza's banked curves in the rear engined Ferrari 156 F2. This was the famous race in which the British teams did not compete because the event was held on the full 10 km circuit — the road section plus the high speed ring — which they considered dangerous for their light, rear engined cars. The race was won by Phil Hill in a traditional Ferrari 246, the Scuderia's only championship victory that year and the last in F1 by a front engined Maranello car.

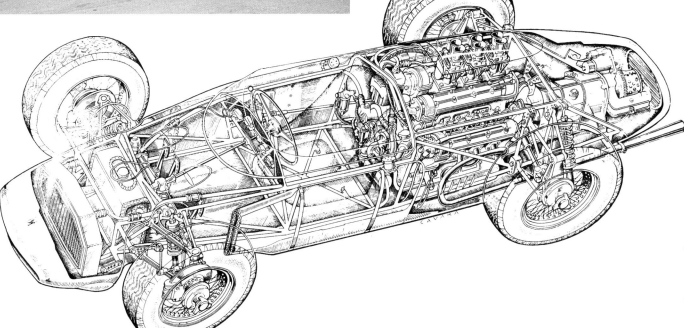

GP of Monaco, 29 May 1960: the Ferrari 246 P, the Scuderia's first rear engined car, made its debut driven by Richie Ginther and is shown here with a front engined 246. Also making his first appearance in the Ferrari pits was a 25 year-old engineer named Mauro Forghieri, even if just as an observer.

Below: a cutaway of the 246 P, which first took to the track at Modena one Sunday evening (22 May), four days after which practice for the GP of Monaco was to be held. Against engineer Carlo Chiti's advice, Enzo Ferrari decided the car would compete at Monte Carlo and it put up the same time as the tried and tested front engined 246 with a lap of 1 minute 38.6 seconds. Pole position went to Stirling Moss in a Lotus 18 with 1 minute 36.3 seconds.

mendatore became a decisive influence on my future. 'What do you want to go to American for?" he asked. "It's clear you like cars, given the subject of your thesis, and here you have a modern factory where you can start right away. When he was alive, Fraschetti spoke very well of you. Everyone says you are a positive sort of lad and that you graduated very well. Come and work with us and begin to gain experience, at least while you wait to be asked to go to America".

And that is how I joined Ferrari in January 1960, even if as an external employee for the first two months. Ten days after that, Gian Paolo Dallara, another new graduate, arrived from Parma. He soon became my friend and someone

I still see with great pleasure, even though we worked in totally different sectors of Ferrari and I didn't see him very often. He joined the technical office, which was then under Carlo Chiti, and he worked on gearboxes, chassis and suspensions. I was also responsible to Chiti, but I was told to do engine calculus and worked mainly with technicians Rocchi and Bellei. I also looked after the test room engines, together with the head of the department Taddei, so I was close to Cavalier Luigi Bazzi, who had always worked for Ferrari, first as a mechanic and then as chief technician. He was a very practical person who loved his work and was able to solve a huge range of problems. We shared the same desk in a triangular shaped office that measured just

3x2 metres where we were often visited by Vittorio Jano, the celebrated technician who Ferrari brought from Fiat to Alfa Romeo in the Twenties. Jano was a special consultant to the Commendatore and Bazzi's friend, but Chiti didn't like him because he was given the right to poke his nose into any project. And frankly, I don't blame Chiti in the least.

Anyway, it was an important period because Bazzi passed on much of his wide technical experience to me. But under no circumstances could either Dallara or I express our opinions on technical decisions. Chiti, a cultured man, refused to delegate and wouldn't make room for anyone. That irritated me a great deal, but it was a fundamental lesson, because I have a

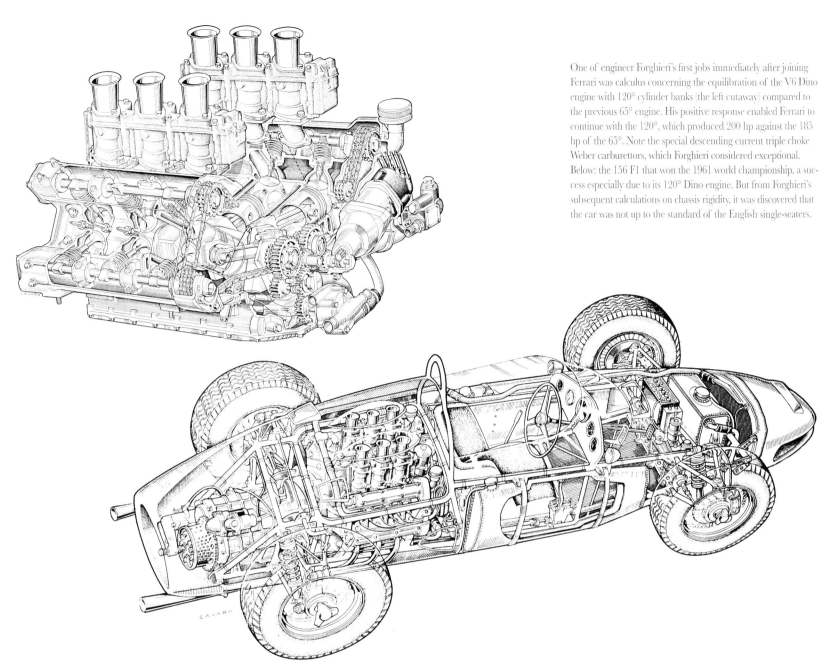

One of engineer Forghieri's first jobs immediately after joining Ferrari was calculus concerning the equilibration of the V6 Dino engine with 120° cylinder banks (the left cutaway) compared to the previous 65° engine. His positive response enabled Ferrari to continue with the 120°, which produced 200 hp against the 185 hp of the 65°. Note the special descending current triple choke Weber carburettors, which Forghieri considered exceptional. Below: the 156 F1 that won the 1961 world championship, a success especially due to its 120° Dino engine. But from Forghieri's subsequent calculations on chassis rigidity, it was discovered that the car was not up to the standard of the English single-seaters.

similar character trait, but I learnt to use collaborators, trying to make them feel responsible and putting them right when they made a mistake. That's the only way a company can function. But engineer Chiti did allow me to collaborate on one futuristic but strange idea nothing to do with racing: it was a gas turbine exhaust to recover some of the power an engine loses. But, faced with the necessity of financing the project, the Commendatore stopped it.

I began to understand that Ferrari was a consolidated but small entity and the money available for new projects was markedly less than outsiders believed. For that reason, the Scuderia was able to invest very little in research: there was no analysis of chassis rigidity, although the

engines were robust but heavy, with almost total cooling, including the cylinder sleeves: technology that was decades old. So there was an immense but useless quantity of water in circulation and enormous radiators. Obsolete, but the financial situation made updating the cars difficult. Later, I realised that Ferrari's ambitions were greater than the facilities available to him, a situation compensated for by the factory, its employees and their extraordinary wealth of experience.

Ferrari won the 1960 World Sports Car Championship and the following year it did so again, as well as winning the Formula 1 world title. Rear engines arrived at Maranello fast and furiously after the 'lesson' of the Coopers and a

lot of technical decisions seemed to me to be outdated. So much so that in the discussions that took place between us young engineers, we allowed ourselves to cast doubt on what we were supposed to do: Dallara on the question of chassis and me on engines. It was not presumption on our part, but the result of the universities we attended having shaped our critical minds. However, we couldn't even mention those doubts to Chiti and after a bit we found it hard to tolerate the situation. That's why Gian Paolo Dallara joined Maserati after little more than a year at Maranello. After that, he moved on to the newborn Lamborghini and established his own racing car factory about 10 years later, which would go on to enjoy such incredible

success. I was also very close to leaving Ferrari. I had received an offer from Lancia, but I was dissuaded from doing so by the practical lessons I was constantly being given by technicians Luigi Bazzi and Vittorio Jano. They may not have completed their studies, but they possessed an enormous amount of experience and information after about 40 years and one on which I could openly draw.

To increase my experience, I was sent to races together with the motor sport director of the day Romolo Tavoni, a fine man. They were long journeys by car, perhaps five of us squeezed into a Fiat 1100. I made my debut at the 1960 GP of Monaco, where the Dino 246 P, the first rear-engined Ferrari, competed. I had no specific task,

except to look and learn. That race meant Ferrari's definitive abandonment of front-engined F1 cars, a difficult decision and one I experienced from a long way off, because it was taken before I joined the company. As always, different schools of thought were for and against and it's true that the Commendatore initially supported the latter. "I have never seen a couple of oxen push a cart, but pull it, yes...". This famous remark of his has become part of motor sport history, but to give weight to his comment he recalled that in the Thirties the celebrated Auto Union GP car with its engine at the rear could only be driven flat out by aces of the calibre of Tazio Nuvolari and Bernd Rosemeyer because it fishtailed violently under acceleration.

1962 GP of Monaco: reigning world champion Phil Hill took second place 1 and 3/10ths seconds behind winner Bruce McLaren's Cooper-Climax. The Ferrari 156 had changed little from 196, except that the rear track was slightly wider, so the difference between the chassis of the new British single-seaters and the Ferraris was evident. Among the 156's problems was its kerb weight of 490 kg, about 40 kg more that the best of the opposition. But the technical office run by engineer Forghieri was able to take a 156 with a revised chassis to the GP of Germany, its weight reduced to 455 kg. For Phil Hill, the Monaco podium position was the best performance in a season that was marred by a series of metal worker strikes in Italy, with consequent difficulties in preparing the cars and missing the GP of France.

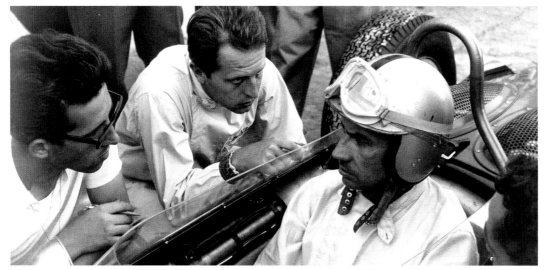

Left, top: Monza, 10 September 1961, Grand Prix of Italy, the Ferrari 156s of Richie Ginther, Phil Hill, Ricardo Rodriguez and Wolfgang von Trips pulling away from the parabolica on the first lap. A lap later at the same spot, Jim Clark's Lotus crashed into the back of von Trips' Ferrari; the German's car flew off the track and killed 14 spectators as well as the driver.

Left, below: 1962 Italian GP at Monza, driver and tester Willy Mairesse talking to engineer Forghieri and Giancarlo Baghetti. The Belgian is sitting in the cockpit of a much modified 156 that could be recognised by its oval front air intake in place of its previous double inlets, its general weight reduction, its lower, more relaxed driving position and its chassis, some parts of which were in small diameter tubes but with a reinforced trellis front and back to make it more rigid. Other modifications were made to the suspension, especially the stabiliser bar mounts and spring-damper group, which was moved more inwards. It was only towards the end of the race that Mairesse lost third place, taken by Bruce McLaren with just four tenths of a second between the two of them.

Below: a cartoon by Marino (alias Marino Guarguaglini) from the Guerin Sportivo. The caption reads, "NUVOLARI" Don't you worry, brother, they're all leaving but their brains are staying behind". It jokingly reflected the situation at Ferrari after eight of the company's executives had been fired on Thursday 26 October 1961. They were engineers Carlo Chiti and Giotto Bizzarrini, who were respectively the technical director and head of GT car development, the motor sport director Romolo Tavoni, Fausto Galassi, who was in charge of the foundry, Ermanno Della Casa, administration director who later returned, Federico Giberti, director of supplies who had been with Ferrari since 1934, Enzo Selmi, director of personnel and Girolamo Gardini, commercial director who rejoined soon afterwards. The sackings were the result of a registered letter sent to Ferrari by all of them in which they complained about the interference – even at the race circuits – of the Commendatore's wife Laura. Later, ex-motor sport director Tavoni explained, "Ferrari knew the facts, but believed it was the place of us executives to react in an appropriate manner. From his point of view he was right, because an executive cannot go to the boss and complain: he must take care of the situation himself. We showed immaturity and, therefore, there was no more trust". Ferrari allowed the weekend to pass and then on Monday 30 October he called Mauro Forghieri and made him responsible for all motor racing and testing.

Even if the Commendatore wasn't a technician, he understood perfectly well that there was no turning away from the lesson of the Coopers. He only tried to put the decision back for fear that a successful rear-engined Ferrari could negatively influence the sale of his road cars, which were all front-engined. Then engineer Chiti, supported by his colleague Bizzarrini, put his foot down and stopped any further discussion on the subject.

In 1961 I went back to the Monaco GP, where I admired Stirling Moss's 'driving lesson' as a result of which he won in a Lotus that was much less powerful than the Ferraris; then I went to the GP of France at Reims, which was won by debutante Giancarlo Baghetti, and at Monza in September, when Phil Hill won the drivers' world championship. A double victory deeply scarred by that awful accident in which von Trips, another one of our drivers, and 14 spectators lost their lives. It was a terrible day.

I was fascinated by the technical challenge of motor racing, but due to the difficulty of trying to dialogue with Carlo Chiti I really wanted to change jobs. I had good relations with him, in fact I respected him as a technician; he himself sent an extremely positive internal note about me to Enzo Ferrari after my first year with the firm. But the confines of my job were too limited. My salary of 60,000 lire a month, working on Saturdays, Sundays, Christmas Eve and many other public holidays, also spurred me on to wanting a change despite opposition from my father, who advised me to be patient.

L'otto senza timoniere

Ferrari

NUVOLARI — Non ti preoccupare, fratello, vanno via tutti, ma il cervello rimane!

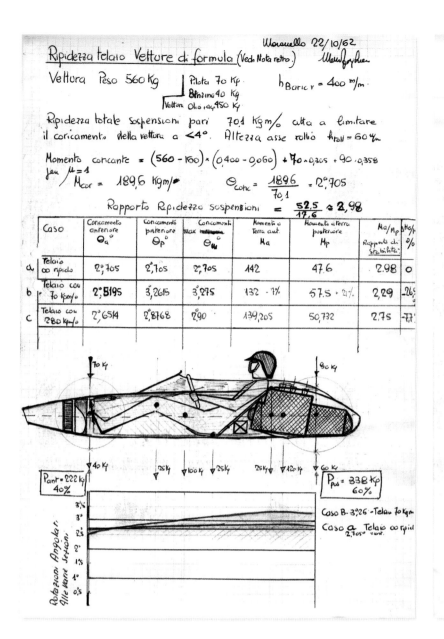

This hand-written document by Mauro Forghieri is dated 22 October 1962. It is the result of an analysis he carried out on the 156 F1 car's chassis, the car in which Ferrari and Phil Hill won the 1961 world championships, and was part modified in August of that year. The engineer wanted to understand the car's limit when cornering with more or less rigidity of the chassis and suspension. To obtain his results, he used not only technical analyses but also question and answer sessions with the drivers, among whom Willy Mairesse made a significant contribution.

It was a personal study, used together with other similar initiatives to design the chassis of the 1963 cars. The notes also deal with the car's set-up.

Then, on 30 October 1961 – it was a Monday – my life was turned around completely. Ferrari called me and got straight to the point. He said, "From this moment on you are responsible for all the motor sport activity and testing". A statement that invited no reply. I was amazed, agog, but I was able to maintain a certain lucidity and explained that I was only 26 years-old and had no experience of that kind. Later, I was to learn that when Ferrari had taken a decision it was impossible to change his mind. He just added, "You must simply do your job; you have to be the technician. Do your job and I'll do the rest".

The decision was the result of firing engineer Chiti and the other seven executives, among them Giotto Bizzarrini: it was an earth-shaking deci-sion that gutted the technical office, but I knew very little about the situation. People talked of the group's complaints about Signora Laura, Ferrari's wife, who often accompanied the team to races at the time, while her husband was notorious for maybe appearing at Monza for Grand Prix testing. One knew that the complaints – itemised in an official letter to Ferrari – were caused by the lady's interference with the racing team: true or exaggerated? In my position as a junior, there was no way I could have known; but I have to say that Signora Laura, who I got to know during my earliest trips with the team, was always very kind to me. It was an attitude that never changed, not even afterwards when she continued to accompany us to the races beyond the mid-Sixties,

Lorenzo Bandini became involved with Ferrari progressively during the 1962 season, and later, due to his outstanding abilities as a technician and test driver, he would take the place of Giancarlo Baghetti. Left: Bandini next to a 'traditional' 156, which he drove in the GP of Italy at Monza. During the summer, he contributed to the development of the car's Forghieri-modified chassis. He then drove the car in the GP of Germany at the Nürburgring, but was involved in a minor accident. Above: the standard 156s driven at Monza by Baghetti (2) and Phil Hill (10).

although with a much more substantial presence imposed by the Commendatore.

I had not overstated the case in playing down my experience at Ferrari: for many months. I was mainly occupied with calculations for the new F1 V6 1500 cc in both the 65° cylinder bank and the subsequent 120° versions, which were for the 156s that won the 1961 world championships. But I made my mark, because I concluded that the 65° engine was as equilibrated as the 120°, even if in a different way: so the initial doubts were overcome and the cars could be built. Anyway, none of the juniors had carried out these calculations and Gian Paolo Dallara was highly competent in doing others for the gearbox and suspension – especially the roll centres, which were something new at the

time – but he was not yet up to doing so for engines. On the other hand, I was lucky enough to study under Professor Morandi at the University of Bologna and he demanded a perfect knowledge of calculus on the equilibration of engines. Importantly, Dallara and I tried to integrate our knowledge, studying outside work. In the evenings after dinner, I read technical magazines and various other publications, mainly those of the Turin and Milan polytechnics, but I was looking for articles of the foreign origin because there was not much of that sort of thing in Italy. That's how I pushed myself into solving problems that I had not come across before. Fortunately, the university offered a wide range of cultures at the time, but we were not specialists like the Americans and in some cases the

Germans. We started with a human development culture, which gave us an excellent basis. The only work I did completely on my own at the time at Ferrari was to update the test room engines: an extremely noisy workshop that was open to the outside with exhaust pipes in view and close to my tiny office; it was so noisy that I had to work with cotton wool in my ears! The work concerned the cooling and correction of data provided by the test benches: technically irreproachable but modest work. I noticed it was normal procedure to round off the tables on engine power as well as possible and deliver them to Ferrari to avoid his explosive reactions. Habits that amazed me and that I immediately stopped, together with engineer Bussi when he became the head.

Test room boss Taddei was a friend of my family and apparently he had also talked to Ferrari about my work. But later he understood that I had passed my test with Vittorio Jano and Luigi Bazzi from whom I had learnt a great deal about racing cars, at least from the practical point of view. They in turn were impressed with my avant garde ideas and they understood that I reasoned in a different way to the Ferrari tradition and that I had a great desire to become deeply involved. They told the Commendatore that was the case and then he began to have some small technical discussions with me. All in an apparently casual, perhaps standing around outside the office. Later, I realised that he wanted to test me with those talks, to understand how I reasoned.

But involuntarily, even Ferrari was a little more open with me from the technical point of view: I started to get to know him and realised he wasn't really that interested in the chassis of the car and understood little about it. But he was passionate about engines, and when he became a constructor he surprised people with his accurate instinctive intuitions. There is no doubt that, when those dramatic sackings took place, Ferrari's appointment of me was certainly avant garde, but it was also somewhat unavoidable: Dallara had gone and I was the only one left who could take on the job.

So I began to take day to day charge of the technical office, where everyone knew me. More than anything else I sought general collaboration, initially just giving advice and remembering that I had before me technicians of experience who were extremely good at their work. Ferrari's particular strength was in the 'central sector', where I came in, starting to operate by grades and with a bit of sensitivity. Perhaps I didn't have much, but I knew how to use what I had.

From the technical point of view, the sports racing car sector didn't worry me much, but I wasn't sure about the F1 156. The 1961 victories came from the greater power output of the V6 engine compared to the 4-cylinders of the British cars. Yet many at Maranello, starting with Enzo Ferrari, were certain we would still be competitive in 1962. Judging by the British teams' projects I didn't think that would be possible. I couldn't

Spring 1962: the move to Great Britain

In the spring of 1962, I had to convince Enzo Ferrari at all costs to change the technical direction of Maranello, especially as far as the single seater chassis was concerned. It was no easy matter, because I was still inexpert, so I wasn't very credible. But I was helped by the agreement that Ferrari had personally negotiated with Stirling Moss for the 1962 season: the great English driver was to drive a Ferrari entered by a private team. That was a major success for the Commendatore, who had to cope with the departure of seven of his executives from the racing department.

The debut was fixed for 12 May at the International Trophy race, which was not a round in the World Sports Car Championship but all the top line British teams would be there. The Moss agreement was to have been secret, but Ferrari was especially proud of it and he let a few details slip. That was a typical attitude of his on such occasions.

Ferrari had an enormous respect for Moss and the Briton, for his part, had decided to forget that he was left without a promised Ferrari for the 1952 Grand Prix of Bari after travelling all the way from London to southern Italy to drive the car. Maranello had decided to assign the third 500 F2 it had entered for that GP to Piero Taruffi, not Moss.

It was all part of one of the many astute moves by Enzo Ferrari: not only would he use the greatest driver of the moment, he would have a precise answer to just how competitive the car was from someone without any interest in the Scuderia at all. Obviously, the new motor sport director, Eugenio Dragoni, knew about the arrangement and I asked him to support me in transforming the initiative into an accelerated course in the world of the British constructors. It was useless to deny it: the school on the other side of the English Channel was producing cars based on a wealth of new technical ideas and constructional methods. Moss was the driver of Rob Walker's team, which was to have run the 156 on its debut, and his father Alfred was the boss of UDT-Laystall. Both ran Lotus 21s and 24s, which attracted my technical curiosity but, entering into their world, I would have the chance of studying the Britons' whole range of their cars.

With Dragoni's backing, I was able to convince Ferrari to transform the trip into a study of the British technical world, their methods of work and their mentality. Vittorio Jano, the great technician and an extremely positive man, came with me as di Franco Rocchi and Walter Salvarani, respectively specialists in engine design and transmission, people who would be fundamental to my entire period at Ferrari. Unlike Jano, I also had the advantage of not being known in the GP world, so no way was I obstructed as I photographed the more interesting details of their cars.

We left Maranello a few days early and were like a group of students who had to learn.

Unfortunately, we knew that Stirling would never have driven a Ferrari in F1: on 23 April, he and his Lotus 24 were involved in a terrible accident at Goodwood and that signalled the end of his career. But there was still the contract with UDT, which fielded a second driver, Innes Ireland, who was no ace but he was courageous and fast. He was also very pleasant and fun to be with, so much so that we worked together a lot. In line with Ferrari's instructions, once again the 156 remained untouched by the regulations of the Chiti period. Ireland finished fourth but a lap down on winner Graham Hill and he pulled no punches when he gave us his opinion of the car, which he compared to the Lotus and Cooper, both of which he knew well. Only the gearbox was considered 'exceptional' by the Scot, while he believed the engine was potent but the torque was too high and forced the use of gears that were too low. He thought the chassis was just about OK, but that the car's capabilities were generally 'substantially inferior to the opposition'.

All of which was confirmation that we had to really get moving and sort the car. When we returned to Maranello, we took these problems to Ferrari, backed by Vittorio Jano. It didn't take a lot to convince the Commendatore, but I am certain he had also just received a 'private report' from Colonel Ronnie Hoare, Ferrari's concessionaire in Britain and a good friend of Ireland's. During our visit to the UK, we discovered a way of working that was completely different from our own and I realised there was a lot to learn from the British methods. All the teams (BRM, Lotus, Cooper, Brabham and Lola, Ed) had new cars and equally new V8 Coventry Climax or BRM engines, both developed with the support of the British motor industry.

The meeting with Tony Robinson, technical director of UDT, was extremely important. He was working on the new BRP which, with its BRM engine, would have raced in 1963. And not only that, Robinson also collaborated with Tim Parnell, the owner of Team Bowmaker, who raced Lotus-Climaxes and had John Surtees as his number one driver. But at that time, Parnell built the Lotus 24 under licence (it was Jim Clarke's official car, Ed) and I had the opportunity of visiting the workshop and seeing all the different cars under construction. My travelling companions also told Maranello about the technical level of the English, so it was easier to open up a new direction for Ferrari. The trip was an important experience, at least for the near future, even if I knew that in the technical world nothing is ever definitive and that I would have to make it on my own.

count on the help of the drivers, because Giancarlo Baghetti was relatively inexperienced in F1 and Phil Hill, despite being pleasant in human terms, was no different from all his colleagues: he would never admit that they won the previous year due to the engine.

In reality, the chassis, suspension and rigidity were all our weak points. But that was no surprise: in Italy there was no school at all for that sector. It was the advent of the rear engine that created a large number of new problems, because front engined cars were far less demanding on the roadholding front. I didn't know much, but partly due to my university studies and partly because of the lessons I was given by engineer Fraschetti when I was an intern, I – together with

my colleague Gian Paolo Dallara – knew that the 156's chassis would not deliver the necessary rigidity. And during the winter, I knuckled down to study of those weak points and I realised that, among the various problems, the chassis twisted more than the stabiliser bar and, therefore, it was unable to transfer the rear end torque to the front, causing a driving crisis.

The situation was complicated by Willy Mairesse winning the GP of Brussels on 1 April, not an F1 World Championship race but one at which I made my debut as technical head of the Scuderia. Before we left, Ferrari threatened, "Don't even think about touching the chassis adjustments, because you don't change a car that wins. And don't forget that the person who selected you is

May 1963: John Surtees test drives the 156 'Aero' at Monza. The car was completely revised from the 2962 cc version. With the Briton is Mauro Forghieri, who seemed indifferent to the rain, as were the Maranello mechanics, among whom are Giulio Borsari and Ener Vecchi. During the first test, Surtees got down to 1 minute 40.3 seconds, the time with which Jim Clark took pole position at the 1962 Italian GP in the famous Lotus 25. But in another test immediately afterwards, Willy Mairesse went below that at 1 minute 38.4 seconds. The new 156 also had light alloy rims instead of the spoked variety even though the hub nut had been retained. Apart from being lighter, the alloy rims obviated the previous limited rigidity and problems with transverse vortices of air, which contributed to reducing speed. Previous page: Enzo Ferrari, Franco Rocchi and engineer Giancarlo Bussi at Monza.

more expert than you are…" I don't remember whether or not I obeyed completely, but I don't think so. Anyway, the new driver/tester Mairesse won with the new car ahead of the English, beating Stirling Moss in particular and he was driving a Lotus 21 with the debutante Climax V8. They were beaming at Maranello, while I forced myself to explain – but it was difficult – that we won for a series of circumstances, not least of all the courage of Mairesse on a really dangerous road circuit. A few days later, I found out that Ferrari was expecting the definitive opinion of Stirling Moss on that car as part of the secret programme and to which I refer elsewhere in the book. A programme which, fortunately, coincided with my desire to change many things.

During the same period, the Scuderia was being subjected to a positive transformation of its organisation by the new motor sport director, Eugenio Dragoni, a man I was very much bound up and who supported me on various occasions. Dragoni, a middle aged Milanese who was a cosmetics industrialist, was a great enthusiast of Scuderia Sant'Ambroeus, of which he was the secretary, heart and soul and had achieved important results with private drivers. It was he who gave the most modern turnaround to our organisation which, until 1964, went ahead with just one department, with racing and road cars together. An illogical situation justified by financial savings and suited only to Ferrari at the beginning. To shine again in F1, Ferrari not only needed

It had to be the transition car until the new 156 V6 and 158 V8 were ready, both of them with monocoque chassis, yet the 156 Aero driven by John Surtees, shown above at the Karusell, scored right away by winning the GP of Germany at the Nürburgring after a close fought battle with Jim Clark. That same season, Surtees set the fastest lap time at Monaco and Silverstone. Opposite page: a spring test at Monza with the same car: with Forghieri (back to camera) are John Surtees and Mike Parkes, who were testing the 250 P on which Giulio Borsari is working. In the absence of official Ferrari data – apart from the general 156 and 158 designations – the exact definition of the Ferrari F1 car of the 1963/5 period was the subject of confusion, so much so that often the monocoque was called Aero, a term which was official and suggested by the mechanics, but it was only for the 156 with a direct injection V6 engine and a tubed chassis with a 'skin' of riveted aluminium, that competed during 1963. From the GP of Italy that same year, the 156 designation was also attributed to the real monocoque (it had the same engine as the Aero), which became the 158 once it was equipped with the 8-cylinder. A flat 12 was also installed in the monocoque chassis and that spawned the 512, often called the 1512 outside Ferrari, probably to distinguish it from the 1970/1 sports racer of the same designation.

a modern chassis, it had to update the Dino V6 engine and put its money on the new 8-cylinder. And it had to move on from traditional carburettors to fuel injection, a system unknown to Maranello and already in widespread use among the opposition.

Partly as a result of Michael May's technical advice, we chose direct fuel injection for which a specific pump was needed and the choice was limited. We were using a Bosch unit designed years earlier for the Mercedes-Benz SL coupé, when the president of the German company, Herr Goesche, wrote to Ferrari saying that the system and the pump were covered by a patent. It was a difficult moment, because Ferrari would never have agreed to pay to use it. If we had given in

I would have been in a lot of trouble, so I suggested Ferrari should send an ambassador to the president and say that the pump would only be used in F1 and not on production cars. I must have been convincing, because Ferrari chose me as the ambassador and I did well, boosting my reputation with the Commendatore.

Injected engines were essential if we were to win in F1. At that time, the championship was for the 'small' 1500 cc cars and just a few horsepower more – from 200 to 210 hp, Ed – or a better generation of power made an enormous difference. The V8 Climax used by many of the British teams, had indirect injection, like BRM. We were frighteningly ignorant of the matter, and we even started with the most complicated type of

Above: a spectacular picture taken at Monza in 1963 by Franco Varisco during testing of a 156 V6 Aero by John Surtees. This excellent photograph reminds us that pictures of this kind were also shot at the request of Mauro Forghieri, who tried to extract some extra data from them about the performance of the car when cornering, especially about the suspension components. The 1.5-litre V6 120° engine of the Aero generated 205 hp at 10,500 rpm with Bosch direct fuel injection, at the time the real jewel in the crown of Ferrari. Working on the development of the Scuderia's engines, Forghieri spent time at Shell's research centre in Chester, not far from Liverpool, England. "One lived in a decidedly spartan way", recalled the engineer, "but the colleagues of that centre had a great deal of experience of direct fuel injection development, especially the aeronautical sector. It was an extremely positive period that was fundamental to the subsequent work carried out together with engineer Michael May on the first Ferrari injection engines".

The eve of the 1963 Grand Prix of Italy: under the direction of Mauro Forghieri, work is going ahead on the 156 V6/63 Aero to be driven by Lorenzo Bandini (2) and the new 156 V6 monocoque for John Surtees. Among the interested o onlookers is the bearded Denis Jenkinson, correspondent of the monthly Motor Sport. The two cars had the direct injection V6 engine in common, but the monocoque, which was conceived 'around' the new 8-cylinder engine for 1964, had an aeronautically inspired chassis. It had a transverse hoop in sheet steel and double lateral covering in aluminium, in this case riveted and empty inside. Rubber fuel tanks had been envisaged on both sides of the car for that space, conceived in line with safety criteria. Four reduced diameter tubes were also placed inside – two on the right and another two on the left, which made everything more rigid but their task was to direct the cooling liquid and oil from the engine to the front radiator. Surtees took pole position with this car with a time of 1 minute 37.3 seconds, beating Graham Hill's BRM by 1.2 seconds, but John was forced to retire on the 17th lap with an engine problem.

direct injection in which the nebulised petrol was squirted directly into the combustion chamber with advantages in both combustion and fuel consumption: from the Nineties the technique went into general use on road cars. We used injection to improve the power and torque of the V6 with cylinder banks at 120°: output went from 190 hp at 9500 rpm to 205 hp at 10,500 rpm. We did the same for the V8, which was sketched out by Bellei in early 1963 and which he then developed together with Vittorio Jano, who had helped me so much as always.

A Swiss born in Stuttgart in 1934, engineer Michael May was an expert consultant in setting up the injection and was enticed to Maranello in a joint operation by Ferrari and Dragoni. May, who

was also a good racing driver, was a genial and pleasant sort of man and always generous with his experience. He turned out to be an excellent collaborator, pleased to give us everything he had learnt and experienced at Bosch. He became my friend and worked closely with Giancarlo Bussi, the young Trieste engineer who joined us at the end of 1962. Bussi had no great experience, but he was highly intelligent and extremely well organised. And he had a critical mind, a useful characteristic at decision time. He worked in the engine section, experimentation and testing. We were very much in tune with each other and I worked really well with him. Unfortunately, he was kidnapped while on holiday in Sardinia in October 1978 and we never saw him again; he was

The 1964 season brought great success to Ferrari, but it also demanded an enormous effort due to the double commitment of F1 and sports car racing, the latter with a new challenge from the giant Ford. Even so Mauro Forghieri, pictured with John Surtees and Franco Rocchi, was still the youngest technical director of all the teams in the history of the sport to win the Formula 1 World Championship. Below: Lorenzo Bandini driving the 156 V6 in the 1964 Grand Prix of Monaco.

47 and it is a matter that still causes me great pain today. Bussi never liked to call attention to himself and rarely went to the races – the 24 Hours of Le Mans and not much more – but he made a determinate contribution in many sectors, among them the development of the 12-cylinder that made its F1 debut in 1970 and which was used until the advent of the turbos in 1981. Bussi was much respected by Enzo Ferrari and motor sport director Eugenio Dragoni.

In the meantime, our group was transformed into a cohesive team, which enjoyed the confidence of the Commendatore. Between 1963 and 1964, the atmosphere was frenetic but strangely serene, one of the reasons why we achieved such good results with the V8 engine (which gener-

ated 210 hp, Ed) even if we did have trouble with the Bosch pump.

The pump was in fact an adaptation: to begin with, it was installed upside down. That was so that we could have shorter feeder tubes and precise injection phasing for up to 11,500 rpm. It was an engine that revved really high for the period, more than the British Coventry-Climax.

The development of the V6 and V8 engines with direct fuel injection certainly didn't detract us from the central problem at Ferrari at that time, which was the creation of new chassis for F1, able to compete with the non-stop development of the British cars. The Lotus 25 appeared during the 1962 season and was the first car with a monocoque in aluminium and, I must say, we were dumbstruck.

Compact, light and potent (210 hp at 11,000 rpm), the 158's 90°
V8 above during a Monza test with mechanic Bruno Solmi at
work. The engine was fed by a Bosch pump with direct fuel injection designed by Ferrari. A unique decision during the period
of mainly Lucas injection systems. The advantages in terms of
power, torque distribution and lower fuel consumption would also have their influence on future Ferrari cars for racing and subsequently those for road use (from the Nineties, all high level cars
boasted this type of fuel feed system). For the development work
Bosch requested a one billion lire contribution, but no way could
Ferrari come up with that kind of money at the time.

I much appreciated the support of John Surtees in my re-launch operation; he had joined Ferrari at the end of 1962 and was a driver of class, a complete tester and champion as well as a good technician. John had already won seven motorcycle world championships with MV and it was probably for that reason that he had a unique driving style that I have never found in any other racer. In that period, steering wheels deformed a lot under driving stress, but only Surtees' was deformed him by 'pulling' them against himself. The other drivers 'pushed' them towards the nose of the car. Perhaps it was because he was used to pulling the handlebars to straighten up his motorcycle coming out of a corner; anyway, he was outstanding for his exceptionally effective driving and for his char-

acter that led him to putting everything into what he did, a man to be greatly respected. Dragoni and I had followed his career for some time and we were especially impressed with what he did at the GP of Germany on the deadly Nürburgring during a cloudburst in 1962 driving an only moderately competitive Lola Climax; he drove the car into second place, 2.5 seconds behind Graham Hill (BRM) who was to win the world title.

Surtees also had the advantage of being able to speak good Italian, which he learnt during his time with MV. A help in his relations with the mechanics and also with Enzo Ferrari, who spoke French well but not English. But then, the Commendatore had a great respect for ex-motorcyclists, starting with Tazio Nuvolari.

I had a good feeling with John, open and sincere, at least in the early stages of his time with us. The same goes for Lorenzo Bandini, who had become the second driver by that time and there never was any negative rivalry between them. Lorenzo was intelligent, had worked hard to get into F1 and understood that his English colleague was of a superior class, even if the Italian scored a number of great results more than once. Then there were the endurance races, in which victory was associated with an enormous number of unknowns, even if the class of the driver certainly counted. Winning a 24 Hours of Le Mans was almost as important as becoming F1 world champion.

Chassis development began before John Surtees arrived at Maranello and in this area, too, I had to

impose my point of view, which was not immediately shared by everyone. We were all fascinated by Colin Chapman's Lotus 'monocoque' and everyone would have followed his lead. Even Enzo Ferrari intended to do so, probably convinced by some of our men – Rocchi and Salvarani in particular – who came from Officine Reggiane, where the remarkable RE 2000 aircraft were built. In the past, they had used technology at Maranello for designing fighter plane fuselages, which turned out to be relatively useful.

An absolutely right concept, but it needed a great deal of time and would not have been ready before the start of the 1963 season. So I suggested a divided approach: the technical office would work on a monocoque while designer Farina and

I would do the same, but for a more traditional chassis capable of being competitive in '63. And once again, Vittorio Jano supported us in convincing Enzo Ferrari that this was the right path to take.

And that's how the 156 Aero was born, with a 6-cylinder engine with Bosch direct fuel injection. It had a chassis of modern rigid tubes, with triangulation especially designed to distribute the stress well. Most importantly, it was entirely covered by a 'skin' of riveted aluminium over the tubes, which gave exceptional general rigidity. It was a new technology that was invented at Ferrari that would be stay in force right through to the start of the Eighties.

The subsequent monocoque was entirely built at

Maranello – I also studied aeronautical technology – and was an excellent result. It was a splendid car, designed with care and a fundamental detail that made all the difference against the already famous Lotus 25: the load-bearing engine that acted as part of the chassis at the rear end. It was a concept that would later become the basis of all F1 cars from the second half of the Sixties right through to today. The Lotus had a chassis with a lengthened the rear to support the engine and gearbox. On the 156 and 158 monocoques, which were 6 and 8-cylinders respectively, there were only two light edges that supported the motor during the installation stage but, in practice, they did nothing: the chassis was replaced by the engine.

Opposite: spring 1964 and the definitive version of the Ferrari 158 'monocoque' is being tested on the Modena circuit. Engineer Forghieri is talking to a half-hidden journalist with head of the Ferrari engine test room Taddei just behind the rear wheel. Also there is technician Franco Rocchi, concentrating on the job in hand. Born in Reggio Emilia in 1923, Rocchi worked at Ferrari from 1949 until 1978 and was one of the extraordinary designers, in his case of engines, who transformed Forghieri's ideas into reality. But the 158 is attributed to Angelo Bellei, who worked at Ferrari from 1946 until 1987. Bellei, an intuitive and rapid designer, worked in close cooperation with Mauro Forghieri, who always emphasised the collaboration of the highly expert Vittorio Jano, who was a Ferrari consultant at the time. Behind Rocchi is young engineer Cocozza, who later became the head of the production department but who lost his life in a road accident while testing a Daytona. Also there are mechanics Borsari – to Rocchi's left – Ener Vecchi and Dino Pignatti.
Above, right: the 158 being driven by John Surtees in the 1964 GP of France.

Monza, 6 September 1964, Grand Prix of Italy: a triumphant day for Ferrari and Surtees, seen here chasing Dan Gurney's Brabham-Climax, which he overtook without problem. After his first win in the GP of Germany with the 158, Lorenzo Bandini scored Ferrari's second victory at the GP of Austria in a 156 'monocoque' and after that a podium place at Monza. The supremacy of the 158 at the Italian circuit was unquestioned, it having also take pole with eight tenths over Gurney's Brabham despite Surtees being unwell. The future F1 world champion was recovering from a rather violent accident at Goodwood, where his Ferrari GTO overturned in a fast corner; the driver got out of it unhurt but was admitted to hospital with severe shock.

But we did notice that the advantage of the monocoque was not determinant. A comparison was quickly made, given that the V6 was installed first in the Aero and then in the monocoque which, among other things, was slightly heavier at engine parity. Who knows what results we expected, but we certainly noticed that the previous 156 Aero in which Surtees won the GP of Germany at the Nürburgring ahead of Clark's Lotus and for the whole 1963 season was the British car's and was no way inferior to a valid monocoque. I would also like to underline the effectiveness of the 25, which was made even more so by Jim Clark, who I regard as one of the greatest drivers of all time. The 1963 GP of Germany was also important because it was my first victory in a world cham-

pionship race. I was really happy, but we didn't get too carried away because for a number of months we had understood – especially Salvarani, Rocchi and I – that the 156 was absolutely valid and just had to make its mark. Starting with the engine, it had various good qualities, including its suspension, which could be changes in just a few minutes. Surtees did well with the car as early as the GP of Monaco, where he came fourth, took second behind Clark in the British GP and won the German at the Nürburgring. The whole racing department dreamt of a complete success, encouraged by Surtees' positive opinion, which rather reflected everyone's view, starting with Enzo Ferrari. At the 'Ring after practice (second fastest behind Clark) the mechanics tried

Top, left: spring, 1964, Mauro Forghieri and John Surtees taking some improvised shelter from the rain under the tailgate of the racing department's Peugeot 404 Familiale Grand Lux. In the background is the Commendatore's 250 GTE, which he loved to drive himself, always accompanied by his driver Peppino Verdelli, who sat in the passenger seat at his side or even on one of the small rear seats if there was a guest on board. Ferrari particularly liked Peugeot, both for the company's compact family industrial management and the models they produced. He drove a 404 saloon for some time and liked its comfort and roadholding. But once he entered the world of Fiat he had two cars produced by the Fiat Group, apart from the ever present Ferrari. The only exception was a Renault 5 Turbo of the early Eighties.
Bottom, left: John Surtees in the 158 carrying the colours of the cars entered by an American team. The story is well-known: Ferrari importer Luigi Chinetti's NART team competed in the GPs of the USA and Mexico and not Ferrari, who had an Italian licence. The Commendatore's controversial gesture was to emphasise his disappointment at the lack of support from our motor sport federation for the homologation of the 250 Le Mans by the international federation.

to speak to John to get to know what he expected of the race. But as was often the case, the answer came from his pleasant, patient and beautiful wife Pat, whom John loved even if, like many great champions, he was decidedly egocentric. It was Pat who gave me hope. She said, "My dear Mauro, I can assure you that John is also sure he will win". Fast and aggressive, that day Surtees was implacable and he pointed that out himself after the race. He said, "I was simply perfect". John wasn't exactly modest, and would often really indulge himself.

That was the Grand Prix in which the rivalry between Surtees and Clark, two absolute number ones, fully emerged. They respected each other but they were not friends, yet Surtees did not get

on well with his British colleagues, partly because of his prickly personality and partly because he came from motorcycle racing. On top of that, he literally lived with Ferrari, with which he identified himself. He never ever left the group, which was unique for a driver; for instance Clark was synonymous with Lotus. In my opinion, the two were equal as far as speed is concerned, but sometimes John was colder than his rival.

Unfortunately, the race that united them in a single legend, in my view, was not a round in the world championship, although all the top drivers were there. It took place at the Solitude road circuit in Germany in July 1964, an 11.4 km track with really treacherous undulations. After practice, Clark (Lotus 25) and Surtees (Ferrari 158)

were separated by just two tenths of a second, with Graham Hill third three seconds behind them. It was raining heavily and Surtees was fantastic: driving flat out in the middle of woods, he took 19 seconds off Clark. The others just didn't exist. When the sun came out again, Clark went after Surtees, who was hampered by worn tyres, and managed to win but the organisers decided the lap of honour should be driven by both of them. It was a kind of pre-coronation for John, because two weeks later he won the GP of Germany and that was his first real step towards the world title. That discovery concerning the validity of the monocoque was somewhat of a disappointment and, as there were no major benefits, I convinced myself it was not worth pursuing that path as I

This famous shot by Franco Varisco clearly expresses the series of thoughts, doubts and hypothesis that the technical director of an F1 team is trying to put in order during practice. To reflect and, perhaps, to seek a minimum of peace, Forghieri slipped into a 158 cockpit 'parked' outside the Zandvoort pits in Holland. Even though he loved to drive, the engineer never allowed himself to cover even a metre at the wheel of the many F1 cars he designed and which were often shifted from one place to another by the mechanics, among whom one of the regulars was Giulio Borsari. The quick runs from Maranello along the Via Giardini through the villages to the Modena circuit 15 kilometres away in F1 and sports racing cars were well-known and only came to an end in the late Sixties. That was why there was a 'Prova MO 49' number plate on the cars, issued by the local authorities. Practicality and time reasons demanded such runs, which were probably tolerated rather than being considered lawful.

Note the strange arched component in front of the hoop and dashboard of the 158 the bodywork of which has been removed; it was not part of the chassis, which is monocoque with riveted aluminium panels, but connected the two fuel tanks on the car's flanks with each other.

had no factory with aeronautical experience available to me. And then there was the high cost, plus much longer construction times. In fact, when I was working on the new cars for the 1966 season (with 3000 cc engines, Ed) I continued to use the 'Ferrari system' I had developed: it gave us a sufficiently rigid chassis that were easy to build and repair, which was impossible with a monocoque. Naturally, I talked about this with Ferrari for a long time. The monocoque satisfied his pride, because at the time that technology was the jewel on the crown of the constructors. But of costs, he had no doubt: the choice brought enormous financial advantages, given that a monocoque chassis cost up to 50 times more! Don't forget that at the time Ferrari was facing none other than the giant Ford

A Franco nel mondo dei momenti simpatici passati mi pure per il mondo, lui con il click io con i pensieri

Previous page: another shot of engineer Forghieri in a 158 cockpit at Zandvoort. The picture has been dedicated by Forghieri to Franco Varisco saying, "To Franco, remembering the pleasant moments we have enjoyed travelling the world, him with a click and me with my thoughts".

Above: Grand Prix of Holland, 18 July 1965, Zandvoort circuit: a photo souvenir of John Surtees in the 158 and for all the understaffed Ferrari team. In picture from the right are Pat Surtees, the driver's wife and timekeeper, Mauro Forghieri, motor sport director Eugenio Dragoni and chief mechanic Giulio Borsari. On the pit counter is Lorenzo Bandini. In the race, Surtees was held up by the uncertainty of Graham Hill and took a modest seventh place.

in the World Sports Car Championship with fairly substantial financial risk and no outside help. And on top of that, we had to do everything in-house while the British teams commissioned their chassis from aeronautical companies, which was unthinkable in Italy at the time. Both the Aero and the monocoque were the result of some excellent work by the Ferrari mechanical workshop of which my father Reclus was the head. He gave me considerable help during the chassis' construction: without a good workshop we would not have been able to revolutionise a section like that in such a short time.

Naturally, we refined the technique: the first chassis were built with round tubes, but later we used micro-structures, small 10 mm tubes on which the aluminium skin was glued and then riveted. We used brad rivets, which also gave a good aesthetic effect. For almost 20 years we used chassis for both F1 and sports car racers which resulted from our experience, which we gathered quickly. And they could be repaired in the case of an accident: we just cut out the bent area and welded on new pieces.

We could also carry out operations like that at the circuits with excellent results: in one non-championship race in Ontario in 1971, Mario Andretti dramatically crashed his 312B1. It seemed like there was nothing we could do, but chief mechanic Giulio Borsari and his men literally rebuilt the car in the pits, and on the Sunday Mario won the race in it! Another advantage of our chassis

was that they didn't deteriorate, while with time and use the monocoques lost some of their rigidity, probably because of current eddying currents that corroded the rivets.

John Surtees won the 1964 Formula 1 World Championship driving a Ferrari 158 after a much alternating season fought out against Jim Clark and his Lotus 25 and Graham Hill in his excellent BRM. Surtees won at the Nürburgring and Monza, two circuits with diametrically opposed characteristics. Yet in the same period, the British driver insisted that we develop the new 512 F1 quickly, a car that was added to the 158 and built around the new flat-12 engine.

"With the 1500, the power difference between the various engines is very limited", Surtees main-

tained. "The flat-12 could give us 10 hp more, which could make all the difference".

And that was not wrong, but it was a rather traditional flat-12, designed without internal aerodynamic study and with a very wide angle of the two valves; nothing like the flat unit of five years later. Personally, I was perplexed because on paper it had to have a few more horsepower than the V8, but it was a heavy engine with fuel consumption that was quite a lot higher. But at the time, Enzo Ferrari and various other technicians didn't have the slightest doubt and talked about using the more powerful engine anyway. That's why the project was combined with the 158 operation.

In the beginning, the new 512 F1 gave us nothing

but disappointment, yet it was the car that helped Surtees become world champion.

It happened at the 1964 Grand Prix of Mexico, the last race of the season and the event at which the title would be won by either Surtees, Clark or Hill. Naturally John drove a 158, but with the 1965 season around the corner we assigned a 512 F1 to Lorenzo Bandini. We wanted to continue to test the car to see if we could make it competitive.

To compensate for the low air pressure – Mexico City is 2,000 metres above sea level – we worked out a set-up for the 12-cylinder, considerably lengthening the aspiration trumpets using rubber tubes. An improvisation and not a very attractive at that. However, the engine began to work perfectly: it produced an excep-

Previous page: Enzo Ferrari without his usual dark glasses dominates the Monza pits on the eve of the Grand Prix of Italy on 12 September 1965. Two 512 F1s were entered for John Surtees (above) and Lorenzo Bandini (right, with mechanic Carlino Amadessi). The development of the cars with their flat 12-cylinder engines was pushed by Ferrari at Surtees' behest as they were sure that a few more horse power than the V8 from which the 512 F1 took its general characteristics, would be an ace up our sleeve against the British V8s. Maranello gave the new car's power output as 220 hp and the V8 as 210 hp, but Forghieri never fully shared that conviction because the flat-12 was conceived too fast and in line with concepts that he himself had overtaken. The technical director and Enzo Ferrari agreed to disagree, but the new 12-cylinder was excessively heavy and consumed more fuel.

tional thrust and Bandini was really happy. In the race, Lorenzo was very competitive, more so that Surtees as it certainly was not his day. He was far less brilliant than usual, seeming almost resigned and not so responsive, perhaps because he had started badly due to the engine initially being hard to rev. But Bandini was so fast that he was able to snap at Graham Hill's heels and tried to overtake the Briton on a slow curve on the return. In an episode that is now part of F1 history, Lorenzo defended himself but Hill ended up against the guardrail and ruined his car's exhausts. Then, after being 'invited' to do so by a pit signal, Bandini allowed Surtees to pass him so that the Englishman came second (ahead of Dan Gurney in a Brabham-Climax, Ed) to win the Formula 1 World Championship.

Quite honestly, if that engine had not turned out to be so competitive on the Mexican circuit at such an altitude, perhaps history would have been written differently. But John deserved the title for all the good results he had produced during the season. However, it's curious that the flat-12 was not developed much in 1965 and was not successful in its sports-prototype races before the move the following year to 3000 cc engines. Yet from that unit we derived the famous 2000 cc with alternate distance between the cylinders, which scored victories and brought us an incredible amount of satisfaction in the European Mountain Championship.

A V12 behind the driver
The golden years of sports car racing

Between the end of 1961 and the beginning of 1962, I was mainly involved in setting up the GTO together with my colleagues in the technical office in which engine specialist Rocchi was outstanding, as were Salvarani, Farina, Bellei and Maioli. Excellent people to work with and with whom I immediately began a relationship of reciprocal esteem and friendship, which continued down the years. It was a fundamental starting point for me, and one that contributed to the serenity of the office. The GTO had just been designed, as were the 196 SP-286 SP and the 248 SP-268 SP rear engined sports racers, which were the first after the F1 cars to adopt that technology. We only planned to use V6 and V8 engines, because at Maranello at the time it was considered crazy to build sports rac-

ing cars with the classic V12 behind the driver. The engine was thought to be too big and bulky, an opinion I immediately opposed and I turned out to be right 12 months later.

The GTO operation was a rather delicate one, because that now famous grand tourer was to be sold to the public; 39 were built and they were extremely important to Ferrari. The car was derived from the 250 sports coupé that first appeared in 1959. It was developed by Giotto Bizzarrini, who had resigned and didn't finish the job.

The car prototype was test driven by Stirling Moss at Monza in September 1961 and he turned in some very promising lap times, but it was also this test that created a series of doubts. The new Ferrari was to have been introduced together with

all the others for the upcoming season at the press conference 'show' on 24 February 1962 – Ferrari's first – recommended by Eugenio Dragoni, who had some modern ideas on the subject. But the GTO had been homologated by 1 January and major modifications could no longer be made.

The first thing that set the alarm bells ringing was a serious accident on the Bologna-Florence section of the Autostrada del Sole with driver and tester Willy Mairesse at the wheel. There was no speed limit, not much traffic and the motorway's curves were ideal for testing cars at top speed so much so that the A1, as it is designated, was a sort of test track used as an alternative to circuits like Monza. Mairesse was immediately blamed for the crash as he was good but impetuous. I was sure something

had gone wrong from the mechanical point of view and Gaetano Florini, the man who looked after the private entrants' cars, agreed with me. The prototype, the body of which had just been modified by our technical office, was tested at Monza by Bandini, Baghetti and Mairesse. Nobody got close to Moss's time, so it was clear that it was due to the Englishman's bravura, a man who could have dominated any car. Bandini said he found the GTO unstable, especially in fast corners. At that point, we carried out an analysis together with the department's technicians and we decided the rear axle, which was held by only two semi-rods and a spring-damper group on each side, was not under sufficient control and moved in large curves to create erratic steering.

It was a dramatic situation as the car had been homologated, and we couldn't change anything. Eventually, we fitted a Watt's parallelogram anchored to the differential box but kept the coil springs, which could not be eliminated because they appeared on the homologation fiche. But we selected a minimum diameter wire, which was a ploy because the springs no longer performed any function – they were just left there to respect the homologation.

There was a certain tension when we went to Monza for the final test in front of Enzo Ferrari in early March, and we sighed with relief when Bandini recorded a faster time than Moss, confirming we had solved a complicated problem. Ferrari was satisfied and I had earned a little more

Previous page: Monza, September, 1961: the debut of the GTO driven by Stirling Moss, who broke the circuit's GT record but said the car was 'difficult to handle'. With modifications designed by Mauro Forghieri, the Ferrari went back to Monza in March 1962 for its final test: the faces of Forghieri, Ferrari and Dragoni (in the picture on page 87) say it all. Above: other photographs of that fateful day. Below: Lorenzo Bandini describes what the car was like in action, as confirmed by the look on the faces of Forghieri and Ferrari.

Mauro Forghieri seldom wore casual clothes, but he did so at Monza to watch Richie Ginther testing the Ferrari 246 SP in 1961. The model was turning out to be the key to Ferrari's growth, not just because it was Maranello's first sports racing car with its 2417 cc V6 in the rear. It was also used to carry out Ferrari's first aerodynamic tests, aimed at improving its handling in corners. On its debut, the 246 had a large rear fin that should have improved its speed on the straight, but test driver Ginther said it was markedly inferior and nothing like as good as the previous year's identically powered V6 246 F1 when cornering. They even tried to test the car without the rear bodywork and, incredibly, Ginther reported it to be more stable in corners. With those results engineer Carlo Chiti, who was Ferrari's technical head at the time, took a different route on the aerodynamics front, partly at the insistence of Vittorio Jano, Ferrari's super-consultant. In fact, Forghieri remembers that Jano advised the mechanics to create a rear flap in aluminium, which produced excellent results and was blended into the body of the definitive 246.

of his confidence. That in turn increased the esteem of my group, in particular giving us greater autonomy that was fundamental with the Commendatore, who was always extremely well informed about our work.

I also remember the panic before the start of the season due to the gearbox used by the 246 SP and 248/268 SP sports racers, designed by Carlo Chiti and only evolved with the clutch of the new engines: there were the usual V6 uprated to 2862 cc and a new 2458 cc V8 (2645 cc, later) that wasn't very successful, but it became the basic engine for Ferrari road going sports coupés many years later. The two cars were to make their debut at the 12 Hours of Sebring, but they ran the risk of not being able to leave Maranello. A month before the

race, we discovered the clutch inherited from the previous sports racers and the 156 F1 and fitted to the end of the gearbox had excessive inertia. I was never convinced of the effectiveness of that solution, which we used for reasons of time. In a test at the Modena Autodrome, the gearbox turned out to be useless due to the inertia increase; as the drivers tried to put the car into gear, there was a grinding noise but no gear engagement. It was a dramatic moment that we only overcame because of the incredible ability of all the mechanics, people who could quickly solve any problem. Salvarani, Rocchi, Maioli, Farina and I sat around a table and we sorted out everything, reducing the inertia. Salvarani designed a completely new gearbox and, one by one, we took his drawings and pulled all

the individual elements together. My father and his lads in the workshop gave us a great deal of help, so that we were able to send the cars to Sebring even if it was at the last moment.

The GTO was also one of the first to have an aerodynamic flap attached to its tail. With the now widespread use of such concepts, there is often a lot of confusion over who was the first to come up with ideas on this important new trend of aerodynamics. Personally, I remember having seen Vittorio Jano give advice in 1961 on how to cut sheet metal to create flaps for the 196 and 248 SP sports racing cars, work that was supported by racing driver and tester Richie Ginther during the evolution of the GTO. The car was then modified in line with that concept, because he lacked

adequate knowledge of that kind in the beginning. My life soon became frenetic. For instance, I had to travel to England to contact and evaluate Mike Parkes, a Rootes Group engineer who was a good racer and drove for Colonel Ronnie Hoare, Ferrari's UK importer. In August 1962, I went to Germany to see the Grand Prix at the Nürburgring. Late that night, I boarded a DC3 together with a group of Britons including Colin Chapman, Bruce McLaren, Graham Hill and other drivers: the aircraft's cabin wasn't even pressurised, but it was flown by Battle of Britain pilot John Cobb. We landed after 2 am at Gatwick, which was rather spartan in those days, and Col. Hoare was waiting for me. When we reached London, I only had time to shower followed by the usual huge English breakfast before

leaving by car to meet a number of Ferrari suppliers. It was a long trip, because Col. Hoare had the habit of stopping every now and then for a gin and tonic, but he was impeccable at his work. He was a relative of Queen Elizabeth II and always travelled with spare cuffs and a change of collar for his shirt – white, of course – which he wore on all important occasions. That afternoon, we arrived at Brands Hatch to watch Parkes in a Ferrari GTO and a 246 SP. I had to work out what I was going to say to the Commendatore about Mike possibly working for us as a road and racing car technician and driver.

The whole thing was an incredible tour de force, but my opinion was favourable and the tall engineer turned out to be very useful to Ferrari: he

raced well and had excellent ideas from the technical standpoint. We became friends and I was extremely upset when he lost his life in a 1977 road accident.

At the wheel, Mike made a great contribution to the development of the prototypes, which were more important to Maranello than F1 cars in the early Seventies. Enzo Ferrari was sure endurance races like the 24 Hours of Le Mans and the 12 Hours of Sebring were essential to selling his road cars and that was true, especially during the Ford challenge from 1964 onwards. The fact is that every year until mid-June, the racing department was more committed to sports prototypes than single seaters, and that certainly stopped Ferrari enjoying even greater success in the F1 world championship.

24 Hours of Le Mans, 15-16 June 1963: Ferrari 250 P number 21 (above, right) started the event with Lorenzo Bandini at the wheel, but the joy of crossing the finish line as the winner went to Lodovico Scarfiotti. The bottom photograph shows there are five more minutes to go in this punishing race.

The win was Ferrari's first at Le Mans with a rear engine car. The previous year, Maranello had won with the classic Testa Rossa powered by a 4-litre V12 up front, although the car had been updated, especially its aerodynamics. The arch at the drivers' shoulders stood out and that was the first attempt to exploit the air to reduce turbulence, achieve more speed and increase downforce. Theories that led to the design of the 250 P a year later. Centre: engineer Forghieri in the pits with John Surtees and Willy Mairesse, who led the race in 250 P number 23 until the 18th hour. After refuelling, the petrol breather pipe wore and a small quantity of fuel trickled through to the pedal area. When Mairesse braked, a spark from the stop button created a flare-up and the whole car burst into flames, seriously burning Mairesse's face and hands. But the experienced driver walked back to the pits and explained what had happened to Forghieri who, though disappointed, grew to respect the courageous but unlucky Belgian even more.

My first approach to the two-seater cars was a gradual one, because in 1962 the 246 and 248 SPs with their engines amidships were entered for the event and they were designed during the Chiti era. Apart from tails that were too high, these cars were fairly good, despite having a chassis similar to that of the 156 F1, as their shape and increased width enabled them to achieve an acceptable torsional rigidity. But there was a power problem: neither the 2.4 V6 nor the 2.5 V8 could produce more than 275 hp, so for the 1962 24 Hours of Le Mans we had to 'invent' a traditional front engined Testa Rossa for ourselves, but with a 4-litre V12 engine.

Everyone at Ferrari was certain a 12-cylinder rear engined sports racing car would be techni-

Justifiably proud, Enzo Ferrari poses with John Surtees and Mike Parkes, who joined Maranello from the UK in the autumn of 1962. The decision to give Surtees, seven times motorcycle world champion with MV, the responsibility of bringing the F1 world title back to Ferrari turned out to be the right one. He was extremely fast and charismatic and became one of Mauro Forghieri's close collaborators. The same can be said of Parkes with sports cars: the 1.91 metre Englishman had completed his engineering studies and was not only a fine racing driver, but also a talented tester. The photograph was taken in front of the private 'petrol station' that Shell, one of Ferrari's key technical sources, had installed in the factory's courtyard. Engineer Forghieri remembers that to give a first opinion on Parkes before the Briton was taken on, he had to put up with a plane journey in a veteran DC3, which took the British teams, drivers and technicians back to the UK at night after the 1962 German GP. Accompanied by Colonel Ronnie Hoare, the Ferrari importer for Great Britain, on the Monday the engineer went to the Brands Hatch circuit, where Parkes was to race a Ferrari GTO and a 246 SP. The Italian noted that the youngster was a competitor of great courage, who sometimes drove over the car's limit; that did not happen with Surtees, who was really fast and classy, but didn't risk more than was necessary.

Left: Willy Mairesse, who was paired with John Surtees, winning the 1963 1000 Km of the Nürburgring in a Ferrari 250 P.

cal madness. "It can't work with all that weight in the back", the Commendatore maintained, as he was one of the most resistant to changing ideas. However, I was sure it would be successful and proposed we built a car with a rear end weight of no more than 55% of the total. It was a bit of a gamble in the winter of 1962/3, but in the meantime John Surtees joined us and he was a driver of tremendous technical lucidity: he supported me, as did Eugenio Dragoni.

And that's how the 250 P, a slightly modified 248 SP, came about with its 12-cylinder GTO-type engine that was another derivation of my very first project for Ferrari, developed a little by myself and by Vittorio Jano. It would be considered a road car today, but at the time 300 hp with an equilibrated torque and dry sump lubrication made it suitable for racing.

I think we probably had a little luck, which helps in technical matters despite seeming to be a paradox, because we got it all right simply by putting the concepts we had in mind into practice. The car went really well and at the end of the winter I went to Monza for the final test, during which Surtees literally shattered the track record. I was pleased, because a number of new aerodynamic features on the car had worked and that sports racing cars would benefit from a much higher downforce than the single-seaters due to their greater body surface areas near the ground. I asked Ferrari if I could use the 1:1 scale wind tunnel at the University of Stuttgart, and on that occasion he was decidedly long sighted. Due to the cost – despite working hard at night to save electricity – tunnels were not used much at the time. Because of their tradition in aerodynamics derived from the aircraft industry, the British exploited such theories more than anything else. Ferrari understood that it could be an advantage and even in Chiti's time a rather simple wind tunnel was built at Maranello for reduced scale models.

Later, the Commendatore gave me a 4-cylinder engine with which to power the new "tunnel's" fan in a fairly well developed wooden structure. But there was a basic problem – we had no data and a data bank is fundamental to such work to create a comparison with a new model. It was an extremely specialised job for which we were unprepared.

But engineer Pottof, head of the Stuttgart University's wind tunnel, was able to provide us with an enormous amount of material for comparison purposes, and he also became a non-stop source of useful suggestions and advice. He was a great man who contributed to the development of the 250 P, for which we had studied a new line similar to the one that became the definitive Targa. Similar because of the aerodynamic arch that ran the whole width of the body immediately behind the driver's shoulders, and was also an effective roll bar. It was a solution that gave its name to a Porsche model years later, but the initial idea was Ferrari's.

The aerodynamic advantage began with the shape of the windscreen, which had to be wrap-around,

while it had only been slightly curved on all the other cars.

We went crazy trying to achieve that shape, which was absolutely necessary if we were to avoid turbulence. That way, the fluid air streams were captured by the glass so that they did not disperse with the Targa system but were crushed – and that is no exaggeration – by the rear flap so that the pressure centre increased fivefold.

That way, rear downforce was substantial and the car was much more driveable at high speeds.

At the time, this early foray into aerodynamics was an industrial secret of considerable importance, so much so that we decided not to speak of it to anyone – not even the drivers or mechanics. But in that kind of situation it was difficult to keep things se-

Monza, Wednesday 16 December 1964: the first important test of the brand new Ferrari 330 P2, with John Surtees driving and Mauro Forghieri in the pits. It was a totally new project compared to the 1963/4 P series, designed due to a formidable attack on sports car racing by Ford. It was a real racing car with more extreme features than the P series: the picture shows an intermediate two-seater version used to evaluate its aerodynamics. The new car was powered by a V12 engine with twin overhead camshafts, a layout that had been dropped by Ferrari for the big sports prototypes after 1957. Both the P and P2 were raced in 275 3285 cc and 330 3967 cc versions, but the twin overhead camshaft engines enabled us to extract much more power from the units: 350 hp against the P's 320 hp and 410 hp to 370 hp respectively.

Sebring, 21 March 1964: Ferrari took over the entire podium at the 12 Hours, which was a round in the International Prototype Trophy. The winners were Umberto Maglioli, shown on the right in the 275 P, and Mike Parkes. Below, right: Maglioli again, this time driving the 275 P at the 24 Hours of Le Mans, which he shared with Giancarlo Baghetti who had returned to Ferrari after a period with ATS. Baghetti was the involuntary cause of the car's retirement, as he was involved in an unlucky accident when the Peter Bolton/Jack Sears Ford Cobra had a blow-out. The race was won by Nino Vaccarella and Jean Guichet in a Ferrari 275 P, an important victory because it was the first time Maranello faced a strong challenge from Ford. Surtees and Bandini played the hare and immediately went on the attack, so that after just five hours all the Ford GT40s had dropped out.

cret: enthusiasm cancelled out all reticence. Only designer Casoli knew about it, but he said nothing. Ford, which became our deadly rivals in sports prototype racing, achieved something similar but they were not happy people (cracked glass, Ed) because they had not found the right balance. The 250 P won the 12 Hours of Sebring – its debut race – driven by John Surtees and Lodovico Scarfiotti, an excellent crew because no way was Lodovico inferior to his celebrated English colleague when racing the big prototypes. Scarfiotti came from a prominent Marches family related to the Agnellis, who own Fiat among other things; he was a gentleman first and foremost, but also a complete, highly professional driver. His family was against him racing, so much so that he had considered competing under a pseudonym, but that was a bad idea because he soon became well known. Dragoni, a man who did a lot for Italian drivers, brought Lodovico to Ferrari. Together with Bandini, Scarfiotti won the 1963 24 Hours of Le Mans, which was a fantastic victory for Italy. They were called the Spring Team – even if that same name had been used by a Fifties F1 squad – and they were excellent in both competitive and human terms, one of the best that ever competed for Ferrari. There were Vaccarella and Biscaldi as well as the foreigners, all new drivers who were well prepared and conditioned by the presence of Dragoni, an extremely strong minded man, even hard, but an excellent organiser. He was also a talent scout and among his projects was the involvement of the 20-year-old Franco Patria, who Dragoni believed would be a major F1 star, before he was killed at Montlhéry.

I personally had a great relationship with Dragoni, as I have already noted, partly because he relieved me from having to deal with the press. If he hadn't, they would have always contacted me and that was an extremely delicate job, which Enzo Ferrari kept constantly under control.

Every year, the most important event to Ferrari was the 24 Hours of Le Mans, which had become internationally famous. And Ford, which had attempted to acquire Ferrari in 1963, wanted to beat us in all the endurance races we entered, both sports prototype and grand tourer (the Ferrari GTO 3000s came up against the fearsome 7-litre Ford Cobra

7000, Ed). It was a clash that became legendary in time, and started with Enzo Ferrari's refusal in April '63 to allow the Americans' acquire his company after long negotiations.

It all started because of the financial difficulties Ferrari faced, especially due to its motor sport programme. The factory grew, the brand was established and the number of road cars produced each year increased. But that wasn't enough to pay for Maranello's involvement in the Formula 1 World Championship and sports car racing. Inside the organisation, we didn't exactly realise what the situation was like even though all expenditure, no matter how small, had to be approved by the Commendatore himself. So Ferrari could have accepted a partner that committed itself to his company financially, but at the same time giving him a certain freedom, especially in racing.

Faced with a significant Ford offer the Commendatore agreed to negotiate, but he would never have sold his company to the Americans as one often read. As Enzo Ferrari explained, it was an agreement, not a sale; perhaps an informal one, assuaging our anxiety caused by the comings and goings of Ford men to Maranello in the spring of 1963. Even after the transaction, Ferrari would have kept his job. But on the day everything was to be tied up, when he was still doubtful, he was told he would be free to make any decision he thought fit to an expenditure limit (450 million lire a year for racing, Ed). Above that, the Detroit executives would have to give their approval. That brought

Modena Autodrome, Tuesday 13 April 1965: the Dino 166 took to the track for the first time. It was a fascinating sports coupé conceived as a luxurious complement to the Fiat-Ferrari agreement. Low and light (96 cm and a 586 kg kerb weight), the car had a 1592 cc engine that put out 180 hp at 9000 rpm. It lived an autonomous life and did well in endurance racing. The subsequent 206 version (1986 cc, 205 hp) won the 1965 European Hillclimb Championship, driven by Lodovico Scarfiotti.

In the Sixties, the 1000 Km of Monza always attracted a huge number of spectators. The photograph on the left was taken at the very first event, held on 25 April 1965 when Ferrari won with a 275 P2 driven by Mike Parkes-Jean Guichet, in the foreground with car number 63. Also note the Dino 166 (53) of Giancarlo Baghetti (right, with his hands behind his back) and Giampiero Biscaldi, as well as the Lorenzo Bandini-Nino Vaccarella 330 P2. John Surtees and Lodovico Scarfiotti came second in another 330 P2 and third was the Bruce McLaren-Ken Miles Ford GT40. Ferrari-Ford rivalry would result in some epic battles in the 1966/7 seasons.

The Dino 166 was making its racing debut and set the 12th fastest time in practice, but it developed an engine problem during the race. That disappointed Enzo Ferrari, who had closely followed the 1600 sports coup's progress during practice, when it was driven by John Surtees for three laps. The F1 world champion clipped two seconds off the Dino crew's official time of 3 minutes 02.3 seconds.

everything to an abrupt halt, as Ferrari would never agree to such a condition. I always had a nagging doubt about the Commendatore's willingness to accept a partner and, perhaps, the negotiations took a turn he didn't like after Ford proposed the design and construction of a medium-high grand tourer prototype to add to its own price list.

But I am sure that in the end it was Gianni Agnelli who pushed Ferrari towards a refusal – it seems with the mediation of Pinin Farina - with promises of help from Fiat. That is exactly what happened two years later, when the Turin car maker produced the Dino sports models around our V6, which was then homologated to create the Ferrari F2 car.

It seemed like the end of the world. The Detroit

managers were so thunderstruck by the Commendatore's refusal that, in order to have 'something' of Ferrari's, they offered me a prominent position at the Ford Research Centre in California. But I turned it down as I would never have left Modena and Ferrari, to which I felt inextricably attached. We won the 1964 24 Hours of Le Mans with the Guichet-Vaccarella 330 P, a car derived from the previous year's 250 P, but the Ford challenge convinced us to increase the V12's cubic capacity to just under 4-litres to give us 370 hp. We also made more progress with its aerodynamics by adding a wrap-around laminated windscreen produced by VIS. So we felt fairly confident: despite their extensive means, Ford didn't especially impress us. The following year, though, we began a period of

work that was gruelling to say the least. The Ford challenge had become incandescent, the Dino was being created and we had to begin thinking about a 3000 cc F1 car to meet the new 1966 regulations. We literally worked from dawn until dusk, partly because there weren't many of us: just 160 people in the motor sport department, but that was counting the Commendatore and his driver, Peppino Verdelli, who always say in the passenger seat because Ferrari loved to drive. There were only just over 600 people in the whole factory, where the road car production side was growing substantially. Among my many responsibilities, the most pressing was the new sports racing car. I realised a much more advanced technical project than the 330 P was needed. We had shown a

Nino Vaccarella's autograph leaves no room for doubt: he won the 1965 Targa Florio with Lorenzo Bandini in a Ferrari 275 P2. Above: the 1965 1000 Km of the Nürburgring: top, the winning Surtees-Scarfiotti 330 P2; centre, a similar car entered by Col. Hoare's Maranello Concessionaires for a special crew – Graham Hill and the future three-times F1 world champion Jackie Stewart, but they retired with an electrical problem. The Baghetti-Biscaldi 275 GTB (3) was driven to the German circuit on public roads by Mike Parkes. On the left of the GTB is journalist Gianni Cancellieri, now a prominent author and motor racing historian. Opposite page: a Monza test for the Dino 1600; note Scarfiotti in his driving overalls and coat, engineer Forghieri, who doesn't usually feel the cold, and a well wrapped up Eugenio Dragoni.

certain supremacy over Ford, but we couldn't let it rest there. So the modifications to the 330 P were radical indeed: the P2 was a real racing car – low, with accentuated aerodynamic development and, most important of all, powered by a 4000 cc engine that put out 410 hp, even though it was fed by carburettors but with twin overhead camshafts for each cylinder bank.

We tested the P2 for the first time at Monza in mid-December 1964 and we immediately realised it was right on the money, the smaller engine 275 P2 version having won the Targa Florio and the 1000 Km of Monza. I won't deny that I shuddered a little when we turned up at the 24 Hours of Le Mans. Ford was there with the kind of organisation never before seen at a race, taking care of all the details

and comfort of their drivers and technicians. They even had a satellite ready to transmit the race live to American television, which was rare at the time and a clear sign that they thought they would win hands down. Phil Hill lapped their 7000 cc car at an average of 225 kph in practice, but in the race our confidence soon proved well founded. Ferrari's experience started to get the better of the situation, so that all the Fords had dropped out by the sixth hour while Surtees-Scarfiotti were leading at average of 210 kph. By the eighth hour we had four of our cars in the top four places, but around midnight trouble began. During a pit stop we noticed that the brake pads of the leading P2 were split and that the new ventilated discs we started to use at the beginning of that season were cracked.

The previous winter, I had gone to Girling in the UK as they had acquired Dunlop brakes to carry out some tests before reaching an agreement with their technicians. We found that ventilated discs immediately gave us some tremendous advantages in racing, but we had never tried them in such a long event. So those problems eventually emerged on all the works cars, enough to cause us major concern. What could we do? Retire all the cars or come up with a solution?

Both the volcanic Gaetano Florini, responsible for clients' racing cars, and I had the same idea of taking the discs off the 275 GTB road cars – the latest model to the development of which the racing department had contributed – as they were more or less the same. So we took the discs off

The Way We Were
Ferrari's away races
of the Sixties and Seventies

I don't want to make comparisons with the practices of current Formula1 teams when racing away from their home bases, it would make no sense. But the difference compared with the past…makes me laugh. Back then, you had to be enormously adaptable, partly because tourism in general was nothing like as well developed as it is today, so we organised our trips in the best way we could. We probably touched bottom during the GP of Great Britain at Silverstone, where it was not easy to find decent accommodation until recently, so you can imagine what it was like in the Sixties and Seventies. To avoid having to drive many kilometres through small, tortuous country lanes, Ferrari reached an agreement with a Presbyterian minister, who had a sort of students' residence not far from the track. John Surtees suggested it as a possibility and it turned out to be inexpensive, in line with the British champion's standards. There, we had rather spartan rooms and shared the bathrooms. In the evenings, we ate in a hall with the minister as head of table, but we could not order food; we had to eat what was served and, being English cuisine, there were a lot of unwelcome surprises. We were all a bit spartan, really. For instance, when I was at university I spent part of my summer harvesting beetroot. So we didn't expect much and we never complained, not even about the long, unsociable hours we put in, until I reached a limit in my own case of having to run two races during the same weekend. For example, on 10 July 1965, we made the Silverstone GP podium with Surtees in third place. But I don't think I was there to cheer him, because I had to rush off to Luton Airport about 80 kilometres away. From there I flew to Milan that evening, where Sauro Mingarelli – a well-known mechanic who had a Ferrari service garage in Bologna – was waiting for me. We left Milan for Trento, where Lodovico Scarfiotti

was competing in the Bondone hillclimb, a round in the European championship. I eventually got to bed in the dead of night and the next day watched over Ludovico's 2-litre Dino and, fortunately, he won. That was my life every week of the motor racing season. The cars were almost always tested at the Modena Autodrome until mid-afternoon on the Wednesday under the critical eye of Enzo Ferrari, especially if an F1 race was due to take place the following weekend. It was a slow circuit that only permitted limited checks, but that was our procedure. At the end of testing, which included a spare engine – it was not until after the 1969/70 season that we would have two spares – everything was loaded aboard a Fiat 643 truck that left immediately for the appointed race circuit, driven by mechanic Pignatti; only rarely was a colleague allowed to travel with him so that one could drive and the other rest. Sometimes, he had to drive 1,500 kilometres and without the advantage of today's motorway network, but we were always sure to find Pignatti in the circuit's paddock unloading the cars on the Thursday evening. This excellent mechanic-driver was involved in a 'historic drama' with Enzo Ferrari, who made sure he checked even the smallest details. When Pignatti put in his expense sheet after one of his

trips, the Commendatore noticed the man had 'dared' to drink two coffees after dinner one evening. The driver was not reimbursed for the second cup!

I usually arrived at the circuit on the Thursday evening, or perhaps on the late side, with four or five mechanics, all of us squeezed into the company Peugeot 404 station wagon. We were only allowed to go by air if the distance between Maranello and our European destination was really excessive: otherwise, we drove uncomfortable, interminably long distances. During race weekends, we more or less lived in the pits and had to make our own arrangements for lunch, usually rolls or sandwiches. There was no veto on wine, but a bottle rarely appeared and only then if someone had brought it from Italy. We always hoped we could eat Friday and Saturday night dinner in some restaurant or other, but that depended on how much work we had to do. Quite often, I or a mechanic had to grab a bite at the track, although I always tried to arrange a 'real' dinner for everyone ahead of the traditional time. After that, we went back to work on the cars, but at least we had a 'civil' break. It wasn't an easy or simple life, but before the arrival of motor sport director Dragoni it was even worse. He had our hotels booked in advance and ensured they were of a reasonable standard. He convinced Ferrari that solutions to logistical problems also contributed to improving the Prancing Horse's image. And he concerned himself with the general conduct of the team, with our company clothing, the way we presented ourselves and so on. We started to have a reasonable organisation, something that contributed a great deal to increasing the respect people had for us, whether we won or not.

some of the private GTBs in the car park to adapt them to the 330s, leaving a note under each car's windscreen wiper saying we would replace them, although we had some difficulty finding the right size pads. Then we fitted the new pads on one side of the calipers of each racing car and the used ones on the other.

We lost some time and it was a cobbled together solution, but at Le Mans it is essential to move on, because one never knows what may happen right down to the last minute. With reduced braking power, the drivers had to use their gearboxes and engine brake more and that created some negative consequences, especially for the transmissions. But, fortunately, our honour was saved by Luigi Chinetti's NART team, whose 275 Le Mans

won, driven by Masten Gregory and Jochen Rindt. That same year we won the International Prototype Trophy again, while the equally important GT Constructors' Championship went to Ford and their 7000 cc Cobra. We developed the 1961 GTO, modifying the aerodynamics at the rear (the 1964 GTO, Ed) in line with the technology tried and tested on the prototypes. It was a closed car, but the lengthened roof group gave more downforce in the tail area.

The car was tested extensively by Mike Parkes who did a fine job, but the cubic capacity difference against the Ford was too great. That was the first warning shot that confirmed the American company's progress in motor racing. I could see that their cars had improved

The last of Ferrari's nine victories at the Sarthe was in 1965 and was scored by Masten Gregory and Jochen Rindt in one of Luigi Chinetti's NART team 275 Le Mans. The photograph above shows the bespectacled Gregory in the centre, next to mechanic 'Sparky' Tramonti, who is wearing a cap.
Opposite page: above, the 1964 team of Ferrari mechanics; below, testimony to one of the strangest episodes as told by Mauro Forghieri, the change of gear ratios on the Jackie Ickx Dino F2. It was carried out while the car was still on the transporter in front of the team's hotel in Kensington, London. The race was at the city's Crystal Palace on the Monday and practice was on the preceding Saturday. But the circuit had no means of accommodating the cars overnight, so chief mechanic Giulio Borsari (kneeling near engineer Forghieri, whose back is to the camera) and his colleagues had to work at the roadside.

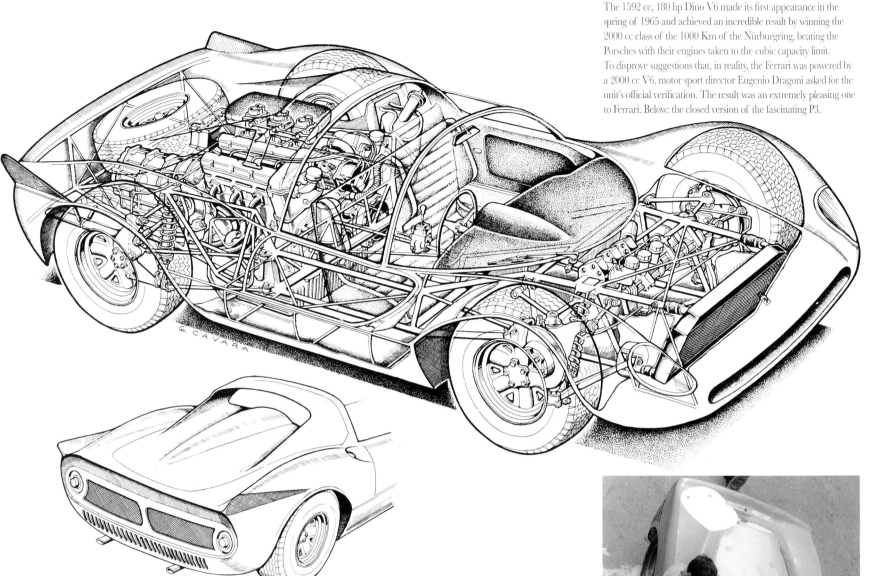

The 1592 cc, 180 hp Dino V6 made its first appearance in the spring of 1965 and achieved an incredible result by winning the 2000 cc class of the 1000 Km of the Nürburgring, beating the Porsches with their engines taken to the cubic capacity limit. To disprove suggestions that, in reality, the Ferrari was powered by a 2000 cc V6, motor sport director Eugenio Dragoni asked for the unit's official verification. The result was an extremely pleasing one to Ferrari. Below: the closed version of the fascinating P3.

considerably and that they would be extremely dangerous once they became sufficiently experienced. Naturally, I talked to Enzo Ferrari about the situation and, as I have already mentioned, his pride became stimulated by challenges, particularly those that were weighted against us. We agreed on a rather complex development of the 330, which was to become the P3. Helped in particular by Bussi, Rocchi and Salvarani, I designed a new 4-litre engine with its sump in light alloy and of more general racing characteristics, starting with the structure of the combustion chamber. And for the first time, we fitted a sports racer with Lucas indirect fuel injection instead of carburettors.

And so began a new phase in which sports rac-

ers no longer descended from road cars, even if the rather contradictory regulations still imposed a space in which suitcases should be stored. In fact, we had to show that our car had the space for a certain number of cases of a stipulated size. So we made room for the 'boot' in the rear of the P3 and Carrozzeria Fantuzzi had to make sure those damned cases were in the car.

When the job had been done, we noticed that the edges of the cases had been eliminated! Fantuzzi himself explained in Modenese that "I have never seen cases with sharp edges". It was an astute move, but not in line with the regulations and Fantuzzi, an exceptionally talented body builder who constructed many of Ferrari's racing cars, had to remake them. At a meeting with Ferrari, he asked

After fielding the Dino 166 and 206 in 1965, in January 1966 Enzo Ferrari unveiled a new Dino at his annual press conference. It was the 206 S with a 1986 cc V6 engine that produced 240 hp at 8800 rpm, the closed version of which is shown above during spring testing at Monza before its race debut. The car quickly became popular, partly because it looked like a smaller 330 P3. It was especially important to Ferrari, because 50 of them had to be built to achieve sports racing homologation before being sold to private entrants. In reality, Ferrari constructed 16 206 S, their chassis numbered from 002 to 032, 13 open versions and three sports coupés, all entered among the prototypes.
Right: the winning Surtees-Parkes 330 P3 in a very wet 1966 1000 Km of Monza, where they beat the Ford GT40s of Gregory-Whitmore and Müller-Mairesse.

me why the car was not ready and he became furious, but then started to laugh.

Among the P3's new developments were its gearbox, which had the same layout as the previous car, and a tubed chassis with the usual aluminium panels, which were replaced in some areas by plastic elements: an innovative system that made the car lighter and more robust. The open and closed versions of the body were new, with more advanced aerodynamics and a much accentuated tail. The P3 was an efficient and fascinating car, so much so that I remember on the day it was presented to the press in early February 1966 Enzo Ferrari showed he was pleased with it, and he was a man who rarely expressed his feelings openly in his relations with those who worked for him.

The P3 was developed without the significant help of John Surtees, who had been involved in a serious accident in a Lola Can-Am at Toronto the previous September. But after months of convalescence, he returned more in form than ever and won the 1000 Km of Monza with Mike Parkes, driving the P3 in torrential rain. Soon afterwards, Parkes and Scarfiotti drove the car to victory in the 1000 Km of Spa.

Ferrari and Ford clashed again at the 24 Hours of Le Mans but we were fairly confident, even though we had heard the Americans had invested something like $10 million (around six billion lire at the time, Ed) in an effort to win at the Sarthe. Madness for the balance sheet of a company like Ferrari, where the Commendatore admitted he

spent 604 million lire on the entire 1964 racing season. However, Ford's logistical organisation – with real rooms behind the pits, a restaurant and an incredible number of staff – was even more substantial than the previous year. They had all that, and we had lost John Surtees, who was fired just before Le Mans.

We also lost our top car being driven by Scarfiotti and Parkes, which went off the track and crashed. Then the Bandini-Guichet and Rodriguez-Ginther cars retired with various problems. There is no doubt that the whole thing was ruined and, even worse, Ford took the International Championship of Makes, but there is no doubt that the P3 was still fully competitive.

We were all disappointed, Enzo Ferrari more than

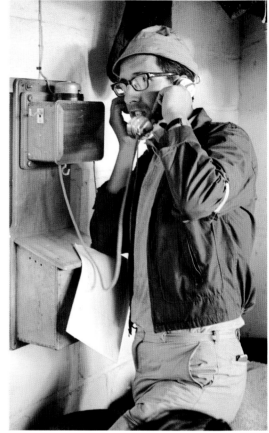

anybody. He wanted a rematch as quickly as possible and that meant at the 24 Hours of Daytona in January 1967. His intention was clear: to beat the Americans on their own doorstep! I must say that Bandini and Parkes replaced our ex-point man Surtees well, while Ferrari supported our preparations from the financial standpoint.

Ford had won Le Mans due to the many tests they had carried out and we had to do the same for Daytona. For us, endurance testing had always been the race itself, but that was not enough anymore; we had to match the opposition.

First of all, we designed and developed the new P4 between October and November, well ahead of time. That suggested a test at Daytona itself for a full 24 hour period two months before the race. It

was going to be an expensive operation, but Ferrari agreed immediately, also due to the support of Dragoni, who had decided to leave the Scuderia at end of 1966. That was one of the consequences of the Surtees Affair and the comments by the press, especially the British, and resulted in a journalist being chosen to take on the job of motor sport director!

Well-known Milanese journalist Franco Lini took Dragoni's place. He was a good man, but I have to say he was not ready for a role that demanded a fighting spirit and a strong personality, both internally in his confrontations with Enzo Ferrari, and externally at the circuits. Dragoni was the perfect man for the job and I greatly regretted him leaving. Anyway, we went to Daytona with the P4, the aer-

Above, right: the telephone line between Le Mans and Maranello ran hot at the 1966 24 Hours of Le Mans. That much is confirmed by the expression on Mauro Forghieri's face as he tells Enzo Ferrari of the P3s' problems when up against the 7-litre Ford GT40 Mk IIs, which took the first three places (top, left). Above: Forghieri talking to Huschke von Hanstein, Porsche's motor sport director. Below: this cartoon by Marino hit the mark. Opposite page: the Scarfiotti-Parkes P3 winning the 1000 Km of Spa.

odynamics of which had been further developed, it had a new engine with three valves per cylinder – similar to the 3000 cc with which Scarfiotti won the 1966 Grand Prix of Italy – that put out 450 hp. We were all confident, me more than anyone because I knew the P4 was really fast and had become extremely reliable. There was no messing about at the 24 Hours of Daytona and we staged the famous victory in which the Ferraris paraded across the finish line three abreast – Franco Lini's idea –way ahead of the rest of the field as our reply to Ford's 1966 Le Mans success. The cars were driven by winners Lorenzo Bandini-Chris Amon, Mike Parkes-Lodovico Scarfiotti and Pedro Rodriguez-Jean Guichet, the latter in a private 412 P. The whole thing was an immense joy to us all. And to think that we

had to work well into the small hours the day before, because Parkes had gone off and destroyed the rear end of his P4 during the last practice session. At the time, nobody took such large replacement components as a car's tail to the circuits and we didn't have a team of over 100 people like Ford, more like 24 or 25 of us. So after dinner, I was watching the body builders and a mechanic working on the damaged car, when I remembered there was a rather proficient body man in the team of our American importer, Luigi Chinetti. Rather slim and lanky, I found him and asked if he would like to work on our damaged car. He agreed right away, even if my extras budget was very low and I could only offer him $150. He worked well and together we put the shape back into the car's tail. I paid

him and he thanked me warmly, after which we all went to our beds. The day after the race, we were at the airport where I saw our 'body man' on the runway, elegantly dressed and wearing a Stetson, walking towards a private plane. Chinetti had said nothing to me, but our helper turned out to be a wealthy Texas oil man who loved to go to the races and always tried to give the teams a hand. I almost died when the smart looking Texan came over to say goodbye and said he would frame the $150 as a souvenir.

Race day was memorable and was a great victory for European industry. Nobody expected the P4 to be so fast and reliable, but it was well designed and developed, light, never caused tyre problems and boasted carefully studied aerodynamics.

Above left: after the great disappointment of the 1966 24 Hours of Le Mans, Ferrari took its revenge right on Fords own doorstep by winning the 24 Hours of Daytona on 4-5 February 1967. The cars cross the finish line three abreast to deliver a crushing defeat. The winner was P4 number 23, driven by Bandini-Amon. Above: one of the many tests of the new P4 at Monza that included a simulated 24 hour race.
The other three photographs on this and the opposite page recall the 1967 1000 Km of Monza of 25 April, which was Bandini's last victory – with Amon – before his tragic accident at Monte Carlo. Left: the winning Bandini-Amon 330 P4 (3) is preceded by the Scarfiotti-Parkes sister car (4) and the Rodriguez-Guichet privately entered 412 P (9): the first two are about to lap the Herrmann-Siffert Porsche 907 as they come off Monza's Parabolica. Opposite page, colour picture: the start of the 1000 Km of Monza, with the P4 of Bandini-Amon followed by the 412 P driven by Rodriguez-Guichet. Destined for private teams, the 412s were updated P3s with carburetors, a fuel feed system that was no longer used on the works cars after the P2. Opposite, above: the Scarfiotti-Parkes P4 in the foreground, with the well-known mechanic Antonio Bellentani beside it.

But Ford made a big mistake over the reliability of its highly modern 7-litre cars: in an effort to thwart our attack, they ordered their drivers to go flat out. The race became more interesting, but the Americans were massacred by breakdowns.

Enzo Ferrari was, rightly, proud of that victory – I have rarely seen him so pleased but, in line with his style, he did not celebrate. Like all of us, he had had his revenge for the Le Mans defeat. And that was preceded by Lorenzo Bandini's tremendous win in the 1000 Km of Monza, where the Italian, paired with Amon, was really fast against the fearsome Chaparral. Sadly, it was Bandini's last victory; he died two weeks later after an accident at Monte Carlo.

We went to Le Mans with four P4s and we were confident, even if Ford did enter 12 cars comprising Mk IVs, Mk IIs, Mirages and GT40s. And that's without counting the even more imposing organisation they had put together, which even included a hair dresser!

But we noticed something was wrong in practice. Ford had problems with their driver crews as some of them had not practiced so, as the regulations stipulated, they could not compete in the race. Our motor sport director Franco Lini raised the matter with the organisers, but he could do nothing. Ford had permission to run an extra private practice session on the Saturday morning to make sure those crews qualified. Something that had never previously happened in the history of Le Mans, although some teams had made similar requests. It was clear that Ford's influence on the event had grown.

But the most incredible episode, which cost us any hope of winning the race, was linked to the official communication of the cars' positions after each lap. IBM systematically distributed communications that corresponded with the results obtained by our time keepers, who were highly experienced members of the Federazione Italiana Cronometristi and mistake proof. From around midnight, we no longer received the IBM communications and were told the automatic timing system was momentarily out of action. Still, we were sure that our Scarfiotti-Parkes P4 was only a lap behind the leading Gurney-Foyt Ford, which was the 'hare'. I remember our satisfaction and also a

discussion with engineer Bussi that we were forcing Lodovico and Mike to drive high pressure laps to keep up, despite our fuel and tyre consumption advantage. At a certain point, Scarfiotti became ill and Parkes had to do a double stint. The Englishman lost a little ground, but according to our time keepers' data we were still just one lap down on the Ford. Yet at dawn, we were bitterly disappointed when the IBM system started to work again and they brought us a communication that said Scarfiotti and Parkes were five laps behind the Ford! That was both incredible and inexplicable, because there was no way our time keepers could have made such a huge mistake.

Naturally, we reacted fast: Franco Lini made his protest and they assured us they had checked

their lap counter, but there was nothing we could do. Later, Lodovico's health improved and he was able to pull something back from the Ford, but the P4 could still only maintain its second place. And all this happened while the leading Ford Mk IV was losing bits of its bodywork due to broken fixings. It was all being held together by sticky tape and there was a real chance that the huge rear end might fly off and injure some spectators. On top of which, the Le Mans regulations said the car had to cross the finish line with its body intact. Franco Lini was about to protest but, supported by Bussi, we were told we had to go directly to Finance, the powerful boss of the Le Mans organisers and a person who had always been close to Ferrari and the Commendatore himself. Finance

listened to me and then gave me a short, sharp answer, *"Mauro, c'est l'argent…"* after which I understood everything.

It may have been a coincidence, but the route was modified for the following year with the important and complex chicane before the finish line which, from that moment on, was called the "Chicane Ford…"

Those were the reasons for our defeat, even though a glorious one, so much so that the top Ford men came to congratulate us. We also took third place with the Mairesse-'Beurlys' P4 – the pseudonym was of the really fast Jean Blaton, which he adopted because of family opposition to his racing: he was one of the top Belgian drivers whose daughter married Jacky Ickx. Their

P4, the Scafiotti-Parkes' sister car, also beat the previous year's record.

Strangely, Enzo Ferrari reacted with less violence than on other occasions when he was told that his team had lost even though it was competitive. I believe he knew everything that had happened on both the sporting front – the extra practice on race morning – and Ford's powerful influence. So it is clear that he had some excellent informants. Anyway, that was the result and a revolution would have been counterproductive, partly because the International Championship of Makes, which Ford had won the previous year, would be decided in July at Britain's Brand Hatch circuit. Controversy would have been useless and would have diverted concentration from the upcoming finale. At Brands,

there would not only be the a number of Fords – not the Le Mans 7-litres, which were developed for ultra-fast circuits, but the fearsome GT40s – and the Chaparral 2F-Chevrolet, the futuristic American sports racer that we beat at Monza. The 2F took its revenge and won in the UK, but we still came second with Jackie Stewart and Chris Amon. It was the first time the future triple F1 world champion had driven a Ferrari and he wasn't even a sports racing car specialist, but he adapted perfectly well to the situation and was exceptional.

Of that race I remember a pit stop when Jackie complained about a slight but unpleasant amount of exhaust gas leaking into the cockpit. Some bulkhead bolts had loosened behind the driver, which was a fairly normal occurrence on

racing cars until a type of aircraft fixing system came in. There was no chance of tightening the bolts at the time, so I broke a small Plexiglas window with my fist to create an exit. An improvisation, but it helped us win the international championship.

At the end of the 1967 season, Ferrari decided not to compete in the 1968 International Championship for Makes. His reasons could have been many, among them that I had been saying for some time that he should make the break; or due to the enormous commitment that would have diverted us from developing the best possible F1 car, which already seemed it had winning potential; perhaps the Le Mans situation contributed to the decision; or Ford's partial re-

tirement. It was the first time Ferrari would not be competing for the sports car championship since the series began in 1953. The decision was officially justified by saying it was due to the International Federation, which had lowered the engines' cubic capacity to 3000 cc. It looked like a gift for Porsche, who were unbeaten in the minor capacity classes. If Ferrari had asked us, we would have quickly readied a competitive 3-litre, but there was something else that made him 'surrender'. So he let us catch our breath a little, but another six years would pass before he finally agreed to favour Formula 1 at the expense of sports car racing. I made some optimistic predictions for 1968, but they turned out to be seriously flawed.

From the departure of Surtees to the arrival of Ickx
The difficult 1966-1969 seasons

Enzo Ferrari was especially intuitive in quickly in understanding the positive side of a proposal, particularly when moving from the project to the practical stage. In my case, he played the fundamental role of a filter, evaluating every decision financially and assuming the responsibility for it himself. Our rapport was a direct one of reciprocal trust, because both of us knew we were working for the communal good: the success of the Prancing Horse. It didn't happen as often as people say, but sometimes I lost my patience and our discussion became a furious argument, with the two of us shouting at each other. Obviously, I couldn't go beyond a certain limit and, at that point, my tactic was to say, "You're the boss. If you don't agree, let's go back and do it the way you want it". But I must say that didn't often happen.

When the discussion was not so "boisterous", I allowed myself to remind him – almost always in the Modenese dialect to ease the tension – that I was the engineer and that's what he was paying me for. That cheesed him off, because he liked to be called 'engineer' himself after receiving an honorary degree in 1960. Mine was not a superior attitude, that would have been all we needed. I only wanted to divide the roles in line with the concept he expressed so clearly when he promoted me to head up motor sport. Ferrari had always called me Mauro and sometimes he surprised me by adding, "You won't be offended if I don't call you engineer…?" Hardly! I liked him calling me Mauro and considered it as a sign of affection, which it was in reality.

This relationship also helped me to overcome the difficult years, like those of 1966 to 1969, even if during the latter – and I will explain why later – I designed for the future without being closely involved with the racing department. During those years, Ferrari only won three Grands Prix; the Belgian and Italian in 1966 and the French in 1968. We were key players (Ferrari achieved three pole positions in '66 and four in 68, Ed), but a number of incidents were added to our normal technical difficulties. They included the huge effort, both human and financial, it took to take on the Ford challenge in sports car racing; the departure of John Surtees in mid-1966; the resignation of motor sport director Eugenio Dragoni – a great drama of coordination with Enzo Ferrari – all at the end of

Previous pages: Monza, 4 September 1966 – a peaceful invasion of
the track by the fans began with the triumph of Lodovico Scarfiotti in the GP of Italy. The crowd was deliriously happy for
the driver from the Marches and for Ferrari, which had entered
three 312s with the new 3-valves per cylinder engine. Mikes
Parkes took second place, but it was also significant that Lorenzo
Bandini was forced to retire. A story of other times, when there
were fewer regulations dictated by the FIA and Bernie Ecclestone, but how much more enthusiasm there was then!
Page 111: confirmation of Mauro Forghieri's common sense as
he works to set up a Dino F2 engine.
This page, above, left: the 36-valve Ferrari 312 during tests prior
to the GP of Italy. In the cockpit is mechanic Giulio Borsari; in
the darker overalls is Marelli technician 'Sparky' Tramonti. The
312 was the first F1 Ferrari designed by Forghieri to meet the
regulations that came into effect on 1 January 1966, which called
for 3000 cc engines.
Opposite page: Testimony to the famous argument between
John Surtees and motor sport director Eugenio Dragoni at the
1966 GP of Monaco. Fiery words flew back and forth as Maranello press office boss Franco Gozzi and his wife Gabriella
look on, astounded. There was no more 'feeling' between Enzo
Ferrari and the British driver, so after that came the divorce, to
which the Italian motor sport weekly Autosprint devoted its front
cover. Losing Surtees was a serious mistake, according to engineer Forghieri.

the same year. Then there was the horrific death of Lorenzo Bandini at the 1967 GP of Monaco and the incredible bad luck of a good driver like Chris Amon, who joined us at the beginning of '67.

In 1965, we worked through the night many times due to our long list of commitments, which included designing, developing and building a new car and engine for F1 in 1966, when the cubic capacity doubled from 1500 cc to 3000 cc. We had nothing on the shelf so we were unprepared, as were the British teams, which still came up with great cars. Our first problem was the engine: it was unthinkable to start a totally new project. We didn't like giving it up, but it was expensive and we had our long tradition of 12-cylinder 3000 cc engines to consider; as the Commendatore reminded me, "we practically have

the engine in-house". In fact, we exhumed an old V12 twin cam power unit with its cylinder banks at 60°, a sports car racing version of which had been used in the Fifties. It still had screw-in cylinder sleeves, because back then head gaskets were unreliable. It was an antiquated engine, heavy and a big step back from the highly modern V8 1500. But I must honestly admit that, if the Commendatore had given me a free hand to design an engine from zero, I would not have come up with the flat 3000, which arrived five years later. I still hadn't thought of it: I would have been happy with a much more modern 60° V12 that was lighter and more rigid than the unit we ended up using. Still, we did what we could to make the old flat 3000 more modern, changing things like the drive shaft and modifying the head,

which had normal gaskets. We also adopted Lucas indirect fuel injection, although I would have preferred to continue with the direct version, which had worked so well on the 1500 cc single-seater and was exclusively for Ferrari's use. But we needed the support of Bosch for the supply of a new injection pump, given that the one used on the V8 was unsuitable. The German manufacturer asked for a contribution towards the pump's design, but Ferrari did not feel he could make such an investment at the time. That was a big disappointment, because we could have continued to have an undoubted advantage for years to come, one that we could also have transferred to our road cars.

Even if updated, the old V12 was still an engine from another era, massive and bulky. We could only re-

duce its weight slightly, because we had to use castings that had been conserved. But there was no uncertainty about the chassis: we went back to the Aero type of construction after the experience with the over expensive aluminium monocoque, while we successfully adopted the suspension layout that had worked so well on the previous 1500.

And that is how the 312 came about, with that heavy engine and, therefore, with a slightly unbalanced rear end. The car's power output – 360 hp on its debut – wasn't bad for the period, but John Surtees was forced into a long period of testing to find the car's equilibrium. Bandini was assigned the 246 Tasmania, which was built for the championship that took place in the southern hemisphere during our winter. That car had a 2.4-litre V6 Dino engine

which generated 280 hp, an optimum power output taking the car's 500 kg weight into consideration (the limit permitted by the regulations, Ed) against the 312's 550 kg, which was mainly due to its heavy engine. The Tasmania's main claim to fame was its equilibrium, but the 312 was also competitive, taking the opposition into account. Surtees started next to pole sitter Jim Clark's Lotus on the front line of the grid at Monte Carlo and then led the race before having to stop with a broken transmission. Controversially, John had asked Dragoni if he could drive Bandini's more agile Tasmania, saying he would win with ease. But at the GP of Belgium on the 14 kilometre Spa road circuit three weeks later, Surtees scored a fantastic victory in the 312.

Despite a few technical compromises, the 312

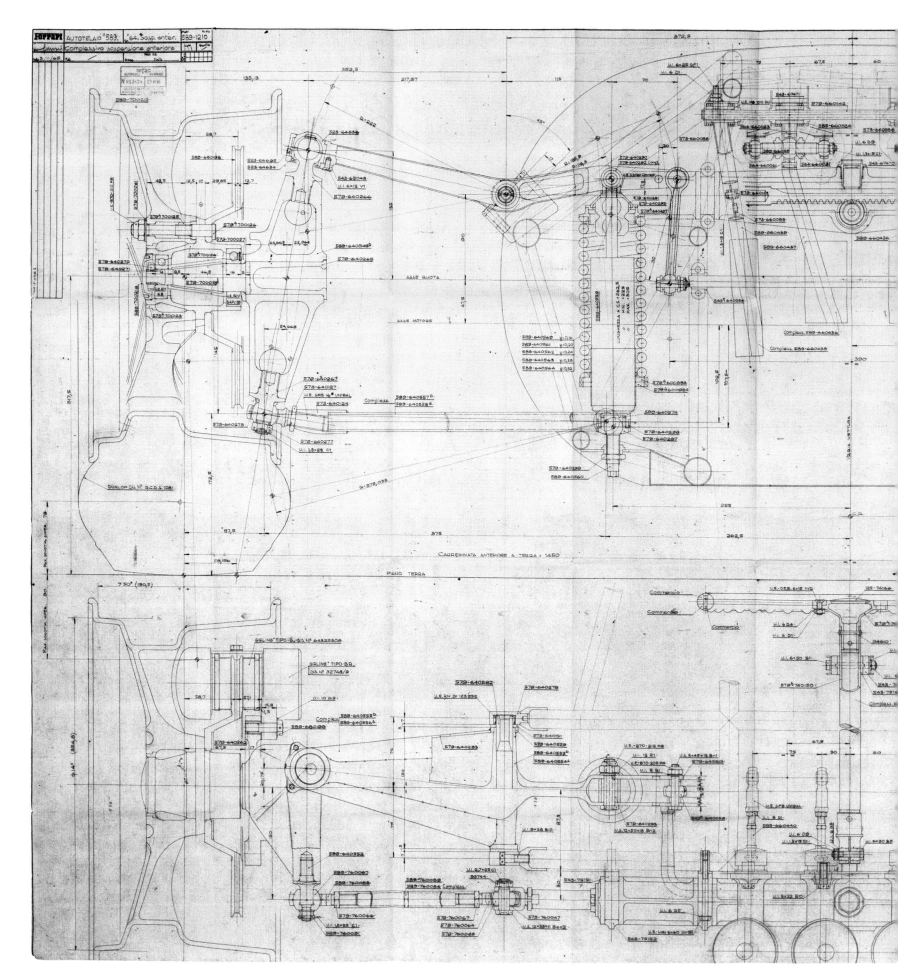

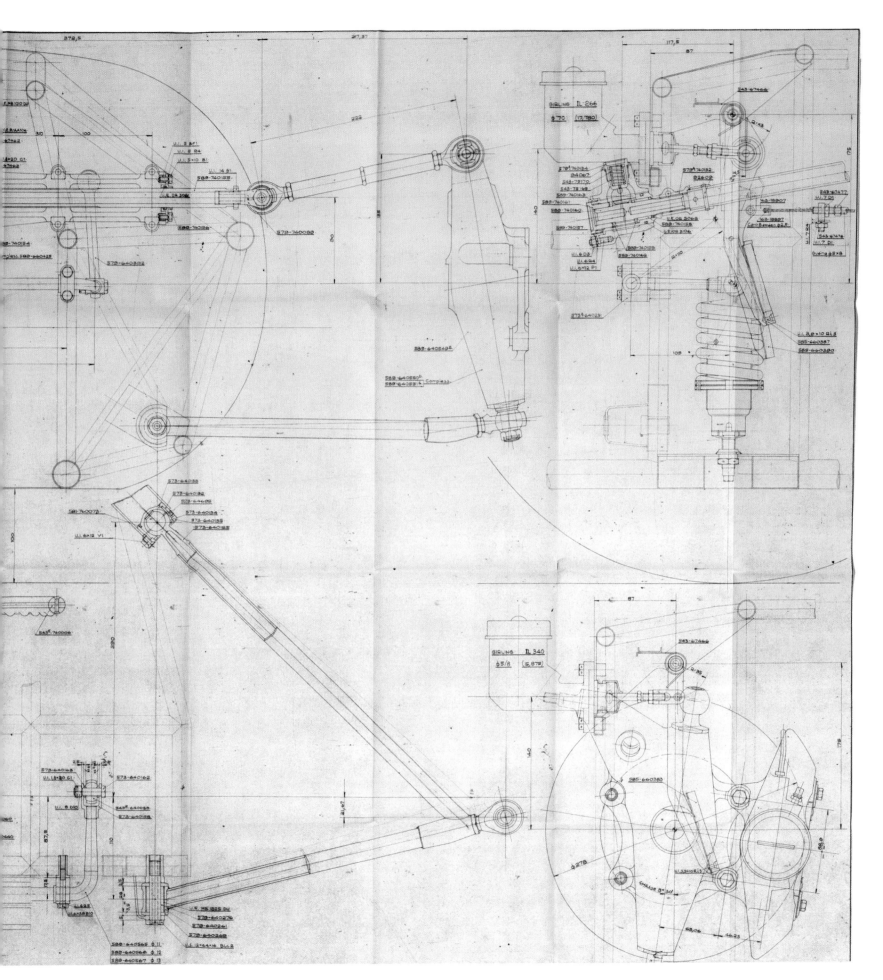

Previous two pages: until the start of the Eighties, Ferrari designers set down their engineers' ideas on paper and were well-known for their precision and notable technical culture. That is confirmed by this fascinating drawing of one of engineer Forghieri's projects, dated 29 June 1966, of the entire front end of the Ferrari 312 F1 car. In the upper part of the drawing is the front view in which can be seen the steering, suspension with spring-internal damper groups, the hubs with the disc brake complex and a rim with tyre. The lower area with the steering wheel shows the same components from above.
Above, left: Lorenzo Bandini and his wife Margherita watching practice for the 1966 GP of France: Bandini took pole position and led the race until the 32nd lap, when he retired with a broken accelerator cable.
Below: even today, the Eau Rouge-Raidillon corner at Spa-Francorchamps is respected by drivers. But back in time, it was a real test of courage and driving ability. Here, John Surtees in a 24-valve Ferrari 312 leads the grid away after the start of the 1966 GP of Belgium, which he would go on to win.

played its part well and Surtees would have been able to aim for his second world title. Instead, the whole thing came to an end with his controversial departure, which nobody expected – and here I speak of us technical people – in spite of complaints from Enzo Ferrari and the hostile attitude of motor sport director Dragoni.

It all started on 25 September 1965, when John competed in a Can-Am race driving a Lola 70 in which he had his serious accident. Surtees and the boss of Lola, Eric Broadley, were friends as the constructor had run John in Formula 1 in 1962 but later became a collaborator of Ford, our adversary in sports car racing. Broadley had developed the prototype Lola GT, which was later transformed into the famous Ford GT40.

Mike Parkes being welcomed by Enzo Ferrari on his return to Maranello, still showing signs of his serious accident in the 1967 GP of Belgium at Spa. Due to a patch of oil from Jackie Stewart's BRM, Parkes went off at the fast Blanchimont corner when he was lying fourth. He was thrown out of the Ferrari 312 and ended up on the track in front of the cars of his team mates Chris Amon and Lodovico Scarfiotti, who were able to avoid him. Result: shock, a broken leg and a fractured wrist.

But I don't believe John raced at Mosport without the permission of Enzo Ferrari, who was possessive and intransigent on such matters. He made an exception just for Surtees, a driver the Commendatore thought highly of for his class and determination at work. The two liked each other, partly because Ferrari could chat with his driver in Italian. When John relaxed he was pleasant and extrovert, although he did have one defect: it was really difficult to get him to pay for the coffee…

Ferrari was most concerned about the terrible accident, which kept John immobile for months. They spoke on the phone a number of times – and Surtees remembered with gratitude that Maranello's insurance covered him, even though he had been driving another constructor's car at the time. So

when John came back to work for Ferrari at the end of the 1965 winter with his first wife Pat, he was welcomed like a prodigal son.

But relations were no longer as before. John's driving talent was intact, but his character had changed: he was less open and more irritable. And that's how a period of disagreements began, even over the most ordinary things. Ferrari had become obstinate and relations between the team and the driver became completely exclusive. They said Surtees had carried out some brief tests during his time in Britain and that he also had an interest in Broadley's factory. John never spoke of such matters with me; anyway I respected him and continued to do so as a driver and as a man. He always made important technical suggestions to me

After the controversial departure of John Surtees in June and a subsequent period of not much success, Enzo Ferrari asked his collaborators for a maximum effort to win the 1966 Grand Prix of Italy. So in little more than a month, the racing department was able to produce the 312 heads with 3-valves per cylinder, which took the V12's power output to around 350 hp initially and later about 370 hp. Lodovico Scarfiotti (6) was a great prototype driver and was competing in only his fourth world championship GP at Monza, where he pulled off a fantastic victory. In a race in which Lorenzo Bandini was continually dogged by small technical problems, Scarfiotti found that only his team mate Mikes Parkes (4) could compete with him, although the Englishman helped Lodovico to contain pressure from Denny Hulme.

and put everything into solving a problem. He was one of the greats, whom I would have no trouble in putting on the same level as Jim Clark.

Yet the Commendatore was intransigent, partly because he feared his ex-driver could take to Lola experience he had gathered at Ferrari, seeing that Broadley was developing the T70 sports racer, which was similar to our P4 even if it was eventually disappointing. A sort of 'spy story' I never believed, but Ferrari was notoriously protective and told Dragoni to make Surtees leave the team.

Even today there are those who believe Dragoni was totally to blame for Surtees leaving, that he himself decided to get rid of a driver who did not comply with the team's regulations. But that is absolutely ridiculous, because the motor sport

director had no power over matters of that kind, about which Ferrari made the decisions and nobody else. In fact, he ordered Dragoni to work out a strategy that would lead Surtees – exasperated by the attitude towards him – to resigning. The moment arrived with the 24 Hours of Le Mans, which was to take place a week after the GP of Belgium at Spa: when listing the crews for the race, Lodovico Scarfiotti's name was put down as Surtees' reserve. Something completely out of the ordinary, as well as offensive that a champion of John's calibre could not tolerate. That is how a relationship dating back to 1962 fell to bits.

Personally, there was no way I agreed with the choice of drivers, but my opinion was only indicative. Naturally, the affair naturally created uproar in

the press, with Dragoni being blamed and Ferrari able to keep himself out of it.

But I had no time to reflect on what had happened, because there was plenty of work to do: developing the 3-valve F1 engine (two aspiration and one exhaust, Ed), the P4 Sport project for the following year, the V6 engine for the F2 car… And with that pile of work going on, we had lost a great driver who could have been extremely useful. I will never forget the following two or three months, when I literally had sleepless nights. Mike Parkes took John Surtees' place as tester-driver, but we were forced to build a 'long' F1 car that matched Mike's height – another complication.

Lorenzo Bandini was promoted to number one F1 driver and there was always Lodovico Scarfiotti,

An arm raised with joy, Lodovico Scarfiotti is about to take the chequered flag being brandished by race director Gianni Restelli that signals the end of the 68-lap, 391 km 1966 Italian Grand Prix. Six seconds later, Mike Parkes crosses the finish line after battling to the end to contain Denny Hulme's Brabham-Repco, which came third just 3/10 of a second after the Englishman. The Ferrari 312 with its 3-valves per cylinder engine was showing its competitiveness, even if Mauro Forghieri would have preferred to go for a more modern unit from the outset. But for cost reasons, Enzo Ferrari obliged him to go back to the concept of a V12 used in sports car racing about 10 years earlier. The Commendatore was particularly pleased with the Monza victory, although he did not demonstrate that fact openly. He would have liked to close the F1 season there and then to concentrate all the Scuderia's efforts on the Ford prototype challenge, which would be on again in 1967. It was only after pressure from his American importer, Luigi Chinetti, that a 36-valve 312 was sent to the US GP at the last minute for Lorenzo Bandini, who drove a fine race at the difficult Watkins Glen circuit; he was leading at mid-race when he had to retire with an engine problem caused by a broken spark plug. Ferrari did not compete in the subsequent Mexican GP or the first race of the following F1 season in South Africa. Engineer Forghieri recalls that the team's results in the second half of the Sixties and beyond were sometimes conditioned by union difficulties, which disrupted the continuity of the racing department's work. Despite the extremely good relations that were always maintained with the workers' representatives, strikes also hit Ferrari, which was forced to slow the development of its projects and at times race engines could not even be overhauled.

another good, fast racer, but I knew we had lost the only champion with a real chance of bringing the F1 world championship back to Maranello. No team stood out particularly, but we had a sufficiently fast 312. In fact, Bandini took pole at the Grand Prix of France and led the race for 32 laps before being stopped by a broken fuel pipe.

The debut of the more powerful 3-valve, which put out 390 hp at 10,000 rpm and was slightly lighter, was brought forward to the GP of Italy on 4 September after pressure from Enzo Ferrari, who had always considered the Monza GP as a sort of personal parade ground. That year, there were also other reasons that 'forced' Ferrari to seek success at home. The departure of John Surtees, who later took second place in the German Grand Prix

driving a Cooper-Maserati, created a controversial backlash, while our subsequent lack of success at the 24 Hours of Le Mans weighed heavily on morale. We had to make sure Ferrari won again; I don't know who worked harder between the test room and assembly, but the decision to race the 3-valve turned out to be a good one. We completely dominated the Italian GP to the sheer joy of the Commendatore, whom I had rarely seen so openly pleased. Throughout the following Monday, he showed his happiness without his usual intimidating air. And he kept joking, letting phrases in dialect slip out about everyone from time to time, but with an underlying threat. *"A la vi messa bèin con cla Vittoria, se no, vo' avrev vest cosa cavcapiteva…"* (So you sorted yourselves out

with that victory then, otherwise you would have seen what would have happened…"). He was also pleased because Lodovico Scarfiotti had won; he deserved that result for all the enthusiasm he put into his racing. In addition Lulù, as everyone called him, was close to Gianni Agnelli with whom he talked about racing and, naturally, this could favour a closer relationship between Fiat and Ferrari. The press wrote about a "great Ferrari", which was quite a complement, but in reality financial problems were beginning to surface that would lead to the agreement with the Turin car maker in 1969. Much of the 1967 budget was swallowed up by the P4 project, so the 312 F1 car was just updated, even if fairly substantially. New developments included a slight lightening of the chassis to 530

Above: final scenes of the John Frankenheimer film 'Grand Prix', which had the support of the leading F1 teams, were shot during the 1966 Italian GP. In the film Adolfo Celi played Commendatore Manetta, a role modelled on Enzo Ferrari, who is pictured talking to his 'double' in the pits.
Far left: Yves Montand, in the cockpit of an imitation Ferrari, talking to Lodovico Scarfiotti, winner of the real Grand Prix, as the Frenchman plays driver Jean-Pierre Sarti, who dies in a Monza accident. Left: Lorenzo Bandini poses with Françoise Hardy, who played Lisa in the film and had a flirt with 'driver' Barlini (Antonio Sabàto).

kg, even if Maranello had never worked in this area with any kind of determination: we only had complete freedom on the dimensions of the engine and gearbox. But there was nothing we could do to improve those elements in the case of the 312. We modified the heads, placed exhausts at the centre of the cylinder bank V to reduce the transverse bulk of the car, which was fundamental to improving top speed at the time and enabled us to return to the much smaller size of the 158 F1.

Unfortunately, the season was marred by the awful tragedy of Lorenzo Bandini's accident at Monte Carlo, but the 312 development did better balance the car compared to the 1966 version. Circumstances forced us to take another look at the programmes, so that after the Grand Prix of Bel-

gium we only ever entered a car for Chris Amon. Mike Parkes had had a serious accident at Spa that meant he was immobile for months with a broken leg. And after the Dutch GP, Scarfiotti did not race in F1 again and was given no explanation as to why not, but one knew his family had asked Gianni Agnelli to intervene with Ferrari so that he only competed in sports car racing. Unfortunately, an incredible twist of fate led him to join Porsche the following year, when he lost his life in a hillclimb. The famous Lotus 49 powered its legendary Ford-Cosworth DFV engine made its debut in the 1967 GP of Holland, a historic motor racing occasion. The car was extremely interesting, but was based on concepts that had already been developed by others, Ferrari included. I was impressed by the

The rapport between Enzo Ferrari and the Italian drivers was not always smooth, but in reality he often appreciated their qualities and put them to the test when a chance presented itself. In early autumn 1967, it was the turn of 26 year-old Andrea De Adamich, who had won the Italian F3 Championship and had then moved on to Alfa Romeo, where he did well with the 33 Sport and GTA. The Milanese driver had already been given a test at Monza by Ferrari in a P2 in May 1965 for a possible place in the team at the 24 Hours of Le Mans, but the matter ended there. In1967, Ferrari tested him again for possible involvement in F1 with a series of tests in the 312 at the Modena Autodrome, Monza and Vallelunga. The picture on the right is of the Monza test, where the 312 was supervised by engineer Gianni Marelli, shown speaking to De Adamich. During the test, the driver seemed fast and safe so that Ferrari entered him for a non-championship F2 event on 12 November at Jarama, near Madrid. Among the many competitors at the Spanish race were the Lotus-Ford F1 cars of Graham Hill and Jim Clark, plus Jack Brabham in a Brabham-Repco. In the finale, De Adamich was beginning to earn himself a good third place until a puncture caused his retirement. But he was confirmed for 1968 and on 1 January he competed in the Grand Prix of South Africa at Kyalami. He was eighth fastest in qualifying, ahead of more experienced colleagues like Chris Amon and Jacky Ickx, but he went off during the race. In March, he was involved in a serious accident at the Brands Hatch in the Champions' Cup event, as a result of which he spent many months recovering, but at the end of the year he won the Temporada Argentina in a Ferrari Dino F2. However, the subsequent technical sports reorganisation at Maranello in 1969 left no room for him at Ferrari and he did not return.

global efficiency of the Ford V8 unit, the clear result of the American company's support of F1. I realised that modern research and new ideas were at the heart of that engine: confirmation of a number of convictions I held together with engineer Bussi on the engines we used for our racing cars. Even if it was not all that clear at the time, the turnaround had begun so that 18 months later it led me to review my role with Ferrari to re-launch the Maranello racing department.

After the Grand Prix of Belgium, Chris Amon shouldered Ferrari's responsibilities in the remaining seven GPs of the season. The 23 year-old was fast, courageous and determined and had a refined technical sensibility but – at least at that time – with a character that was developing. He was

Above: Chris Amon should have made his Ferrari F1 debut in the Champions Cup at Brands Hatch in March 1967, but he was involved in a road accident before the race so he made his first appearance at Monte Carlo in May, the day Bandini crashed and later died. Below: Amon in the updated 4-valves per cylinder Ferrari 312.

great friends with Bandini, who was eight years his senior, so that after the Monaco tragedy he was shaken and disoriented. Chris was a lad with heart and when he saw Lorenzo's 312 overturned and burning, he stopped at the pits for a few seconds to ask for news. It was something that touched us, even though we urged him to get back into the race immediately.

Amon began his Formula 1 career when he was just 19 years-old, driving sporadically for minor teams. He had a reputation for being an incorrigible night owl, but Modena changed him. He put everything into making the 312 shine and took it to four third places in 1967.

Ferrari liked Amon from the start, as he appreciated drivers who didn't try to become big shots and had

real test driving capabilities. In that sense, Chris was a great discovery. He got right to the heart of the matter and gave precise answers without waltzing around the matter in hand like so many other drivers did. And at that time, a tester-driver was essential. We had signed an agreement with Firestone and our commitment had changed a lot compared to when we were associated with Dunlop.

The British tyre manufacturer was the sole supplier to all the F1 teams and every year it simply came up with a compound and type of tread pattern homologated with the famous "M", followed by a number. The arrival of Firestone changed the rapport between the tyre men and the teams: competition between the two tyre companies had led to the continuous development of their products to make

The Ferrari 312 was substantially developed during 1967.
Above: the definitive car made its debut at Monza for the Grand
Prix of Italy: it had a new, lighter, 48-valve engine that produced
400 hp, a more slender body and a total weight close to the 500
kg limit. The new gearbox, which had two shafts and removable
ratios that could be easily replaced, made its appearance at the
German GP and weighed 15 kg less than its predecessor.
Below: Amon testing the updated 312 at Monza.

them more competitive, as had always been the
case until the more recent return to the exclusive
supplier again. So we became an F1 test team
with excellent financial advantages. We were fully
available to the American company and obviously a driver like Amon, who was so accurate with
his diagnoses, was of real value to us. The programme envisaged development work on various
circuits with a preference for the highly technical
Brand Hatch, near London. That track really drove
home to me how Chris was a driver suited to Ferrari. It was the end of 1966 and he had just become "ours", but he was still committed by contract to McLaren as a Can-Am driver and F1 tester.
We tested tyres from 9 am until 4 pm with a short
break for lunch. After testing every set, the driver

gave his impressions to a tyre engineer, who was
a pleasant man. We were all in the same hotel and
in the evening we talked about the day's work with
a comradeship that, unfortunately, died out a few
years later. The engineer said Amon carried out
suitably spaced tests of three sets of brand new
tyres that had identical characteristics during the
course of the same day, but each time he was told
they were new. And his comments on all three sets
were absolutely identical!

It was Chris who cleared up any doubts I had about
the 312's chassis, because in his opinion it was
as good as those of the opposition. But he asked
for more power from the V12, a problem that we
unfortunately knew only too well. As usual, after
the 24 Hours of Le Mans we worked like crazy to

Black day
at Monte Carlo

Without the overpowering presence of John Surtees as number one driver, Lorenzo Bandini felt more at ease at Ferrari. He became more certain of himself and of his abilities. And he had a good relationship with the newly arrived Chris Amon, an excellent driver who was good at human relationships. Lorenzo had a positive character, although he was not a talker but he was open. If he spoke every now and then of future possible successes in early 1967 – like "this will be my year", which he also said to Ferrari, it meant he really believed it.

We didn't compete in the Grand Prix of South Africa in January because we were fully committed preparing for the 24 Hours of Daytona, but we were sure we would be key players in the GP of Monaco on 7 May. Lorenzo was even more certain and he liked the Monte Carlo cir-

cuit, where he came second in two earlier Monaco GPs and third in 1962. He was anxious to do better after the disappointment of the previous year in the 2.4 246, when he was unable to beat Jackie Stewart in the 2-litre BRM P 261. Instead, that 1967 Grand Prix of Monaco was transformed into a tragedy that deeply upset me. Everything began in a serene atmosphere late on the Wednesday afternoon before the GP. We were at the Modena Autodrome for our usual final test session to check the Bandini and Amon 312s and everything was fine. Lorenzo was showing off one of the new Dino Spiders he had been given to test for Fiat and was to drive it to Monte Carlo. He was on his own, because his wife Margherita travelled from Milan to meet up with him in Monaco at the weekend, so I was happy to accept the lift he offered. It was a pleasant trip: Lorenzo drove with ease, but he was never one who had to show how fast he could go on public roads. When we arrived, I was surprised to find a room had not been booked for me at the usual hotel; there was a reservation, but from the following night, which was strange because the Maranello travel office was very efficient. But with the race on the horizon we were optimistic and I didn't get too worked up, even if it was impossible to find a room in Monaco for that night. There wasn't much else that I could do except accompany Lorenzo to his slightly better hotel than those of the Ferrari team and then "go to bed" in the Dino's reclining seat in an area without traffic just above the Principality.

Everything went fine during the two practice days, but at the start of the last qualifying session, Lorenzo went into the Mirabeau corner too

fast, hit a wall and slightly damaged his car's suspension. The 312 was more or less imprisoned on the circuit, but Lorenzo didn't lose his head; he was a good mechanic, so after a quick repair, he brought the car back to the Monte Carlo pits and the mechanics soon sorted the problem. To me, Lorenzo didn't seem agitated, but it was possible that the problem cost him the pole position: he was beaten by Jack Brabham (Brabham-Repco) by six tenths of a second at 1 minute 27.6 seconds to Lorenzo's 1 minute 28.3. In the race, Brabham was involuntarily responsible for the beginning of Bandini's drama. Lorenzo was "charged" and didn't want to risk being tied up in traffic as in other years, so he made a great start. But he only covered the first lap in the lead, during which second placed Brabham's car had a serious engine breakdown after the Mirabeau corner. Unfortunately, he decided to return to the pits and flooded the track with oil. Denny Hulme (Brabham-Repco) and Jackie Stewart (BRM), who were behind the Australian, managed to avoid the slippery trail but on the next lap the signalling was not sufficient to prevent the unaware Bandini from slowing down to avoid the oil slick, a manoeuvre that immediately took him to third place. But that still left another 98 laps before the end of the race and it is not possible that a professional of his calibre lost his enthusiasm.

By the 15th lap he was second after Stewart's retirement, 7.5 seconds from Hulme. We could see no problem with the car and he had not signalled anything to us, yet his lap times were inconsistent so that his distance from the leader increased and then decreased without any logical explanation. At the time, the Monaco GP

ran for 100 laps with short straights, so it was real torture for the drivers, who were always under pressure. Lorenzo was physically fit as well as extremely correct in his style of life, but after three quarters of the race we had no doubts: tiredness stopped him from driving as he should. Thoughts that were confirmed by photographers and spectators along the track. With 18 laps to go, he got into difficulty at the harbour chicane and I have always been sure that the cause of the accident was some kind of collapse. Soon after the accident, an enthusiast brought me a close-up photo taken just before the crash that showed Lorenzo with a tired, dulled look about him.

At that time, the chicane was one of the most difficult points of the Monte Carlo city circuit, because the angulation of the track was much less pronounced than it is now. The cars did about 250 kph on the descent after the tunnel and the best drivers went through the chicane in third gear at about 160 kph, cutting it with two quick jerks of the steering wheel, left then right. By comparison, modern F1 cars get up to 290 kph on the section before the chicane, but they go through it at less than 80 kph.

Those who saw the tragedy told of how 312 number 18 skidded to the left without a correction, hit a lamp post first and then the heavy handrail of the steel steps leading to the hard shoulder below. Dangerous objects that were only protected by a few bales of straw, which added fuel to the fire that started when the rubber aircraft-type fuel tank broke, sheared off by the bar of that damned steel steps. The rescue squad was completely inadequate, even when compared to the general level of the period, anything but high quality.

The hours that followed the accident were terrible, because we had no accurate information about Lorenzo. Nobody could get near the part of the Princess Grace Hospital to which our driver had been admitted, not even his wife Margherita, who was soul-destroyed but went through those hours with great courage. By the time Alexander Onassis, son of the famous arms dealer, offered to accompany me to the hospital it was dark. He was a lad of only 19, very kind and altruistic as well as crazy about Ferrari. With his knowledge, he was able to ensure I spoke with the doctor before the official communiqué was issued at almost midnight. Unfortunately, there was no hope for Bandini, mainly because of the burns.

The death of Lorenzo was painful to us all; we considered him one of the family as he had practically grown up at Ferrari. Always helpful, he remained the same simple young man as when he joined us. He considered himself privileged, especially in his relations with the mechanics to whom he was always kind and generous.

Naturally, we examined every detail of the crashed 312, its gearbox and transmission included, but we found nothing wrong. Unfortunately, hitting some something as unforgiving as the handrail of some steel steps could have nothing other than serious consequences. With the Federation's regulations and especially the technology of the period, the problem could not be solved. Even if a very precise rule was in force at Maranello for which Ferrari was a stickler: we should never reach the limit

in designing a car, a rule that I personally respected to the full.

The Monte Carlo circuit was erroneously considered safe because the average speeds were low, but the total absence of guardrails, which by that time were being widely adopted, made it very dangerous. And, rightly, Enzo Ferrari decided not to send his team to the following year's GP of Monaco to underline this incongruity. It was no coincidence that guardrails were subsequently installed and the race was reduced from 100 to 80 laps. After the Bandini accident, a campaign to improve safety that involved everyone – car manufacturers, organisers, drivers and the Federation – was mounted, even if it was rather slow getting off the ground.

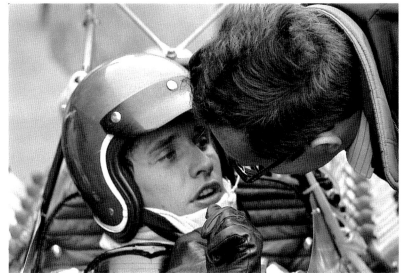

Above, right: Jacky Ickx, seen here talking to Mauro Forghieri, made his Ferrari F1 debut on 1 January 1968, his 23rd birthday, in the Grand Prix of South Africa, from which he retired with an engine problem. Despite the fact that he had only won a single GP in France that season, he was second in the world championship behind Graham Hill when there were only the Grands Prix of Canada, the United States and Mexico to go. Unfortunately, he had an accelerator problem during the first of the three, crashed and fractured a leg.
Above, left: the OM 150 truck, which transported Maranello's cars to the circuits during the second half of the Sixties. It was driven by the legendary Dino Pignatti, who was also a mechanic and pit signaller. The words "Brands Hatch" below the Prancing Horse meant the truck was on its way to the 1968 British GP.

develop a head with 4-valves per cylinder, a modern head with valves that formed a very tight angle with each other. The car was putting out around 390 hp at almost 11,000 rpm so that in the last two GPs of the season Amon, who started the Mexican GP next to Jim Clark's Lotus 49, was the only driver to give the Scot a fight for his money. If we had put all our efforts into developing our F1 car from the beginning of the year, we would have achieved more.

With 1968 in mind, I tried to convince Enzo Ferrari to predominantly compete in Formula 1, like all the British teams. That was the only way we could aim for top results. To my surprise he gave in, but I was helped by Ford's retirement from sports car racing. If they had not, I'm sure Ferrari would have tried

to take revenge at the 24 Hours of Le Mans, even if he was experiencing notable financial problems. As there was now no commitment to sports car racing I made promises that were far too explicit, but I did so with constructive reasons in mind. Chris Amon was a fine driver and the 1968 evolution of the 312, which had started from a good basis, had also been developed to work specifically with Firestone tyres, which were designed in line with the demands of the various circuits. The V12 engine continued to generate its original problems, weight more than anything else, its dimensions and cooling system still circulating enormous amounts of water for no useful purpose and we were studying its internal fluid dynamic problems, knowing that the strength of the Ford-Cos-

worth was in that area. Franco Rocchi did his best, so power output had been boosted to 410 hp at almost 11,000 rpm, the same as the best Fords, but with oil circulation problems in some corners. I had an ace up my sleeve, though: the rear wing that I had been developing for years was sufficiently "mature" to be accepted by Enzo Ferrari without the usual perplexities.

So with the new wing mounted above the 312's gearbox at the GP of Belgium on 9 June, Amon took pole with an enormous advantage over Jackie Stewart's Matra-Ford: 3 minutes 28.6 seconds to the Scot's 3.32.4.

The car lapped the old Spa road circuit at 245 kph, confirmation that the wing had its effect on aerodynamic load on those long curves and, therefore,

Brands Hatch, 20 July 1968, GP of Great Britain: having started from the front row of the grid, Chris Amon was in with a chance of victory throughout the race but finished second to Jo Siffert's Lotus 49-Ford. In just three GPs, Ferrari lost the advantage of its new rear wing introduced by Forghieri at the Belgian GP, simply because all the other teams that were sceptical at first...copied it. Colin Chapman took the risk of fixing his wing supports to the rear suspension of his Lotuses and not the chassis as on the Ferrari. It was a technically valid move, because the wing exploited the air load better, but it was also decidedly risky due to the force exerted on the suspension. The Lotuses were involved in a terrible accident at the '69 Spanish GP and the Federation banned fixing wings to the suspension after that.

the Ferrari's stability. It didn't take long for all the other cars to sprout wings, some way out, and all of that led to aerodynamic research and the next generation of F1 racers. My original idea went way back to the experiences of engineer Michael May, who worked at Maranello five years earlier and who fitted a wing on his private Porsche 550 for the 1956 1000 Km of the Nürburgring with more than just good results, even if the device was initially banned.

I was immediately impressed by the possibility of exploiting the air to better facilitate driving and I thought about it on and off for a long time. I found a lot of data on the pre-war Auto Union and Mercedes-Benz record cars, but I decided to bring out a wing four years later, because it would not

have been be easy to introduce such a drastic revolution to Ferrari. I would have to convince the Commendatore and I had already imagined his reaction when faced with the wing. He would certainly have transmitted a clear message, probably in Modenese dialect, *"Cus' el cal bagai lè..."* (What is that?). Certain things had to "mature" at Ferrari, so we continued to carry out experiments with spoilers and guide vanes on the sports racers and built a data bank that was very useful later. Even the Commendatore was becoming used to the evolution of aerodynamics, making sure he was fully informed, and the results we achieved in the wind tunnel convinced him.

Someone suggested the idea had been copied from the Chaparral, the American sports racer,

Apart from the V12's power output being taken to 410 hp at 10,800 rpm and, obviously, the wing that made its debut at the 1968 GP of Belgium, the year's Ferrari 312 was not very different from the last version of '67. Chris Amon, shown here at Watkins Glen in '68, scored three pole positions and started from the front row of the grid another five times. It was an excellent result for both driver and car, but our only winner was Jack Ickx (opposite page practicing for the Canadian Grand Prix).

which had turned up the year before with a wing. Apart from the fact that the aerodynamics of a closed car are a lot different from those of a single-seater, the Chaparral put its aerodynamic load straight down on the rear wheels. It was a technique copied by Colin Chapman for the Lotus, but which caused a serious accident in the 1969 Spanish Grand Prix. Before Belgium, it wasn't even possible to carry out a wind tunnel test (at the time, Ferrari still had to use the one at Stuttgart University, Ed) so I placed the wing at the 312's centre of gravity. Therefore I did not alter the load ratio of the car and the calculations – there were few of them, to tell the truth – we carried out enabled us to understand that the ratio of weight on the ground was almost unchanged. I knew that,

used in a certain way, aerodynamic load could support an aircraft and that the same profile, up-ended, generates an opposite load that increased the one to the ground. Therefore, the tyres played their part with a higher vertical aerodynamic load and increased the ratio of the lateral load, while the slip angle of the tyres (their tendency to deform in a corner under centrifugal force, Ed) diminished. That way, the car became more predictable and easier to drive.

So Amon was extremely fast during the tests and that was without him forcing himself. "It's fantastic, Mauro", he told me. "I could understand it during the few laps at Modena, but on the long curves at Spa the wing would be marvellous. Let's stop for now, though. I don't want to show the others

the advantage we have created. Otherwise, they'll understand and react".

In the race, Amon was leading until Jo Bonnier's Cooper "fired" a stone at his Ferrari and hit its water radiator. Chris immediately knew he was in trouble, but he continued with one eye on his instruments and then stopped at the pits when he was still ahead of the rest of the field. Naturally, we didn't understand the reason; it seemed like nothing was wrong with the car. I'll never forget Chris, who seemed calm but his face was ashen, taking off his gloves tugging his fingers out one by one. "What happened? Nothing, except there's a hole in the radiator. I tried to stay out of trouble but a stone…"

Jacky Ickx came third in a 312 without a wing, be-

cause it was Amon who conducted the tests so Ickx didn't know how a winged car worked.

That Formula 1 season showed that my confidence in the Ferrari was well-founded. But I had not been able to foresee the events that would torture Chris Amon GP after the GP. It was grotesque: the world of motor racing doesn't accept "bad luck", it only speaks of "something that was not foreseen". But in 1968, Amon started from pole three times and eight times from the front row of the grid, obtaining just a second place in Britain. He was in the lead in Spain by over 20 seconds, but in the finale the Bendix fuel pump broke, a component used by the aircraft industry and well-known for being indestructible. When Giulio Borsari went to retrieve the car out on the circuit, he hit the errant pump

with a tool and it started to work perfectly again: he even drove the 312 back to the pits!

A stone was "fired" into the 312's radiator at Spa ensuring Chris's retirement; he retired with a broken transmission 17 laps from the end of the GP of Canada having led the race from the start, changing gear without the Borg&Beck clutch because the ring that worked the clutch spring had broken. At Monza, he literally flew off the track after contact with a Honda in the melee of the early laps, ending up dangling from his overturned car in the bushes beyond the guardrail. It was a dramatic accident that happened at 220 kph, but Chris walked away from it without a scratch – and I must say the chassis stood up to the impact really well.

In such a sequence of disappointments, it was inevi-

Above: with the 1968 Grand Prix of Italy coming up, Ferrari tested the 312 at Monza on 28 and 31 August. As always, Chris Amon, seen here talking to Mauro Forghieri, bore the brunt of the work because of his especially sensitive test driving gifts. The New Zealander started the race from the front row after a qualifying lap that was just 14 hundredths of a second slower than John Surtees, who took pole with the Honda. Our car and driver were certainly competitive, but the understandable anxiety to win after a soul destroying series of jinxed attempts caused slight wheel spin at the start: it was just enough to relegate Amon to fourth behind Bruce McLaren, Graham Hill and Surtees. Then on the ninth lap, by which time Amon had moved up to second place, came that frightening flight through the air at Lesmo after coming into contact with the Honda at 220 kph. Chris's 312 turned over completely before coming to rest upside down above a tangle of bushes, but his courage and coolness enabled him to unplug the electrical contact lever while he was suspended in the air the wrong way up. He walked back to the pits…

Monza, 7 September 1968, the eve of the Italian Grand Prix: above, the delicacy of the moment is emphasised by sphinx-like expressions of Enzo Ferrari, engineer Forghieri and Chris Amon. There would be no pole position, but the New Zealander would still be on the front row.
Below: Amon at the 1968 Grand Prix of Spain, a race dominated by him and then lost to a simple electric fuel pump breakage. The kind of pump widely used in the aircraft industry that is practically indestructible.

table that the number two driver, 23 year-old Jacky Ickx who came to us from F2, would shine. The Belgian was another who knew no fear and drove with great class. In my opinion – and we were to find out more during his second period with Ferrari – his character was not an easy one, partly because he had obtained everything from life too easily, thanks to his influential journalist father. Jacky was pleasant and we became friends, but humility and the spirit of sacrifice were not among his most prominent characteristics. He won the French Grand Prix on the difficult Rouen circuit, showing that the 312 was completely competitive but provoking incalculable bitterness in poor Amon.

Jacky set the third fastest time, but he was not happy with his car's set-up. An hour before the race, he and the other drivers were to do a lap of the circuit in the Ligier micro-cars so that the spectators could see them. I drove and Ickx gazed at the sky, certain that it would rain. But all the weather forecasts predicted just the opposite and the whole grid would be shod with slicks – with one exception. When he returned to the pits, Jacky stopped in his tracks and asked for wet weather tyres to be fitted to his 312 (hand-cut Firestone R125s, Ed). Both I and Franco Gozzi, who had been appointed motor sport director that season but he was really Maranello's PR man, tried to stop him because the sky was clear but he insisted, so his 312 fitted with wet tyres. He was greeted with general hilarity when he took his grid position; his colleagues and technicians thought he was mad, but it turned out that he was right.

On road and track, the F2 Dino engine

Right from the early Fifties, Fiat had had its eye on Ferrari, partly because it knew Maranello's successes reflected well on all Italian industry. When Lancia gave the Prancing Horse all its Formula 1 cars in July, 1955, the Italian car giant added its own special contribution of 50 million lire to the deal, despite the fact that there was no rapport between the two Turin car makers at the time. Gianni Agnelli intervened with promises of support for the future in the Commendatore's dilemma over whether or not to sell his company to Ford. So when engineer Gaudenzio Bono, managing director of Fiat, visited Maranello at the end of '64 Ferrari could no longer hide his brilliant idea that would soon lead him to conclude a doubly interesting contract with the Turin car manufacturer. The idea was for a 2-litre V6 engine that Fiat could use for new sports car models and from which Ferrari could create a Formula 2 power unit.

F2 regulations in force in the subsequent 1967 called for an engine block derived from a unit of which at least 500 examples were built each year. So without Fiat's support Maranello would never have been able to construct an F2 car. It was an idea that also gave Fiat a chance to broaden its range with the prestigious Dino Spider, Coupé and later the 130 Coupé.

The use of the Dino name, which had been synonymous with Ferrari racing cars since 1958, became a natural part of the contract and between 1965 and 1966 it was made even more popular by the racing exploits of the 166 SP and 206 P with their 1.6 and 2-litre 65° V6 engines. It was a 1986 cc version of that engine with a bore and stroke of 86x57 mm that went to Fiat and that specification was retained by Turin. However, it was partially redesigned to make it more suited for use in a road car, with an eye to lowering its production costs and robustness of all its components. That was a job initially carried out by Franco Rocchi and the Fiat technical office and in particular Aurelio Lampredi, the Tuscan technician who joined Fiat after his years at Ferrari. Probably too many people meddled with that en-

gine, the set-up of which depended only in part on Maranello.

Enzo Ferrari oversaw everything because he wanted to look good in Fiat's eyes, but he was very disappointed when a pre-series 2000 cc, 160 hp Dino Spider was brought to him for testing. The Commendatore drove the car for a while but soon came back to the factory and turned the car down: in his opinion, there was no way the engine had the horsepower measured on the test bench because it lacked acceleration and especially torque. Engineer Bussi took the problem in hand and he soon discovered an unsuitable Fiat engine modification: the exhaust pipes were not of the agreed progression but had been revised for ease of assembly. Changed back to their original format, the Commendatore became more relaxed and the Dino engine went on to produce excellent results, including in its 2.4-litre form.

But we were left with a series of problems concerning the F2 project, which meant that engine became the V6 with the most modifications and tests carried out in the entire history of Ferrari between the end of 1966 and mid-1968.

To begin with, the problems concerned the cylinder head gaskets, the cylinder sleeves and the cylin-

Previous page: Enzo Ferrari being informed of test progress by Casoni, who is at the wheel of one of the four Dino F2s entered for the GP Lotteria at Monza. Left: Mauro Forghieri would have preferred a 4-cylinder engine for the 1600 cc F2, which would have been more convincing in a technical sense. But the Fiat agreement was, obviously, a priority. Powered by its V6, the Dino won its first race at Hockenheim driven by Tino Brambilla (4) in October 1968. Car number 6 is being driven by Derek Bell on the Tulln circuit, which was part of a military airport near Vienna. Below: the 2.4-litre Dino at Monza in 1966 with Giancarlo Baghetti at the wheel is an F1 car but its chassis inspired the subsequent F2 car.

der studs that were revised in a way we didn't like. With its various modifications, the V6 became a Fiat engine and the reconversion was long and complicated as far as its set-up of the car and its normal development were concerned. It was a unit that already revved high in its 1967 3-valves per cylinder version with its very short stroke (86x45.8 mm). At 10,500-11,000 rpm it put out 210 hp, but at those revolutions the ignition of the period – the Dinoplex system by Marelli aka the famous yellow box– didn't work because it was still at an experimental stage. Unfortunately, trouble with the engine stopped continuity testing and we had no concrete answer in terms of modifications. A continuous pursuit which, by comparison, transformed a famous request by Ferrari on the day of Epiphany into an easy job. It was a public holiday but just when the factory was closed, the Commendatore called an inevitable meeting. It was not the order of the day, but at a certain point I mentioned a present for his next birthday, which was on 18 February. He replied, "Instead of the usual present, give me something that would bring me a great deal of pleasure – the Formula 2 car".

We knew Ferrari was rightly grateful to Fiat and was keen to present the single-seater at the Rac-

ing Car Show organised by ANFIA, the car manufacturers' association, which took place in the last week of February 1967 in the halls of the better known Turin Motor Show. But in the meantime there was none other than the 24 Hours of Daytona and the famous revenge we were to extract from Ford, but we still did it in time. Work to make your head spin, even if it was helped along by the use of the excellent 246 Tasmania chassis, a car that was also powered by a 6-cylinder engine. But the worst would come afterwards, because the engine would only be made competitive in the spring of 1968. The bore and stroke measurements were changed (79.5x53.5 mm) and we had heads with 4-valves per cylinder. But these were the envisaged evolutions, combined with the much more complicated resolution of the origi-

nal difficulties. But when the Dino produced 225 hp at 10,600 rpm, which became 232 hp by the end of '68, we were happy at last.

Fortunately, Ferrari never reacted in his usual way: he understood the origin of the problems and he was content with the Turin agreement. What remained was his desire to show he could also win in F2 against teams like Lotus, Matra, Brabham, the Ford-engined Tecno and BMW. But the victories of Tino Brambilla and Andrea De Adamich in the second half of '68 satisfied his pride.

As far as we were concerned we expected a 1969 packed with success, but the Commendatore cut the programme. It was a decision linked to the "policy of the factory" in which I, naturally, was involved. At the end of '67, I was able to convince Ferrari to leave the prototype championship to concentrate on F1: with the materials and drivers available I was sure we would be competitive. But for the many reasons that I shall explain in this book that's not the way it went. The prototypes' supporters – led by Mike Parkes, although I don't believe he did so to spite me – had no trouble convincing the Commendatore to leave F2 for the endurance championship. They designed and development a great car but they got nowhere.

At the start, an enormous black cloud hovered threateningly over the group, soon after which the skies opened up and they ran into a sort of water barrier and could see nothing. Ickx was the first to emerge from the other end of the wall of water, but more than a minute ticked by before the others arrived (pole position was achieved with a time of 1 minute 56.1 seconds, Ed). It was a difficult victory due to the weather conditions, but one that was certainly helped by a gifted choice of tyres.

Unfortunately, we were all saddened by Jo Schlesser's fatal accident on the first lap that day. The pleasant, 40 year-old Frenchman was competing in his first Grand Prix in a real F1 car, the new Honda RA 302, which works driver John Surtees had tested and pronounced as unsuitable for its French debut.

I also remember Chris Amon after that race; as he changed clothes in the van he continually hit his head against the side of the vehicle, cursing the hand he had been dealt. "It's just not possible", he shouted, "because I've put everything into it and I still haven't been able to win a GP. Then along comes a new boy and he has a stroke of luck like that".

He was also furious about Jacky's apathy towards car development work, which was almost all carried out by him, yet that evening he paid for the champagne at the party for that spoilt lad who was Jacky Ickx. Chris was like that.

Despite the "variable" Amon, after the Italian GP and with three races across the Atlantic in which to compete, my bet that season could still have

been a winner. That's why I become annoyed even now after all these years when people talk about the '68 312 being a single-seater with marvellous lines – and that's true – but not very competitive. A historic falsity: after the Grand Prix of Italy, Ickx was just three points down on world championship leader Graham Hill. I have always felt a certain bitterness about that race because I knew Ferrari, who was deeply bound to his home GP, hoped for the win that was certainly within our reach. But after Amon's accident, Ickx wasted his chances because he was unable to understand how to use the wing, which was controlled by the driver from the cockpit for that race. From the pits, we could see Jacky was not getting the angulation right on the straight so his car was effectively braking.

His mechanic, Giulio Borsari, continually made pit signals with the word "wing" written in both Italian (alettone) and French (volet) but he still didn't understand. And when he was asked for an explanation at the end of the race, he replied with one of those expressions of his for which he soon earned the nickname "Pierino the Terrible".

But it was destiny that 1968 was not our year. Practicing for the GP of Canada, Ickx went off due to an accelerator blockage and injured a leg, so our dreams of glory evaporated. I had not kept my promise and for that reason I went through a difficult period. Ferrari was disappointed, but above all it was my collaborators who did not support me at that moment. It was not a real war, but there was a tendency in that direction, headed by Mike Parkes, who played on Ferrari's love of sports car racing, which I had asked the Commendatore to abandon in favour of F1. And it was not difficult to go back to that programme.

I discussed our technical situation with Enzo Ferrari and was able to make him understand that we needed a radical change to our systems to be competitive.

They spoke of my "exile" to Modena, but in reality Ferrari had put all his confidence in me and asked me to look at new developments, as I had suggested. I had my department next to his old office in Viale Trento e Trieste, with five designers, and it was there that the technical revolution of the Seventies began. I did not take any direct interest in racing for the whole of 1969.

1970-1973

The slow return to the top
The 1969-1973 F1 seasons

The Commendatore was visibly pleased when the Ferrari-Fiat agreement was reached in June 1969. It did not cause even the smallest practical change, but it did alter the level of our investment in motor racing, which had been severely restricted in previous years. Unlike in the past, we were no longer embarrassed by having to select which technical area to develop; now, Ferrari could finance the development of the whole package.

It was an entirely new life, even if Enzo Ferrari continued to carefully control expenditure and we could not go over the top.

I didn't work in racing itself and many thought my move to Modena, in the historic building that had been home to Scuderia Ferrari, was a sort of exile, punishment for the lack of results in 1968.

In reality, it was the result of a clearly defined agreement with the Commendatore, who knew only too well that Ferrari needed a major technical shake-up.

I had become the head of the Advanced Studies Office, which was to design a completely new F1 car for 1970. We worked hard, because my team numbered just seven people: as well as me, there was Walter Salvarani, Antonio Maioli, Angiolino Marchetti, Sergio Panini, Franco Lugli and Gianfranco Piccagliani. Marvellous technicians and designers, who were not afraid of an extremely demanding programme aimed at a flat 12-cylinder 3000 cc engine with the development of an aero version (the unit that was, somewhat inappropriately, called the boxer, Ed), 312 F1 single-

seater with two and four-wheel drive and a new gearbox.

What I ran more than anything else was the engine side, because it was from there that the new Ferrari would be born. I emphasised to my people that the V12 3000 cc unit we had used until '66 had always been a compromise. With its increase in power output it became more fragile and, due to its dimensions, it was impossible to arrive at an optimum weight distribution, which was 57% front and 43% rear. In fact, for both Ferrari and Chris Amon the 1969 season had been a disaster, but that was not the fault of Mike Parkes' and engineer Stefano Jacoponi, who had taken over the reins of the racing team.

That V12 was modified for the umpteenth time

Previous page: crowds cheered Clay Regazzoni and his Ferrari 312 B after winning the Grand Prix of Italy on 6 September 1970. It was the first act of a decade that would close with an even more exhilarating scene on 9 September 1979, when the fans cheered Ferrari's Gilles Villeneuve and Jody Scheckter, the new F1 world champion. Uniting the two events was the 312's flat V12 engine, designed by engineer Forghieri to oppose the V8 financed by Ford. Due to the new power unit, the 1970 312 B had a much lower centre of gravity and a rear end that was less bulky, which helped direct air flow towards the wing.
Above, left: the 312 B at Modena, undergoing one of its many tests in the spring of 1970. Note the curiosity of Piero Ferrari (extreme right of the picture).
Above, right: Jacky Ickx at the Tobacconist corner during the 1970 Grand Prix of Monaco, ahead of Denny Hulme.
Below: on the eve of the race, Gianni Agnelli came to see the new car in the Ferrari garage and was met by Mauro Forghieri and Franco Gozzi, the Commendatore's assistant but the motor sport director at the time.

by positioning the exhausts outside, which was well done even if it did follow the open method of other teams that was not justified in our case. I had to put my foot down to stop the tendency of allowing ourselves to be influenced by the competition without a proper technical examination. A rather provincial way of reasoning, which in certain cases helped. Anyway, the engine was always the same and it was from an old generation to boot. Often in those four years, I made spontaneous complaints, perhaps half-whispered reflections, but if the Commendatore was there, he would say, "What have you got to say for yourself?" "Nothing", I would say, "but the engine is old". It was a kind of game to us both, because with time I knew very well that we had to renew

ourselves. However, a single piece of information is enough to understand the new direction in which Ferrari was heading: investment in the new flat engine was five times our expenditure on the old V12.

The Commendatore pushed to combine the new engine with 4-wheel drive transmission. In view of the agreement with Fiat, he was keen to shine with a technically advanced project. At the time other constructors were trying to move in the same direction, teams like Matra, Lotus, and Cosworth which built the Ford V8 F1 engines.

The idea of a 4x4 single-seater came from the need to successfully manage the power output of the 3000 cc engine. I had had a project of that kind in mind for some time, making the front

wheel torque independent of the rears. In general, one used mechanical systems that made the drive brusque. I remembered the simple Ferguson P99 driven by Stirling Moss in 1961, which was based on an idea similar to mine. So I inserted a hydraulic joint into the transmission so that if the rear wheels lost grip under the power load, the excess torque would pass to the fronts. Taking dynamic effects into account, we also decided to allocate 65%-70% of the torque to the rear axle, a system that is the basis of many modern 4-wheel drives today, although the torque would have been distributed progressively with the Ferrari project, while many current 4x4s use regressive systems, which I don't like personally.

Ferrari would have liked to debut a 4x4 version of

They say 150,000 spectators saw the 1970 Grand Prix of Italy. Well, that immense crowd was repaid for their attendance by an exciting spectacle from the first lap to the last. No fewer than six drivers led the race – Regazzoni, Ickx, Rodriguez, Stewart, Oliver and Hulme – obviously due to overtaking and not after unscheduled pit stops.

Above, right: coming off the Parabolica at the end of the first lap, pole sitter Ickx (Ferrari 312 B) and Rodriguez (BRM P153) are not in the picture as they had already started to pull away from the pack. So here we have the rest of the grid being led by Stewart (March 701), Regazzoni and Giunti in their Ferrari 312 Bs, Oliver (BRM P153) and Siffert (March 701).

Below, right: Clay Regazzoni took the lead and scampered away from the rest of the field on the 56th of 68 laps in his hyper-effective Ferrari 312 B. After that came the inevitable "party" on the podium: the Swiss received his trophy from Margherita Bandini, widow of the unforgotten Lorenzo.

the new F1 car, but I did not agree and was able to convince him not to do so without too much effort. In only a few months, we were able to create the new car, engine and gearbox from a blank sheet of paper: if we had immediately opted for the 4x4 we would have been late with the car. It was a good thing we did wait, because all of a sudden at the end of 1969 the Federation banned 4-wheel drive F1 cars!

Another project we did not go through with was the little known plan to develop an aircraft version of the flat engine. Ferrari hosted a visit of a group of investors from the American Franklin company, which needed a refined unit for a small aircraft. The project was also developed in this configuration, making the majority of the accessories so that they could fit into the plane's wing. But when the engine was more or less ready, Franklin went out of business.

I met with Enzo Ferrari every day when we were developing our new project , because it was his habit to spend each morning at the Scuderia's old headquarters in Modena (near his home in Largo Garibaldi, Ed) where we were located. Naturally, I explained to him that I wanted to develop a powerful engine, but one that was very light and compact. The flat unit met our need to lower the centre of gravity and the rear of the car so that it would direct the airflow to the rear wing. Finally, we would conceive a car right on the weight limit, but respecting the chassis's dimensions. It is correct to emphasise that the British teams out-

classed us in that area. They were more open-minded than us in lightening the chassis and suspension, while at Ferrari, quite rightly, the mentality was different. I also aimed for an engine that had all the qualities of the Ford Cosworth which, one must recognise, was the result of a careful study by a great constructor. It stood out for its excellent lightness, balance and torque at low revs but its secret was in the oil circulation system, which avoided dispersion and lapping, negative effects that subtract power. I talked a great deal about this problem with engineer Bussi as it had always been affronted with a traditional mentality at Ferrari and on which there was no updated written background material. To the point that one fine day we put the V12 on the test bench

The 1970 podium at Monza was extremely small, but so much closer to the fans. Among those celebrating Clay Regazzoni's victory in the Italian GP is an unforgettable personality of that period, Vittorugo Tramonti aka "Sparky". He was a Marelli technician, who worked with Ferrari for many years and was well-known for the incredible pranks he organised to lower the tension of the races. On Clay's left are the officials: Gustavo Marinucci, president of the Automobile Club of Italy, and Angelo Ponti, head of the AC of Milan.

– the initial idea was Bussi's – and we tested it briefly without a sump. Madness, apparently, even if the lubricant, naturally, churned up by the drive shaft, created what looked like black rain. To avoid unwanted comments, we decided not to tell Ferrari what happened, although it was important. We knew a considerable amount of oil "turned" together with the drive shaft, corroborating some of our intuitions over the problems of oil pumping and internal fluid dynamics. We knew how to proceed and after a running-in period, the flat V12 turned out to be not only powerful but also robust. We went from the initial 480 hp at 12,600 rpm at the end of 1970, to 525 hp at 12,800 rpm by the end of the unit's career in 1979/80. The engine could rev to 13,500 rpm,

but the ignition and injection systems of the period only worked at lower revolutions. However, it was a power output that was always slightly more than the best Ford units, which were constantly under development, but the difference was never fundamental. More than anything else, I always had the general weight of the car in mind, and with the flat engine we finally reached the limit of the regulations like the best of the British cars. Take the famous Lotus 72, for example; for lightness, that car had two small shafts that connected the front wheels with the internal brake discs that looked to me like two pencils. The flat engine was nothing new to Ferrari: in 1964/5 there was the 1500 cc 512 F1, which was rather traditional in its conception even if it

did have direct fuel injection; then later there was the 12-cylinder 2000 cc, which I had engineer Jacoponi, who later became a fine Fiat technical director, design in 1968. I suggested he should develop it with a differentiated axle base (cylinders that were not all at the same distance, Ed) for a particular balance. The result was excellent and the unit put out plenty of power at 290 hp, with massive torque. Installed in an extremely light 212 E: the combination dominated the 1969 European Hillclimb Championship driven by Switzerland's Peter Schetty.
But the new 12-cylinder was more advanced. My battle was with friction, the loss of pumping and the inertia of the drive shaft's rotation. So I envisaged only four main bearings, a drive shaft that

A close-up of Clay Regazzoni on the Monza grid before his fantastic performance in the 1970 Italian GP, which he drove with great professionalism, even if he had made his F1 debut 10 weeks earlier in the Grand Prix of Holland. Clay had a Latin temperament much liked by Enzo Ferrari, but engineer Forghieri has always denied the suggestion that the Swiss was all heart and not so technical. The fact is that Clay always worked on the development of the cars with enthusiasm, never dodging long test sessions that sometimes began at 9 am and finished at 7 pm, perhaps followed by a technical briefing. He was absolutely scrupulous, even if he did not possess the natural gifts of a test driver like John Surtees, Chris Amon and later in his career Niki Lauda. Clay's decisive driving favoured a precise answer in terms of mechanical resistance. And it was Monza that produced confirmation in the field that the new flat 312 engine was able to withstand over 12,000 rpm that were normally achieved by the drivers. To pull away from a pack of followers and avoid being tricked by their slipstreams, Regazzoni extracted an extra 300 rpm from his engine, which is a lot. Forghieri remembers how Clay's positive temperament was always of great help during difficult moments, in both his first and second periods at Maranello, where he worked for seven years, a record that was not beaten until the Michael Schumacher era in 2003.

turned on two spherical bearings at the extremities and camshafts mounted on small rollers. A version with five main bearings was in our minds in case we came up against difficulties, but fortunately that remained on paper. Another great new development was connecting rods made of titanium (an especially light metal, but difficult to use at the time, Ed). We were the first to try it, but the story goes much further back: our first titanium experiments were carried out in 1965 when Luigi Chinetti, our American importer, sent us blocks of the metal, which was rare in Europe at the time. We made con rods for the F1 car out of it, but we had absolutely no experience with the metal and the rods broke after a 10-hour test. Later, I found a solution, even if it was in an almost novel way.

Below: two weeks before the 1970 Grand Prix of Italy, Ferrari tested at Monza with Clay Regazzoni and Ignazio Giunti, the Roman driver shown here in the pits shaking hands with a girl friend under the amused gaze of engineer Forghieri. Enzo Ferrari gave Giunti his debut in F1 at the Belgian Grand Prix that same year, showing once more his unquestioned ability to select talented drivers. Giunti was already 29 years-old yet he had never raced a single-seater. But he drove the 312 B extremely well, finishing the Belgian GP on the full Spa circuit in a fine fourth place, and that was a track where the average speed was close to 245 kph and where F1 would no longer race due to excessive risk. Sadly, Giunti was killed in January 1971 at the Buenos Aires circuit, a permanent track considered much safer than Spa, after an irresponsible manoeuvre by Jean-Pierre Beltoise.
Right: Mario Andretti's Ferrari 312 B in the pits at the Montjuich circuit for the 1971 GP of Spain.

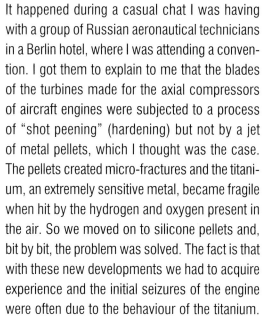

It happened during a casual chat I was having with a group of Russian aeronautical technicians in a Berlin hotel, where I was attending a convention. I got them to explain to me that the blades of the turbines made for the axial compressors of aircraft engines were subjected to a process of "shot peening" (hardening) but not by a jet of metal pellets, which I thought was the case. The pellets created micro-fractures and the titanium, an extremely sensitive metal, became fragile when hit by the hydrogen and oxygen present in the air. So we moved on to silicone pellets and, bit by bit, the problem was solved. The fact is that with these new developments we had to acquire experience and the initial seizures of the engine were often due to the behaviour of the titanium.

But in the spring of 1970 the 312 B started to work really well.

The previous year, we had to lose Chris Amon, which was a disappointment for me both from the human standpoint and for his sensitivity that would have been useful in testing. I remember that he visited me in November '69 and he was rather disheartened. He had signed a pre-contract for 1970 and I suggested he should be confident because the development of the 312 B was going well. Instead, he confessed to me that he was tired of Ferrari.

Unfortunately, he had been negatively influenced by the first test of the 312 B at 8 am on Friday 5 September at the Modena Autodrome. His general impression was excellent, but at the time we were still solving problems caused by the bronze bearings and the test ended with a breakdown. There was nothing I could do to make him change his mind, yet we only needed time: initially, the 312 B was a hard nut to crack, but later the fulfilment was a great feeling.

We got back to winning, finally, with Jacky Ickx – he had returned to Maranello after a year with Brabham, a tough environment that had matured him somewhat – and Clay Regazzoni. We could have won the German GP on 2 August at Hockenheim, an extremely fast circuit at the time; Ickx had set the fastest lap at over 202 kph, but came second for a reason that remained incomprehensible. It was a placing preceded by a real "technical adventure" on the Saturday night and well into

For 1971 engineer Forghieri updated the 312 B, which was renamed the B2. While waiting for the new car to be developed, Ferrari continued to enter the 1970 version, which enabled Mario Andretti to win the first GP of the season in South Africa. All three Ferraris entered for the GP of Spain on 8 April were B1s as they were called at the time, although the designation was not official.

Right: Clay Regazzoni's B1 (5) and Ickx (4) at the Montjuich circuit, where the Belgian led initially and eventually finished second behind Jackie Stewart's Tyrrell-Ford, which is still behind the Ferrari in the picture. The B2 made its debut in the non-championship Race of Champions at Brand Hatch, which was a test bed for the whole team. Regazzoni won without great difficulty, but engineer Forghieri recalls that the rain and Clay's tendency to minimise all driving problems meant he did not realise the B2's new rear suspension, with its horizontal spring-damper group, did not marry too well with the new Firestone tyres.

the early hours of Sunday. Ickx took pole position, but we had some doubts about the bronze bearings. So I asked the mechanics to take out the engine and prepare the cars for the race, then I sent them to bed.

Giulio Borsari and I stayed and opened the Ickx car's engine, which did in fact have some of the connecting rods' bronze bearings a bit stuck. It was a hot night, unusual for that area of Germany, but rather than by the engine we were pestered by millions of mosquitos. Yet there on the grass — inside the garages was like an oven — we first used very fine emery paper, which was made to rub by means of a string and after that a polishing paste which Borsari, a master at techniques like this, operated to polish with em-

ery paper about two hundredths of all the drive shaft's pins. The job would have been difficult enough in the factory, let alone in those absurd conditions! Anyway, after we had replaced the bronze bearings and "closed" the engine we went to bed after 3 am.

However, the job was well done given that Ickx was leading on the last corner of the Motodrom, a few metres ahead of Jochen Rindt in the famous Lotus 72. Then, something incredible happened: just before he was about to cross the finish line, Jacky slowed slightly because he didn't think the Austrian, who won by just seven tenths of a second, was so close! At least that was what he told us, but getting Ickx to explain things clearly was often impossible: he cut short

the conversation with a reply that was not the most polite. I could have killed him. But there again I couldn't, because he was going to get married in Brussels the following day to Catherine Blaton, a beautiful girl and the daughter of "Beurlys", a good driver who had competed in Ferraris for Scuderia Francorchamps.

I will never forget that day because I also went to the wedding, which was held with great pomp and ceremony. Jacky's wife was a member of one of the top families in Belgium and he was a famous racing driver, but also the son of the editor of the daily newspaper "Le Sport". I arrived at the Blatons' villa, on a hill overlooking Brussels, and I delivered the Ferrari gift, a Prancing Horse covered with diamonds.

We drove to the church in a procession of vintage cars – I was in one of them with an extremely pleasant elderly relative who was completely covered in jewels and with whom I laughed throughout the entire journey until we entered the church – where a Dominican monk officiated.

I'm not sure whether I had cooled off after that lost victory, but Jacky was forgiven two weeks later due to his absolute triumph in the Grand Prix of Austria. And I remember with pleasure the congratulations I received from Colin Chapman and Ken Tyrrell, who said in his typically frank English way that he would never have thought that engine could win…

After that, Clay won for us at Monza with Gianni Agnelli in attendance, who watched from above

the pits to confirm that Fiat was with Ferrari. It was a day of alternating feelings, because we certainly couldn't forget that Jochen Rindt had died practicing the day before. Ickx took the pole, but in the race he retired with a broken clutch, while Regazzoni won on a track he considered one of his own. Clay felt at ease in the 312 B and was able to make the most of his forceful driving, which was a bit brutal but effective. At the time, there were no chicanes or the extensive curve after the Monza pits, so the long straight was taken in fifth gear and more or less at top speed. The drivers certainly needed a great deal of courage: Clay never held back and he was also perfect at Lesmo and the Parabolica. He had his very own way of throwing the car into a corner and it was

Jackie Ickx at Monza in 1971 with the Ferrari 312 B2: the lines of the body were flatter and flowed into the rear wing. There were considerable modifications to the engine, with the bore and stroke taken from 78.5x51.5 mm to 80x49.6 mm; the power output went from 450 hp at 12,000 rpm to 495 hp at 12,600 rpm. At Monza, Ickx set the second fastest time but, like Regazzoni, retired due to a broken flexible coupling in the engine caused by tyre vibration.

146

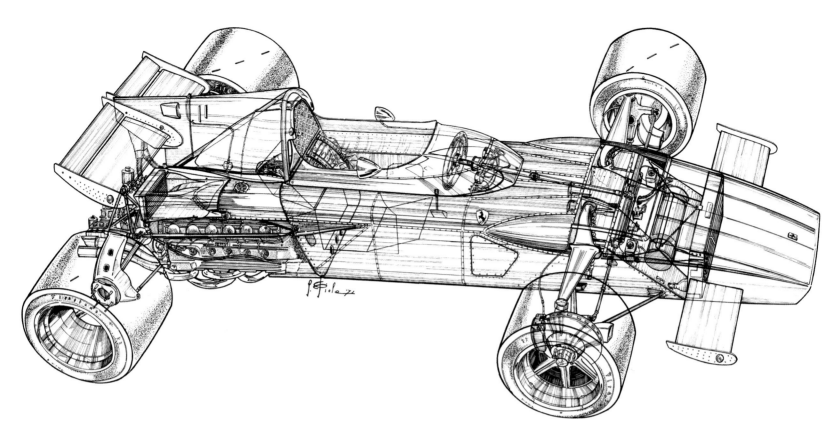

Ferrari fielded the 312 B2 again – above in a cut-away by Giorgio Piola – for the 1972 season, but with a traditional rear suspension. Right: Ickx practicing at the GP of Monaco, where he finished second in pouring rain. Then he won the German GP at the Nürburgring, where Regazzoni came second. It was the only real success in a rather bitter season, at least in Formula 1. That year, Enzo Ferrari was also experiencing serious health problems and Forghieri was moved to the Advanced Studies Department, where he worked on the F1 cars of the future. The Racing Department was assigned to engineer Giorgio Ferrari under the guidance of engineer Colombo.

due to this style of his that he was late in understanding the defects of the new 312 B2.

We won again with Jacky Ickx in Canada at the end of the season and concluded with a victorious Ickx-Regazzoni double in Mexico. We were a little late, but at the time the 312 B was the best car of them all and I had won my bet associated with the much discussed need to start again from zero at Maranello. Ickx was second in the world championship, just five points behind Jochen Rindt and with a hard end-of-season push he could have won the championship if he had not dropped out of the United States GP with a banal injector problem. So the title went posthumously to the Austrian after his death in an accident at Monza caused by the broken brake shafts

of his Lotus 72, the miniaturisation of which had so impressed me.

On that occasion, I was also impressed by a remark made by Jacky, who was most certainly not an altruist. He said, "Mauro, I must say that I'm not really unhappy about this bad luck. The title went to Jochen and he really deserved it…"

A sentiment that did him proud, because Ickx had a rather egocentric character. He had become successful too easily, but if he had worked his way up through the ranks like many other drivers, he could have become one of the greats. He certainly had the class of a champion, but when Ferrari went into a technical crisis he began to consider the situation in a political sense rather than as a driver. He reasoned like Juan Manuel Fangio,

who changed team when he thought his current squad was about to be enmeshed in problems. But the Argentinean changed at the right moment, while Ickx did not have that talent. I remember when we won the 1975 world title with Niki Lauda, Jacky confessed, "I was wrong to leave Ferrari, Mauro. I could have been in Niki's place". Said by someone like him it was really quite touching, partly because from 1971 onwards there was not so much glory in it as far as we were concerned. We had the best car with an engine that gave no more problems at all. Instead of keeping it like that, I modified the rear suspension and that was certainly a mistake but, as I will explain, I made the decision to do so for a number of reasons. Among them was modifying

the spring damper group inside, which had a rational logic – years later. The F1 teams all chose that road and Porsche also produced a similar suspension for one of its sports cars. However, with the modifications the 312 B2 was lighter and it is known that the battle of the unsuspended mass was the basis of all racing and road cars. In addition, we carried out a long test of the modification in the Pininfarina wind tunnel, with extremely positive results. Yet in 1971, we only won the South African GP with Mario Andretti and the Dutch with Jacky Ickx, but both the Belgian and Regazzoni complained about massive rear tyre vibration; it was so violent that the drivers couldn't even see properly.

That year, Firestone introduced its low-sidewall slicks in reply to Goodyear's a little too hurriedly. It was a new developed that transformed itself into a set-up problem, because the other teams supplied by Firestone were not exactly brilliant either. But we were worse off: evidently, the B2 was experiencing a damping control by the tyres that was much less effective than on the B1. But I didn't realise that immediately and in the meantime I tried to obviate the problem by inserting a damping mass onto the hub, set to the frequency of the tyre vibration. However, it only worked well on certain circuits and in some corners as well as with a certain tyre pressure. When the tyres had warmed up, they caused nothing but trouble. We reached the lowest point at the Italian GP. The Commendatore was at Friday and Saturday

In 1972, the earlier development of the 312 B2 meant Ferrari could compete in GPs with greater confidence than in the previous season, even if engineer Forghieri was concentrating on his work at the Advanced Studies Office and was designing the definitive version of the "snowplough" car.

Left: one of Forghieri's last trips was to the Grand Prix of South Africa at Kyalami in March. Here, he is talking to Jacky Ickx as the driver sits in the cockpit of Clay Regazzoni's car, practicing with the 312 B2 with its traditional body, which was different from the one with the wide nose used in the race.

Right, above: Clay Regazzoni in the GP of Belgium, which took place on the Nivelles circuit. Second in qualifying, he was third in the finale when he was stopped by an accident when lapping Nanni Galli's Tecno.

Right, below: it was Galli who took over Clay's car for the subsequent GP of France, because the Swiss injured his wrist playing football with the mechanics during the 1000 Km of Austria weekend.

At the 1972 Grand Prix of Italy, Jacky Ickx set the fastest time in practice, ahead of Amon (Matra), Stewart (Tyrrell) and his Ferrari team mate Regazzoni. The Swiss took the lead early in the race with a consistently high speed, but he was stopped by a banal accident when lapping Carlos Pace's March in the chicane, which broke the pit straight, the first in Monza's history. Later, Ickx retired with ignition problems.

practice and the lack of a good result in front of "his" public put him in a really black mood. The situation was out of control, because on the Friday some of the spectators even gave us derisory whistles, one of the few times I ever saw him so angry, so much so that Ferrari found it hard to hold back. We were even forced to meet one of his requests that, to say the least, was complicated: try a set of Goodyears to understand whether or not the problem was indeed caused by the tyres. Obviously, it was a hurried and illogical test as we were bound to Firestone by an ironclad contract. In theory, we should not have met that request, but when Ferrari ordered something a solution had to be found.

The operation was carried out without hiding anything, but it only created confusion. I had already understood that the fault was in the dampers that were adapted to the new suspension: they acted on one single point, contrary to the B1 which, working on two points, gave a much higher damping effect. The press started more than one controversy onslaught against me and I also had to discuss the matter at length with Ferrari. "I cannot understand why you modified a car that did so well just a few months ago! What were you thinking of…?" The refrain, spiced with a few predictable inserts, was more or less like that. Yet I had not "gone made" as Ferrari asked on these occasions, and he knew very well the reasons why I made the modification: the technical development and the need to unite the F1 engine with

that of the 312 Sport, which the Commendatore himself had ordered me to create.

In the end, a financial question had weighed heavily on a technical decision for the umpteenth time. The flat 12 was born to be also used in an aircraft, so certain accessories like the aspiration trumpets, the distributor of the injection system and that of the ignition – the well-known Marelli Dinoplex – were deployed in a less traditional way. The choice had had no effect on the first F1 car, while we had to find space for those accessories and the engine was modified and unified in the sports racer. But it was obligatory to design a different rear suspension for the 312 B2. And from there began the vicious circle from which I was never again able to break out. So while the

Left: dramatic close-ups of Mario Andretti (3) and Jacky Ickx (4) in Ferrari 312 B2s at Monza in 1972. Born in Istria, the American driver enjoyed maximum regard from Enzo Ferrari who, due to various different sets of circumstances, was never able to have him in his team for a full season. In '72, he competed for the American F. Indy championship and raced in only five GPs for Ferrari. Maranello reorganised its motor sport programme for 1973 and put out a press release on the subject the previous August. Only Ickx and Arturo Merzario, who made his F1 debut in the '72 British Grand Prix driving a 312 B2 and took sixth place, were confirmed and Clay Regazzoni was out. Due to Ferrari's illness, from that summer management of the F1 team started to become hazy and it is probable that Regazzoni, who was extremely sensitive despite his determined appearance, felt this vagueness. That could explain the accidents in which he was involved in simply lapping backmarkers in the GPs of Belgium and Italy, both of which he was leading.
Below: Ickx in the 1972 GP of South Africa at Kyalami. The 312 B2 is fitted with a faired nose, replacing the tapered unit with lateral winglets. That set-up was tested for the first time at the Vallelunga circuit outside Rome in readiness for the South African event and it also appeared at the subsequent Spanish GP but it was not developed further.

1971 International Championship for Makes and the 1972 World Championship for Makes continued to be arenas of great success for Ferrari, the F1 team was dogged by problems we were unable to rationally resolve.

That was the main reason why I was, once again, in difficulty between 1972 and 1973. In the meantime, the Fiorano circuit was opened and, logically, the Advanced Studies Office was transferred to the track complex. Once again I discussed future projects with Ferrari and we agreed on everything. We debated with animosity but I enjoyed his full confidence, despite the "energetic" exchanges of view on the F1 results, which he continually threw in my face saying it would have been better to go back to the old 312 B1. And I always

admitted he was right, partly because the problems continued to arise in '72. During the same period, the Commendatore became rather seriously ill, as he did at the end of 1968. It wasn't by chance that I was put into a difficult situation by some of my collaborators. This time, though, the illness was much more serious and we feared for his life. Naturally, Ferrari was forced to stay away from Maranello for many months; it was a tough period for him because the medical treatment produced serious side effects.

And so Fiat, which had entered Ferrari on tip-toes in 1969 by providing a managing director in Dr. Bellicardi who came from Weber of Bologna – a company that had always had a close relationship with the Commendatore and Ferrari – sent

Above: for 1973, Ferrari's Racing Department, under the direction of engineer Sandro Colombo, designed the B3, shown here at Monte Carlo being driven by Jacky Ickx, the monocoque of which was built in Britain by Thompson. The car was a major disappointment and achieved worse results than the B2, which had been entered for the first three GPs. By mid-summer Enzo Ferrari, whose health had improved, assigned the new Racing Department to Forghieri; in just 20 days, he profoundly modified the B3, which took sixth place in Austria, driven by Arturo Merzario (above).

its man to Maranello. He was engineer Sandro Colombo, who was previously with Innocenti and was to run the Racing Department. He took charge of both Formula 1 and sports car racing, in which we lost badly in '73 after the triumphs of the previous year with a car that was practically the same. But that was nothing to do with me, so I made no comment.

In my Fiorano "exile" I concerned myself only with the future and I had no contact with those responsible for racing; to the point that, if they wanted to visit my department, they had to request my permission.

Ferrari, with whom I talked at times on the telephone, knew that to win again a further decisive technical turnaround was needed. So I established the basics of a prototype that became known as the "snowplough", fundamental to the whole F1 series called "T" cars, which competed from 1975-1980. The snowplough was a car that was even derided within Ferrari itself, but nobody had understood a thing. In addition, I started singing that old chorus that Ferrari was not winning in F1 anymore because it was unable to build a suitable chassis, much less a monocoque like the British teams. This without ever asking themselves how it was that since 1966 we used by choice – and on Ferrari's orders – chassis of small tubes covered in riveted aluminium.

For this reason, too, I was embittered when I found out that the new heads had commissioned the B3's chassis from British specialist John Thomp-

The curious tale of the Ferrari B3 Snowplough

On 15 August 1972, Enzo Ferrari was in the factory or at least at the Fiorano track. It was a public holiday in Italy, but he never took any notice of things like that, despite the fact that he was beginning to suffer health problems, which kept him at home for many months. Meanwhile, men sent by Fiat had taken command of Maranello and I was confined to the Advance Studies Office, which had been transferred from Modena to a building in the Fiorano circuit grounds.

Anyway, if the Commendatore had the intention of creating complete amazement on that humid August day, he certainly succeeded. There was no real presentation, which I was against, just the circulation of a photograph of a car that was called the new F1 B3 at the time. It astounded people as intended, which was understandable as it was even more dramatic due to the complete absence of an explanation from Ferrari, even though the car took to the Fiorano track driven by Clay Regazzoni that very afternoon.

But the car wasn't the B3, it was an F1 prototype that later enabled us to design the series of 312 T-cars (which won three F1 world drivers' championships and four constructors' titles between 1975/9, Ed) and due to which people thought I must be at least half mad. Extremely wide and with a really short wheelbase, the car was later dubbed the snowplough, but it was fundamental to fashioning Ferrari's technical future. Aerodynamics were my mania and, after some

reflection, I realised that the reason why sports racing cars with their covered wheels had a much higher degree of negative lift – the load created by the air that pushes the car down and improves grip, Ed – than F1 cars was because of their vast body surface that passed just a few centimetres above the ground. With sports racers, it was sufficient to create a slight downward "thrust" so that the load became significant. But the F1 single-seaters were always slender and, therefore, there was far less surface running close to the ground.

To test the characteristics of the future T-car, various versions of which were already in my mind, I conceived that prototype with an exposed surface of about 75% of a sports racing car. It had a long, extremely wide nose with an ample wing that flowed into the monocoque, which was equally wide and incorporated the radiators. The centring

of the mass was completely revised compared to traditional single-seaters, with the weight moved between the two wheels of the axles as much as possible, to the extent that the fuel tanks were at the centre and not at the sides. The water and oil radiators were located laterally and traced the line of the body, a concept that has been used continuously in F1 ever since.

The car also had a very short wheelbase (238 cm, Ed) designed to take the elements I had laid down to their extreme: tremendous agility when cornering due to a reduction in the polar moment of inertia. That was a choice made possible by the grip of modern racing tyres. With wheelbase and surface parity, I also achieved another benefit: I calculated the value of negative lift obtained with that aerodynamic configuration. In addition, the short wheelbase enabled me to evaluate how much it would influence the subsequent adoption of a transverse gearbox, which would concentrate the mass within the wheelbase (it was not the same thing, but it was confirmation).

The decision to go for a short wheelbase also came from another idea I had: to build two versions of the subsequent T-car, one with a short wheelbase and the other a little longer. The former was for circuits with low speed curves, the second for faster tracks. It was a highly ambitious project, because two different studies would be needed; it was not enough to shorten or lengthen

With its unconventional appearance compared to all the other F1 cars that competed in 1972 the Ferrari mobile test laboratory, incorrectly called the B3 or Snowplough was not understood immediately by observers. Perhaps because it never raced, although there were rumours that it was to make its debut at the Italian Grand Prix. The car was tested at Monza by Arturo Merzario and Jackie Ickx (previous page) during August and September 1972 with positive results. The aim of this fundamental project of Mauro Forghieri's was to give him and his colleagues the chance of trying out many new ideas, which later led to the concepts that were basis of the 1974 B3 and T-car series.

a wheelbase to modify a car; all the equilibriums would have to be altered.

That is why I had always refused to lengthen a car's established wheelbase, even if it was a widely used method. When I discussed the difficulties of our car on long curves of constant radius, Enzo Ferrari thundered "Lengthen the wheelbase" and I always refused to do so.

Ferrari did not agree with the T-car and its differentiated wheelbase, but only for cost reasons. I also took into account the fact that it would be complicated for an organisation like ours, working 10-12 hours a day, to manage two chassis and their different components. So the T became a compromise (with a 251.8 cm wheelbase, Ed) as a result of which we came across a few problems at circuits that had those long curves; like Anderstorp, where the Swedish GP was held, even if Lauda did win that race in 1975.

The Snowplough underwent a long series of tests in the University of Stuttgart's wind tunnel and it helped me to understand the importance of ground effect long before the introduction of mini-skirts – which were not permitted by the regulations, anyway – on the 1978 Lotus 79. To tell the truth, I discovered the value of aerodynamic load more due to track testing than in the wind tunnel, because such facilities were not equipped to produce certain answers back then. We had to put our faith more in tests and our own intuition. Tests which, after the first one by Clay Regazzoni, continued with Arturo Merzario and Jacky Ickx at both Fiorano and Monza. In fact, I believe somebody in Ferrari had talked about the possible debut of the car at the Grand Prix of Italy on 10 September. But there was no sense in that, because the car really was a mobile test labora-

tory. It is true that a provisional entry was sent for a non-championship race at Brand Hatch on 22 October. But that didn't go ahead either and I someone assumed it was about a spiteful trick by the person who was running the Racing Department at the time, to oppose the Advanced Studies Office. But I just went on thinking about the future and that project, which had given me so much satisfaction. Anyway, the T-car's debut

was scheduled for 1975, so we were able to develop it without rushing. To the point that during the second half of '74 we would certainly have been able to compete in Grands Prix with it and I mentioned this fact to Ferrari. But he immediately dampened my enthusiasm: "Don't even mention it. We have the B3, which is going well. We'll go ahead like that".

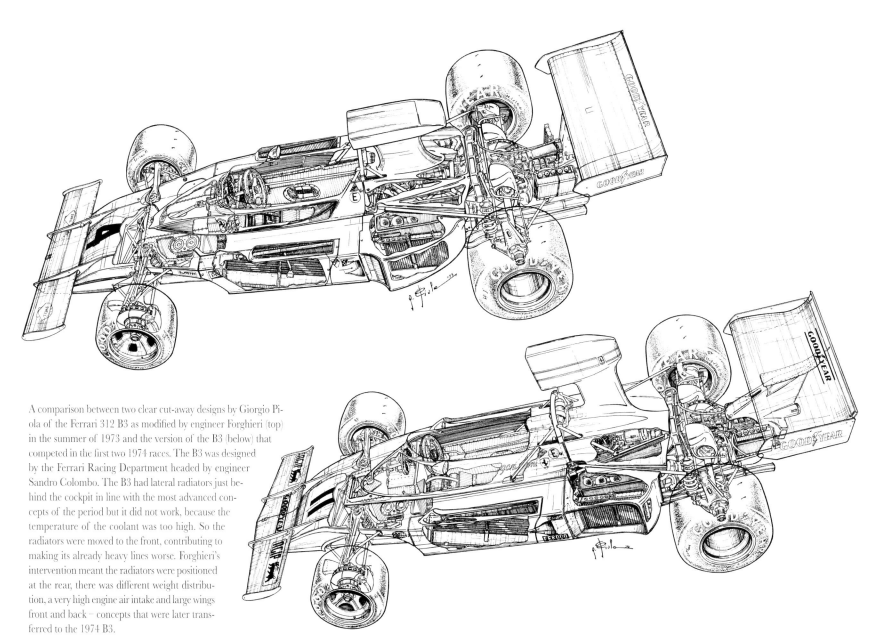

A comparison between two clear cut-away designs by Giorgio Piola of the Ferrari 312 B3 as modified by engineer Forghieri (top) in the summer of 1973 and the version of the B3 (below) that competed in the first two 1974 races. The B3 was designed by the Ferrari Racing Department headed by engineer Sandro Colombo. The B3 had lateral radiators just behind the cockpit in line with the most advanced concepts of the period but it did not work, because the temperature of the coolant was too high. So the radiators were moved to the front, contributing to making its already heavy lines worse. Forghieri's intervention meant the radiators were positioned at the rear, there was different weight distribution, a very high engine air intake and large wings front and back – concepts that were later transferred to the 1974 B3.

son in 1973. Nothing like that had ever happened before; a company like Ferrari being forced to seek expensive help when we had won the 1964 world championship with a chassis completely designed and built at Maranello! It was an incredible decision which the Commendatore was against, but he was not able to oppose it. On top of that, it was a decision associated with a communal location that had caused me an enormous amount of trouble for years. When the British cars won, the "internal opposing faction" maintained that it was a question of road holding. When we won, they said it was because of the engine, perhaps just to please Ferrari who, as we knew, had a weakness for horsepower. But that's not true. Sometimes we won thanks to the chassis, sometimes due to the

engine. And if we lost, the reasons were the same. The famous Thompson monocoque was very well built, but it was also decidedly heavy. Anyway, it was the whole B3 project that was dated after four years. Talking about the "snowplough" I was accused of being too futuristic, but those who had to design the new F1 came up with a car that had a radiator in the nose and aerodynamics typical of cars of a couple of years earlier! Meanwhile, I was aware of the physical improvement of the Commendatore, who returned to his office in mid-1973: he was more effective than ever and took total control of the situation again. He continued to fully run the Racing Department and he called me to his office immediately. He wanted to make up for lost time. "Mauro, this lot are unable to ob-

1973 Grand Prix of Italy, Monza: Ickx competed in his last race for Ferrari in the B3 modified by Forghieri in just 20 days. He only came 14th in qualifying, while his team mate Merzario set the seventh fastest time. Compared to the photograph on page 151, note the radical change in the car's aerodynamics front and back. The large air scoop was also new so that it could feed more air to the 12-cylinder engine, previous versions of which had forced the technicians to shorten gearbox ratios in some cases due to complaints about acceleration from the drivers. The air scoop was in an extremely high position and took the place of the two small intakes, which are behind Ickx's shoulders in the picture on the previous page.

tain any sort of result", he burst out. "We have to intervene immediately to break up this situation, from which there is no way out. Do you think you can modify the B3? I shall be pleased if we can put up a reasonable end-of-season performance…". It was a determined Ferrari, happy to have returned to the place he was used to as absolute head of the Racing Department. I accepted with great pleasure. I simply asked to be given carte blanch and added, "I'll try to do the impossible with a pre-edition of what should, in my opinion, be the car for next year. Just give me the opportunity of working with Merzario (Ickx had almost left Maranello, had competed in a GP with McLaren and was in the midst of a major controversy with the previous Racing Department

management, Ed), who is a good driver. He's also a good lad and I can manage him easily".
So between July and August, I modified the B3. Among the many new elements were lateral radiators just behind the driver's shoulders, the large front wing and an extremely high air scoop. Merzario broke the Fiorano record with the car and Ickx said the B3 was well updated. It was a job that was carried out quickly, but due to various problems we scored no points in the Austrian or Italian GPs. However, we were back as contenders and Ferrari, who always looked ahead, was more at ease, because we had taken the first important technical step towards the following season.

Last world championship before the goodbye
Epilogue of the Prancing Horse in sports car racing

It is well-known that Ferrari was not expansive after a victory but on one occasion, with his drivers in the top two places, he asked me over the telephone after the race, "Why is it that we were only 20 seconds ahead of the third placed car?" A joke? A small one, perhaps; his desire to understand the behaviour of his drivers and cars was paramount, because if not he reacted immediately. At the start of the 1969 season, we realised that the new 312 P would not have an easy life in the International Championship of Makes. And, inevitably, Ferrari put on trial the technicians who had criticised my suggestions of six months earlier to devote our time solely to GP racing.

In that period, I was deeply involved with the new flat engined F1 car project, but I was on the alert because if Ferrari had a new idea nothing was holy, you just had to transform it into reality as quickly as possible. Sure enough, the phone rang. "Continue with the F1 project, but you have to take the prototype sector in hand too. Have you seen how the new 312 P is going? We're not competing in the 12 Hours of Sebring and the tests they do simply increase doubts about the car".

To tell the truth the 1969 312 P, designed and developed by engineer Jacoponi with Franco Rocchi doing the engine along the lines suggested by Mike Parkes seemed correct to me, even if not very innovative. But it was run with little conviction and often just one single car was entered against a hoard of Porsches.

So between one thing and another, I embarked on an adventure with so many unknowns: it was to create a prototype with a 5,000 cc engine of which 25 examples had to be built. So I would have to ensure competiveness was in harmony with cost and the practicability of series production. On the other hand, the old financial problems were a long way from being solved and Ferrari was not all that certain that an agreement would be reached with Fiat. Finally, that situation was resolved at the end of June and we were able to produce the much desired 512 S. The Commendatore was keen to show Fiat that Ferrari was involved on various fronts, in case the innovative 312 B did not turn out to be a winner in 1970. Even so, I have always asked myself why Ferrari

wanted this car, apart of course from the Fiat agreement in relation to an anti-Porsche move; the Stuttgart brand represented various German manufacturers that were the Turin company's competitors. The Commendatore did not love the 512 in the same way that he did other sports racers. And that was not because the car wasn't a great winner. From the start, he defined it as "an absurdity wanted by the anachronistic sports regulations". He was miffed by the obligation to have to build 25 of them, which had no sense even if the six works cars and those for privateers (being sold for 24 million lire, Ed) plus the spares, were finished by the end of a fateful January 1970. We were forced into an absurd tour de force, instead of which I would have preferred to use more time

to develop the 312 B F1 car, which was close to my heart. We still had nothing by the spring of 1969, but on a foggy day in mid-November we satisfactorily tested the 512 S for the first time at Modena. The drivers were Ferrari debutante Ignazio Giunti and Arturo Merzario.

As the project's starting point, we put the 612 Can-Am and its V12 4993 cc engine under the microscope and the 512 S was created in a single month. An engine that produced 550 hp and decidedly positive, as was the gearbox. The chassis and aerodynamics were fairly conventional for both reasons of time and because Ferrari had to build a series of them. Without difficulty, we immediately designed a car that was lighter and more extreme in some areas: the operation was

carried out with tremendous professionalism a year later in the USA by Team Penske for a private 512 S-M, the famous and fast Sunoco racer, which was also built with the experience we had gathered with the subsequent M evolution that I transferred to the American team.

But during the period in which we developed the first 512, we never had the time to put it into the wind tunnel, not even for 30 minutes. A ridiculous situation in the case of such a complex and potent racer with a top speed of well over 300 kph, and we knew it. So it was inevitable that the 512 S suffered from various problems during the 1970 season. Yet on its debut at the 24 Hours of Daytona in January, it set the fastest time in qualifying and amazingly won the next round, the 12 Hours of Sebring,

Above, left: sixth round in the 1970 International Championship of Makes was the 1000 Km of Spa, where the Ferrari 512 S confirmed its competitiveness against its Porsche 917 rivals, which had an entire year of technical advantage, an increase in engine power from 4.5-litres to 5-litres and especially a limited commitment to the championship, as Ferrari was about to debut the 312 B in F1. All of which meant that the Stuttgart manufacturer's cars managed the race better. Jacky Ickx (above, number 20) was once more the best Ferrari driver at Spa, sharing the car with John Surtees, who had returned to Ferrari for three races with the 512 S. The ex-world champion was 36 years-old and was no longer the star he had once been, especially in terms of race rhythm. Ickx set a fastest time of 3 minutes 21.6 seconds to Surtees 3 minutes 23.9 seconds. A logical difference on a road track of 14.1 kilometres, but the Belgian was more constant; he and Surtees still took second place, beaten by the Siffert-Redman 917 but ahead of another similar Porsche.

Chris Amon also returned to Ferrari for two races in the 512. His contribution at the 1000 Km of Brands Hatch was excellent, taking pole position and leading the race until he was stopped by a backmarker's mistake.

Above, right: Ignazio Giunti in the helmet and Peter Schetty, the latter the 1969 European Hillclimb Champion with a formidable Ferrari 212, who contributed to the early tests of the 512 S in which he competed in seven races in 1970.

Even without any wind tunnel testing, the basic aerodynamic configuration of the 512 S wasn't bad at all, in that it was only corrected with two small spoilers on the tail. I must add that Franco Gozzi, who was the motor sport director at the time, assumed the responsibility for moving Mario Andretti to the highest placed Ferrari of Giunti-Vaccarella. Mario, whose 512 S had broken down, showed he was faster and put up a stupendous performance. Giunti, a lad who had just arrived from Alfa Romeo and I considered was good, would have probably have won, but he would have had to take on too much responsibility.

After the American 12 Hours, I never had a moment to take any more interest in that car. We competed in the 1000 Km of Monza, but that was a disaster. We thought we were inferior to the longer running Porsche 917 which had been competing since 1969, but not at that level. Unfortunately, I did not know that its front aerodynamics had been modified. The lower area of the nose no longer had end plates, it was empty. It had been conceived that way to favour the front aerodynamic load. But a plate with reinforcement occupied the whole lower zone. So the car was faster on the straight but it was penalised in the corners, and especially the front and rear aerodynamic load ratios were different. We did badly and that hampered development as well as creating an unsustainable situation. Ferrari was furious and continued to repeat that he would never

understand how the technicians – including me – could have destroyed a winning car.

A difficult moment, because a I had the weight of the new F1 car on my shoulders, which made its debut a week earlier at the Grand Prix of Spain (19 April, Ed) without me being able to personally follow the progress of the prototype team, tortured by the Commendatore's complaints. The 512 S also had a commercial aspect to it among the privateers and there was no way we could abandon it, but I was especially hurt by Ferrari's words and I wanted to demonstrate that the basis of the car was sound. Fortunately, the 312 B immediately confirmed it was a winner and that gave me a little breathing space. So together with Rocchi and Salvarani, I found the time to finally

develop functional aerodynamics for the 512 S with tests in the Stuttgart wind tunnel, added two flaps to the tail and made other minor changes. With its power output taken from 550 hp to 610 hp the car, now called the 512 M, was markedly more competitive, demonstrating that sometimes at Ferrari programmes didn't achieve full success because they were based on impossible timing, certainly not inability. And the 512 M immediately won at the 9 Hours of Kyalami – ahead of the 917s.

I was pleased with the result, but Ferrari immediately put paid to that. "The official 512 programme is terminated; we're not interested in it any more", he said. "Instead, work on a Sport with a 3-litre engine derived from the F1. The

Top: 25 April 1970, 1000 Km of Monza: Chris Amon getting ready to lap the veteran Porsche 907 of Nicodemi-Williams. The New Zealander's race was notable; with Arturo Merzario he took 512 S number 1 to fourth place after an accident in practice with the Italian driving. So for the last hour he drove the Giunti-Vaccarella car number 3 with the task of catching the leading Porsche 917 again. A difficult job that became impossible later, because fire broke out in the car as he was starting it to leave the pits.

Above, left: one of the early tests of the Ferrari 312 PB in 1971, when the car took to the track in world championship events, among others, showing it already had enormous potential, which was confirmed the following season.

Above, right: Spaniard José Juncadella in Scuderia Montjuich's yellow 512 M at the first Interseries Cup race at Imola on 2 May 1971. The Spanish team was extremely active with their bright yellow Ferrari 512 Ms in both 1970 and 1971.

Above: the last race in which a works 512 competed was first Interseries Cup at Imola from 2 May 1971. The car was an M version in which Arturo Merzario won, seen here on a lap of honour with mechanics aboard. The 512 Modificata was the result of a series of innovations designed by Mauro Forghieri and his team during the second half of 1970 to improve the car, which forced Maranello to make an enormous effort at the end of 1969 to produce the 25 necessary for the homologation. The power output of the M's 4993 cc engine was taken from 550 hp at 8500 rpm to 620 hp at 8750 rpm, while the overall weight dropped from the original 870 kg to just under 800 kg. Many aerodynamic modifications were made, among them the design of the rear and the doors, after the team had finally been able to take the car to the University of Stuttgart's wind tunnel. In that configuration, the 512 M made its debut driven by Jacky Ickx and Ignazio Giunti in the 1000 Km of Austria on 11 October 1970. Their car was in the lead by mid-race with over 20 seconds on the works Porsches until it was stopped by a banal battery problem. Success finally arrived for the M on 8 November, when it won the 9 Hours of Kyalami, in which Ickx and Giunti beat the two Porsche 917s. That could have been the launch pad for 1971, but Enzo Ferrari put a stop to the programme and went for a new prototype powered by an engine derived from that of the 312 F1 car. But the 512 S was transformed into the M and continued its career with private entrants. For instance, that was the case with Gianpiero Moretti's open top car, which competed in the 1971 1000 Km of Monza together with Teodoro Zeccoli (below, right).

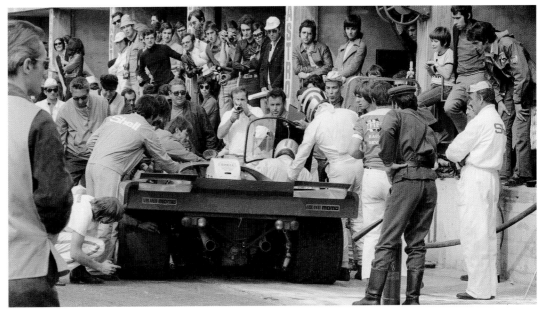

regulations coming in for 1972 seem very interesting to me". I was disappointed and I tried hard to get him to change his mind. But I was unable to do so: he had fallen in love with the "small" sports racer of which I had produced a rough design, starting from the 312 B project, and he wanted it ready by January 1971 – way ahead of its first race.

In effect, I was also fascinated by that project because there had never been a sports racing car with a flat V12 engine and, therefore, with a very low centre of gravity and a general layout more similar to an F1 car rather than a closed wheel racer. So I organised the team – as always comprising Franco Rocchi and engineer Bussi, with engineers Marelli and Caliri on the chassis and

aerodynamics – to firm up on the project and "domesticate" the F1 power unit, even though its output ended up just slightly less than that of the GP car at 460 hp against the F1's 470 hp. It was the usual rush: the car was ready before Christmas, so we immediately took it to South Africa to try it out, as always invading the villa of our friend Otello Nucci, a Tuscan who had immigrated to Johannesburg.

The 1971 312 P is among the three cars that gave me the most satisfaction, even if I wasn't able to follow so many of its exploits on the track. Unfortunately, that situation is also linked to a sad memory, the death of Ignazio Giunti at the 1000 Km of Buenos Aires, where the car made its debut. Ignazio managed to take the lead at the start

Opposite page, above: among Mauro Forghieri's memories of the Ferrari 312 PB was the terrible accident in which Ignazio Giunti died during the 1000 Km of Buenos Aires on 10 January 1971. With co-driver Arturo Merzario, Giunti set the second fastest time in qualifying in car number 24, behind the Rodriguez-Oliver Porsche 917. By the end of the first stint, Giunti was in the lead because the two 917s had just refuelled. In the corner leading to the straight, the Italian came up against the Matra of Jean-Pierre Beltoise, who intended to pit after running out of fuel. It was a prohibited and irresponsible manoeuvre by the Frenchman and, unfortunately, was not dealt with immediately by the race officials. A collision was inevitable, from which Beltoise saved himself by leaving his car. The Maranello two-seater was making its debut after an initial test at the Modena Autodrome. It was taken to the Kyalami circuit before Christmas for a real test with Peter Schetty. Engineer Forghieri recalls the solution cobbled together to resolve a major problem that arose at the South African circuit: the shape of the oil reservoir was wrong. So in Otello Nucci's garage – he always hosted the team when it was at Kyalami – they built a new reservoir using a large tomato tin. It worked perfectly and the correct reservoir, which was made at Maranello, was identical.
Below: a shot from the successful 1972 season. Ronnie Peterson driving the 312 PB during testing at Monza. Partnering Tim Schenken, the ultra-fast Swede won the 1000 Km of Buenos Aires and of the Nürburgring.

This page, above: after the Ferrari 312 PB almost totally dominated the 1972 season with a remarkable 11 victories out of 12 races, the car found 1973 hard going and was unable to win the World Championship of Makes for a second successive year. It only won two races – driven by Jacky Ickx-Brian Redman in each case – at Monza and the Nürburgring. These pictures were taken at the first two races: above is the Carlos Reutemann-Tim Schenken car with the Argentinean in the driving seat and waiting to get back into the race after adjustments by the mechanics. Below: low and compact, the 312 PB was in fact the covered wheel version of the 312 B F1 car, with the same engine that was slightly detuned to put out 460 hp in 1972 and 475 hp in '73.

of the race ahead of the more powerful 5000 cc Porsche 917s, when he took a blind corner only to find the Beltoise Matra in front of him, which the Frenchman was pushing with unequalled irresponsibility. It was an absurd accident that was also due to the thoughtlessness of the organisers. After a look-see season, in 1972 the 312, now called the PB, won the World Championship of Makes, dominating all 11 races in which it competed. I personally delivered the car to the team, which then only had to manage it as practically a turnkey project. As the technician with the most experience of certain types of tests, I also kept an eye on the car when we went to the Turin-Savona motorway, which was closed to traffic, with the long tail version to check on its aerody-

namics. One could do that at the time and Arturo Merzario easily exceeded 300 kph. Ferrari was very pleased and I had shown that we were able to construct a car of that kind with avant garde criteria. But that was not enough to avoid the disappointment of the F1 car in 1971/2 being discussed.
The PB also competed in the World Championship of Makes in 1973, but because of the various modifications made to it I could no longer consider it one of my cars. With the team assigned to engineer Sandro Colombo, it lost the world title and the Commendatore became rather bitter and, apart from anything else, he had just recovered from an illness that had forced him to eke out his visits to Maranello.

1974-1979

Seasons of Glory
Happy days: world championships with Lauda and Scheckter

Enzo Ferrari always liked Clay Regazzoni. The Commendatore appreciated his "old school" driver character, cheerful and full of verve. He was seldom in a bad mood, always ready to race whether in a competitive car or one in which he had little hope of success. He was also a good test driver, but his feedback was useful for a car's general set-up. He wasn't so reliable when evaluating a chassis or tyres.

But Clay was unique in human relations terms and the Commendatore took him back with great pleasure at the end of the 1973 summer, after their separation the previous year due to the momentary reorganisation of Ferrari's F1 programme.

Clay could also take the credit for having insist-ed that he should bring Niki Lauda to Maranello, even if many people claimed they were the ones who discovered the Austrian driver. Ferrari was deciding who to put with Regazzoni and he was thinking about Jean-Pierre Jarier. But when the Swiss returned to Maranello to sign his contract, he spoke in highly flattering terms of Lauda, whom he knew well because they competed to-gether in the BRM team. "Commendatore, don't look at the results that Niki achieved this year", Regazzoni suggested. "Believe me, he is a driver of many good qualities, which would be drawn out by the right car. He could be one of the greats…". A rare admission among colleagues. With Enzo Ferrari back in absolute command from the start of 1973, more than ever proud and determined, I also returned to a level of most intense work, with the cohesion of the whole technical team. The Commendatore gave me, once more, the compete management of both the Racing Department and the Advanced Stud-ies Office, and with me were the usual great de-signers that comprised the two organisations. One morning at the end of June, Ferrari called me and talked of another person who was to become extremely important to the team's man-agement. His name was Luca Cordero di Mon-tezemolo, a 26 year-old Bolognese who lived in Rome and who – the Commendatore em-phasised – was close to the Agnelli family, es-pecially Gianni Agnelli. Ferrari explained that he had been in contact with this young man for

several months and that he would become the Commendatore's personal assistant and motor sport director, a title that minimises the real responsibility of the person concerned. On his arrival he would take on the motor sport management of the team, but also many other external aspects, starting with press relations. Luca played that role with considerable ability, partly due to a particular sensitivity that has always impressed me and which he has maintained down the years: when I meet someone, I quickly perceive which is the best way for us to confront each other, how to communicate together. Luca's work was a great help to me personally. We were building a team with new drivers, new cars, the atmosphere had changed and

Luca not only positively influenced things, he was also able to solve thorny press problems, as journalists did not have good relations with Ferrari for reasons that harked back to the past. Personally, I never really understood why: it's true that if we didn't win we tried to limit press criticism, but that was our right. Luca managed these relations with tremendous ability, maintaining serenity within the team and avoiding possible reactions of the boss, who was always well informed about everything.

Motor sport director Dragoni also assumed that role years earlier, but there was an abyssal difference between the two. He was born in 1914 and tended to keep the press at a distance, but Luca, who was young and brilliant, was even

Previous pages: two Ferraris ahead of them all on 7 September *Previous pages:* two Ferraris ahead of them all on 7 September 1975 at the Grand Prix of Italy. A pictorial summary of two exhilarating F1 seasons, which culminated at Monza with Niki Lauda winning the world championship. In qualifying, the Austrian (12) set the fastest time, but in the race a hard charging Regazzoni was in a GP of his own. Having won four events – and he would go on to also win the GP USA - Lauda came third at Monza and he only needed one more point to take the world title. It was a supremacy helped along in no uncertain terms by the 312 T, a car created from experience gathered with the "snowplough", Mauro Forghieri's strange-looking F1 mobile laboratory that few people understood. The technical sector having found harmony again, the reorganisation of the team was the responsibility of Luca di Montezemolo.

The photograph on page 166 shows the young lawyer with The photograph on page 166 shows the young lawyer with Niki Lauda in front of the small building at the Fiorano track. Montezemolo is leaning on crutches, because he was hit by Ronnie Peterson's Lotus in the pit lane of the 1975 GP of Holland. The re-launch of the Prancing Horse started the previous year, when the 312 B3, which had been totally revised by Forghieri, went into action.

Opposite page, above: the team began well, with Lauda taking second in Argentina and Regazzoni third. The Swiss won the German GP at the Nürburgring, where Niki made a mistake as he was accelerating away at the start (right, the two drivers during the German race). Clay also made a much discussed error at Monaco (photo page 167) but he still came fourth.

friends with the journalists and often went to lunch with them.

Luca also knew how to handle the drivers well despite the criticism – unwarranted in my opinion – that was levelled at him at the end of the 1974 season. It was said he liked Lauda more. It's true that the Austrian was immediately able to put in something more in performance terms, but in my role as head of the team I can confirm that he never intervened in the slightest way in favour of the future world champion. Perhaps he favoured Niki in human terms, but only because they became friends; they met up outside racing, but Luca's relations with Clay were also excellent. And, as I will explain, what happened at the GP of the United States, where Regazzo-

ni was unable to win the world championship, was for completely different reasons, nothing to do with Luca's new role as motor sport director. He was a man who knew how to inspire the team and created an atmosphere without human problems, creating a freedom that had been unknown in the past. It gave me pleasure to help him grow and shine in his role, even if he never noticed it. The team needed a person like that, rich in external attitudes, a man who never ever hid his visceral enthusiasm. There is no doubt that the reason why we all became more pleasant was due to him.

In 1974 Ferrari at last said goodbye to sports car racing, something on which I had insisted for at least six years. As usual, the Commenda-

tore was uncertain but, thanks also to Fiat which pushed for an involvement limited to Formula 1, we devoted ourselves solely to the car that continued to be called the 312 B3, even if I thought it would be more correct to call it the B4. Apart from the engine and gearbox (evolutions of the group that first appeared in 1970, Ed) only the B3's monocoque remained, the one made in Britain and which, quite honestly, was of excellent construction. Ferrari had got us used to never wasting material, provided we never compromised a chance of success. But that monocoque was completely rebuilt: we even changed the weight distribution, moving the driver further forward and changing the position of the fuel tank. It was a delicate job, almost a desperate

one (with me there were the ever-present Rocchi and Salvarani) with separation of part of the plate that was subsequently fixed with the same technology as that used by the British specialists. It was Arturo Merzario in particular who told me that the B3, much revised in those 20 days during the summer of '73, had problems with its mass distribution. Arturo was fast and a good test driver, but unfortunately he was not confirmed as a member of the team, not due to any fault of his own but as a result of the restructuring that had cancelled out the previous period. In particular, the 312 B4 also had that strange wing that was a sort of advanced notice of the subsequent T-car I was creating at the same time as the B3. Sometimes, when he was anx-

ious to see something new on the track, Ferrari insisted on the debut of the T-car in mid-1974, the drivers helping me with enthusiasm from 9 am until darkness fell: we just about wore out the Fiorano track! But the T-car was not ready and, fortunately, he became convinced of the B3 and what was achieved during winter testing by Lauda and Regazzoni. Apart from some retirements caused by problems with the engine's injection and distribution system, we could have won the world championship seeing that Niki and Clay were in excellent positions right through to the finale. I was also pleased with my idea of dividing the mechanics into two teams: the one headed by Giulio Borsari had always looked after Regazzoni and the other, run

by Ermanno Cuoghi, worked with Lauda. It was something new in racing and was later copied by all the other teams. Technicians responsible for the two teams were appointed, and they were Antonio Tomaini and engineer Tommaso Carletti, who were also key to our success.
At the penultimate Grand Prix at Mosport, Canada, Regazzoni was ahead of Lauda in the world drivers' championship, but the Austrian was not able to help him chase the title, in line with that theory that causes controversy every now and then. Lauda took the lead in the GP and would certainly have won if he hadn't retired, skidding on sand put down on the track by Jochen Mass after going off on a blind corner. So Niki wasn't able to let Clay take his place – that there is

Large cutaway: the main characteristics of the 312 T stand out in this line drawing: the transverse gearbox is inside the wheelbase. Below: in the grey area shows the location of the two fuel tanks at the sides of the monocoque, integrated with the smaller one behind the cockpit. The water and oil radiators are split and of contained dimensions, fanned out in the front and behind at the side of the monocoque. Below, left: engineer Forghieri next to the 312 bodywork.

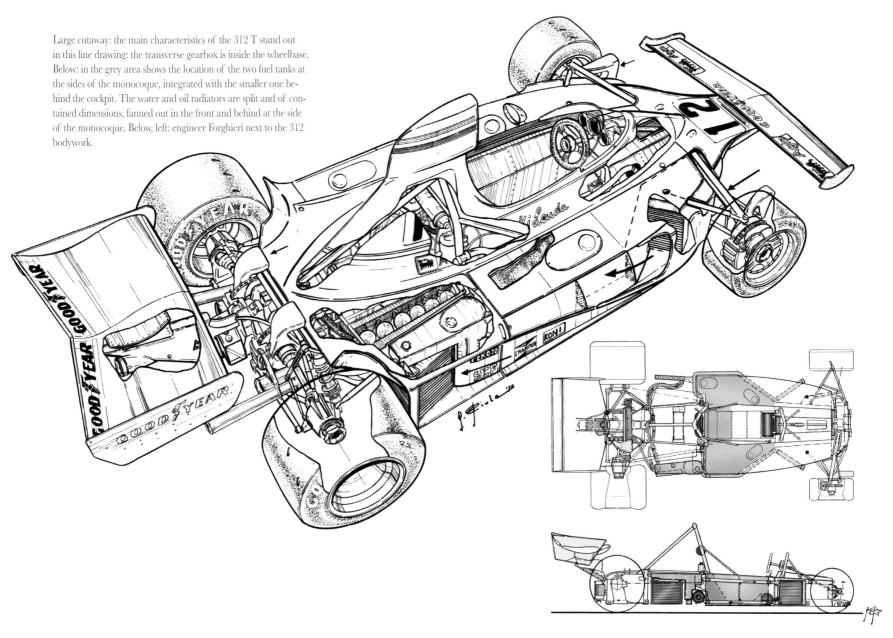

no 'sporting morality' is beside the point as all team sports operate like that – simply because in second and third places were Emerson Fittipaldi and Jody Scheckter, who were also in with a chance of winning the title, while Clay was fourth. Fittipaldi won, after which it was time for the famous epilogue at Watkins Glen for the GP USA with the Brazilian and the Swiss in a points tie. I returned from Mosport to work on the T-car because tests had been planned to take place right after the season had finished. Pre-tests had been planned for the week between the two races, but Clay had an accident on the wet circuit: the car was destroyed and he had a bruised right heel. Fortunately, there was a reserve monocoque at Maranello which

was sent by air and assembled at the circuit. I left on the Thursday, but at Milan Malpensa Airport I discovered my United States visa had run out. It was a strange situation for us at Ferrari, because our logistics secretary took care of such matters and was extremely efficient. The American Embassy in Milan renewed the visa but, after rushing back to the airport I found there were no more direct flights to New York, not even leaving from other European cities. So I took a plane to Chicago, about 1,000 km from Watkins Glen. After an unspeakable journey by car in the middle of a snow storm – on 4 October! – I didn't arrive at the Glen until the Saturday afternoon when qualifying was over and it had not gone well for us. I immediately no-

ticed that Regazzoni was not the usual Clay. He was pessimistic, the accident had demoralised him somewhat and he felt the weight of his responsibility. And with no good reason but just to meet the drivers' rather unclear requests at that GP, in my absence engineer Giacomo Caliri, head of the team, substantially modified the basic set-up of the cars, which had worked well throughout the year.

But in the race Regazzoni didn't use his usual heavy right foot. If he had come second the title would have been his, but when I saw him come into the pits for a banal problem (he continued, but came 11th, Ed) the bottom fell out of my world. We had made a gift of the title to Fittipaldi, even though he only came fourth in the race.

Luca di Montezemolo was pretty annoyed about the modified set-ups, so much so that once we were back at Maranello he wanted to propose that Ferrari fire Caliri. I don't believe the Commendatore would have agreed, and I thought it would be unjust if he did. Caliri did what he thought was his duty, but Luca would not be moved, even if he could only suggest a decision which, anyway, was Ferrari's to take. In agreement with Ferrari, I offered Caliri a job working with me at the Advanced Studies Office at Fiorano. Unfortunately, he left after six months later to work for Fittipaldi's team and that was acceptable. Less so was the fact that he even took the talented engineer Marmiroli with him. In his first period with Ferrari, Niki Lauda gave the impression of being a

Monaco, 11 May 1975: above, after the previous year's bad luck, Niki Lauda was back dominating the GP of Monaco in the Ferrari 312 T. The management of the men from Maranello was excellent, as they switched from rain to dry weather tyres at precisely the right moment.

Below, left: a true Viennese gentleman, Niki kissed the hand of Princess Grace before she and her husband Prince Rainier presented him with the spoils of victory to him.

Below, right: the cool days of Monte Carlo enabled motor sport director Luca di Montezemolo to wear a rather heavier jacket, created by the sponsor for the 1975 season. Enzo Ferrari had some singular remarks to make about Montezemolo at his press conference after winning the title. He said, "…the motor sport director of Ferrari does not exist and has never existed. There is my assistant, who divides his time between the responsibilities he had in Turin and those at Modena".

Above, left: just before the 1975 Italian Grand Prix, Ferrari went to Monza for a test with Lauda and Regazzoni. A couple of days earlier, on 24 August, Clay had won the GP of Switzerland at Dijon in the 312 T, a non-championship race but still one of high level. After the success of the T-car, engineer Forghieri considered using De Dion suspension front and back. That was a completely new technique in modern Formula 1 and was suggested by the advantage of keeping the tyres' footprint on the asphalt in critical conditions as much as possible, which is achieved with the most recent F1 cars with excursions of the suspension kept down to a minimum. A T-car with a De Dion set up was successfully tested at Fiorano, but Goodyear's total support would have been needed to continue, building tyres with five different tread compounds especially for the Ferraris while continuing to produce normal tyres for other teams. An arduous commitment they felt unable to make so they rejected the idea – and Ferrari understood the reason.

Above, right: The AGIP advertising hoarding transformed into a gallery for fans, who certainly did not want to miss the 1976 return of Lauda to Monza after his dramatic Nürburgring accident.

placid type. He and Clay were real friends and they worked magnificently together, both on the track and in the long meetings during which Niki literally pushed himself to understand the cars' behaviour. He invested more time in generally understanding the cars, while Clay leaned more in the direction of always driving them on the limit. When we had developed the 312 T, they split the task of setting up the cars down the middle, even if Niki had been quite fantastic in the 1975 GPs, taking nine pole positions, five victories and the world championship. The triumphant gallop of Lauda began at the Grand Prix of Monaco where we had not won for exactly 20 years, even though we were key competitors the previous season. That time, too, the win seemed

a natural complement to our work: we expected it, which is why I would not put it on the same level as the incredible victory of Gilles Villeneuve in 1981, about whom more later. It's curious to note that the mechanics, sensitive interpreters of the state of the drivers as they are, forecast a Regazzoni win despite Lauda's pole. *"Clay l'è più purtè a buttèr deinter la machine in del curvi…"* (Clay is more likely to throw the car into the corners…) was their somewhat instinctive concept when comparing the Swiss with the cleaner driving style of Lauda.

Anyway, the 312 T really was the top car, and I remember that season telling the drivers not to risk making mistakes, considering that the car was competitive and reliable. Yet I realised

Regazzoni was less on the ball than the previous year. With that character of his he never complained, but I'm sure he came out of the accident somewhat affected by the '74 season's experience. Someone had whispered in his ear, saying that he had lost the world title due to Luca Montezemolo favouring Lauda. A load of rubbish, because the motor sport director could certainly not interfere with the cars, which were absolutely identical. I have already explained that the drivers started at the same level, but I'm sure Clay had this so-called favouritism going around in his head and that it influenced his driving.

Lauda also changed little-by-little with his success. Having won the world title, he started to enjoy all the benefits his notoriety could bring him, but basically it was his separation from Mariella Reininghaus, with whom he had lived for a number of years, that was at the root of it all. She was a delightful girl, a little Hapsburg-like in her mental outlook, but that's why she had such a positive influence on Lauda the driver. She knew how to contain him and she was even more methodical at work than Niki. He literally changed his life when he fell in love with Marlene Knaus, a beautiful woman who was engaged to the famous Austrian actor Kurd Jurgens. And because Marlene was extrovert and sunny (much different from Mariella) she loved living in Ibiza for most of the year, so Niki bought a twin-engined jet and commuted to and from

Above, large picture: it's not a public protest of the Seventies, but a celebration of Niki Lauda's first Formula 1 World Championship. At the time, the driver was engaged to Mariella Reininghaus, an Austrian whose mother was Italian and lived in Trieste, which the couple often visited. The two met while skiing in 1969 and to be with Niki, Mariella stopped studying the history of art. A book on the subject entitled simply "Austria" was published recently. In '76, Lauda married Marlene Knaus with whom he had two children. The couple divorced in '91.

Above and left: immediately after the 1975 Grand Prix of Italy won by Clay Regazzoni and with Niki Lauda's world title in his pocket, Enzo Ferrari held a press conference announcing among other things his confirmation of the two drivers for '76. "We have already agreed", he told journalists. "We shook hands on it before Monza. They did not ask for a single penny more...". He also spoke of the power of the 312 T's engine. "With a conic torque of 9.8 cm in diameter (he was talking of the T-shaped gearbox's advantages, Ed) we are able to transfer 500 hp. We do not have a single horse power more than 500, but the secret of our engine is that it permits us to exploit it from 6500 rpm to 12,500 rpm. In practice, we now have an excursion of 6500 rpm". The famous "torque" for which engineer Forghieri had fought so long and hard since the early Sixties!

Bologna Airport. Lauda's ability as a great driver and tester were intact, but he was less willing to sit behind the wheel or to put up with in technical briefings. I had to manage him with astuteness, even if he sometimes made me fly off the handle: he arrived, ran through the day's programme and noted what was to happen, let's say a four hour test. At that point, he would telephone his personal pilot (he did not fly solo as he did later, Ed) telling him to be ready at 3.30 pm because he would arrive half-an-hour later. After five minutes, I was the one who telephoned the Bologna Airport control tower, asking if they would kindly advise Mr. Lauda's pilot that he wouldn't be able to take off before 5 pm. I was forced to descend to his level, but I had

to make sure he left later so that we could finish the test without rushing. Ferrari knew about the tantrums of his driver and sneered, but never intervened. It was the team's job, and then there was his great satisfaction at having led a person who had never previously won anything to the world title.

With the 312 T partially revised and really competitive, Lauda would also have won the world title in 1976 if he had not had that terrible accident at the Nürburgring. At the end of the lap that preceded the holocaust, Niki had stopped to change his wet weather tyres, with which he had started, for slicks. He came across a wet patch at Bergwerk, smashed into the rock on the edge of the track and Brett Lunger's Surtees crashed

into his Ferrari. Unfortunately, a fuel tank on one of the sides of the car ruptured. Only afterwards did we begin to place the tanks in the centre, between the driver and the engine, after the first crash tests that we at Ferrari and Brabham designer Gordon Murray had requested. Lauda's accident at least taught us which road to take for safety purposes.

After the first two or three days of worry Niki's life was no longer in danger, but the drama of the fire had affected public opinion (Lauda was the world champion, it is necessary to add: with less prestigious drivers, public reaction would have been different) and Ferrari wanted to be completely reassured about the safety of his cars. Among other things, someone had said the

There was a certain continuity between the 1975 Grand Prix of Italy (Lauda became world champion, Regazzoni won the race) and the last win of the Ferrari 312 T the following year at the GP USA-West on 28 March by Clay (above with Lauda on that occasion) in the States. Presented at Fiorano on 25 October 1975, the T2 began its career at the Spanish GP on 2 May 1976. The car was designed to meet the new technical regulations starting from the first European GP, in which Lauda came second, but he had already won the GPs of Brazil and South Africa in the T-car. Opposite page, above: Enzo Ferrari with Niki Lauda and Clay Regazzoni with the T2; conspicuous by its absence is the high engine air intake, the most significant modification to the new car, which also had semi-fared front wheels, fairing that was not used in races.
Below: an overall cutaway of the 312 T2, and on the right a comparison with the 1975 T-car in both profile and from above.

suspension on Niki's car broke, which is why the Commendatore insisted on making an official statement. So through the CSAI (the Italian Motor Sport Commission, Ed) he asked for an external inquiry, which completely exonerated us from blame. In the meantime, we didn't compete in the Austrian Grand Prix and only Regazzoni drove the Grand Prix of Holland, in which he came second, less than a tenth of a second from winner James Hunt in the McLaren. Meanwhile at Maranello, under pressure from Enzo Ferrari, motor sport director Daniele Audetto – a Fiat Group man who replaced Montezemolo – was busy looking for another driver to compete with Regazzoni in the Grand Prix of Italy. Niki got to know what was going on and took

the driver search as a personal affront, a lack of confidence in him, partly because he didn't get on well with Audetto. The word was to take Ronnie Peterson and I must admit that in certain ways I would have been pleased if he had joined us, because I was one of his great admirers. Then up came the name of Carlos Reutemann, who eventually took Clay's place but not until 1977.

At Monza, we witnessed a stoic return of Niki Lauda, who was deeply affected and not just by his injuries. He was annoyed with Ferrari because the Commendatore had "dared" to think of replacing him. In my opinion, it was perfectly correct, because Ferrari was only trying to defend its driver's place in the world champion-

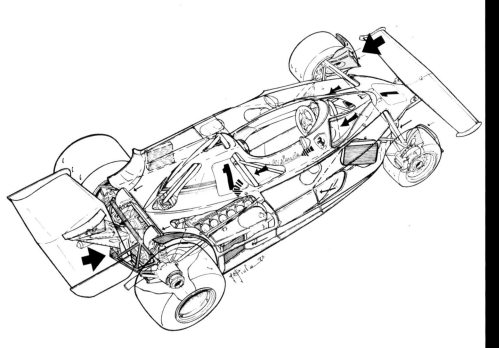

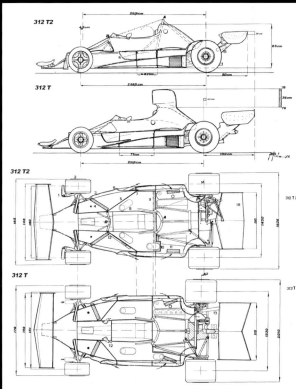

312 T2

312 T

312 T2

312 T

ship. Together with Regazzoni, either Peterson or Reutemann could have "stolen" points from Hunt and his McLaren, who were moving up the table fast.

When I saw Niki with his wounds still open and his morale undermined, I realised we were committing a terrible mistake. It had never been my job to manage the drivers, but on that occasion I was completely against allowing a man to compete in a GP in that condition. I said so clearly to the Ferrari but there was nothing I could do, although the Commendatore did ask Niki if he really felt like competing in the Grand Prix. Lauda, who was passed as fit after an obligatory medical check, wanted to race at all costs to spite Reutemann and it was an ordeal. If he had been

taken care of himself better and had come back in Canada three weeks later having rebuilt his morale, I am sure he would have won the world championship. Niki was a much more complete driver than his rival James Hunt and the 312 T was superior to the McLaren-Ford. But in the last three races, the Englishman had battled against this debilitated Lauda for whom the fourth place at Monza did more harm than good.

Now, we come to the Grand Prix of Japan, where a drama that embittered me a lot took place. Given the mad weather conditions and the danger of the Fuji circuit, most of the drivers decided not to start. They were to do a lap of the track and then return to the pits. Lauda knew that, and he was at ease with it. But a few minutes before the

Opposite page: above, Niki Lauda with Daniele Audetto, the motor sport director who took the place of Luca di Montezemolo. Audetto came from Lancia, where he began in 1971 as a navigator with various drivers including Montezemolo in a Fulvia HF. Below, Monaco, 30 May 1976 and the first victory of the of the Ferrari 312 T2 with Niki Lauda.

This page, above: the GP of Sweden at Anderstorp, where Lauda came third. Despite winning in 1975, engineer Forghieri considered the Swedish Grand Prix rather a bugbear for the 312 T due to a unique detail of that track: some constant radius curves did not favour a short wheelbase car.

Right: a picture taken at the Nürburgring on a dark day for Lauda and for Ferrari, 1 August 1976, the day on which the world champion, seen here talking to technician Antonio Tomaini with Regazzoni and Audetto, was involved in his terrible accident.

Left, below: Lauda in the 312 T2 just before the start of the 1976 German Grand Prix. Given the clear superiority of the T2 during the early part of the season, Mauro Forghieri was not in the pits at the 'Ring, but at Maranello working on the development of the car that would compete in F1 the following season.

start, the other drivers told him that they would race. That caused a psychological effect in his mind which was unquestionably negative: he had not completely recovered from his injuries and he started the race with a downcast facial expression.

He came back to the pits after two laps and was extremely honest. "Do you want us to say your car had an electrical fault?", I asked him. Quite the contrary, he asked us to say that he had retired because he didn't feel like racing, in part due to the behaviour of drivers he considered his friends and who had sold him down the river. Later, I heard that pit signals were made to James Hunt by a number of British teams to guarantee him third place, which gave him the

point he needed to win the world title. That was one of the less attractive sides of Formula 1 in action, but in the previous two years Lauda had done nothing to earn their friendship. And such things matter when you need a favour. He always thought of himself as no longer bound to them, not even to Clay Regazzoni who had brought him to Ferrari. But it should also be said that Clay was not a great help on the track after Lauda's retirement, when he could have contributed to blocking Hunt. At Maranello in the days that followed, I had the impression that Regazzoni was putting himself in the dock somewhat for his opaque performance at Fuji. It's true that Clay did not drive in the same way in the wet as he did in the dry, and he had also been subjected

to the psychological effect of Lauda's situation. Clay certainly wasn't an insensitive person, despite his often bold behaviour: quite the opposite, he was extremely sensitive to certain situations, even a little too much so at times.

But Regazzoni was forced to emigrate to Williams and Reutemann arrived at Maranello. In 1977 our 312 T2 was still the top car, even if the Lotus 78 with the great Mario Andretti as its driver had returned in to the top. And Niki recovered his enormous class quickly, but his character had changed again and this time very much for the worst. He had become touchy, suspicious and had a ferocious aversion to Reutemann, convinced that Ferrari had given the Argentinean the number one driver spot. That was

a pure invention, motivated by jealousy that he had felt since Carlos' name had been mentioned prior to the 1976 GP of Italy. It was a shame, because we had dominated the season, but often amid useless spite.

Symptomatic of the situation was the episode of the new wing we took to Brazil. It was a "twisted" type wing, with an aerodynamic connection angle, variable from the exterior to the interior, our idea that was later copied by everybody else. We only had one wing and I suggested Niki should test it, but by then he had set the fastest time in practice and he refused. So I had the wing fitted to Reutemann's car and he did a better time than Lauda. Then the sky opened up! Lauda wanted to use the wing in the race. And I

Mauro Forghieri pedalling fast in the Monza pit lane during the usual test which preceded the Grand Prix of Italy at the beginning of September. They were days of agitation and not because of the 312 T2, which had already won six times during the season and was fully competitive, but due to the extremely delicate situation that was created after Niki Lauda's serious accident on 1 August. The Austrian, who was still at the top of the drivers' world championship table despite having had to miss two GPs, wanted to return at Monza on 12 September, but his condition was a long way from normal. Meanwhile, to defend its position Ferrari contacted Argentinean Carlos Reutemann, who had driven the 312 T2 at Monza on 2 and 3 September. He was a logical choice and Ferrari had to cover its back at the very least, but in doing so it had injured Lauda's pride and that made him want to return to the track even more.

Above, left: with his burns not completely healed, his head still bandaged and his troubled look, Lauda's return to F1 at the Italian Grand Prix was premature, as Forghieri always maintained. It is true that the Austrian was able to take fourth place and, therefore, add three more points to his world championship score, but he paid a high price for it in terms of his psychological condition.

Above, right: after practicing in the wet in the 312 T2, assisted by his chief mechanic Ermanno Cuoghi, Lauda candidly admitted he had been frightened, a factor that probably affected him until the end of the season. A quieter return in better physical condition would have enabled him to immediately compete at his usual high level.

Bottom, left: but there was Reutemann, who competed in the Italian GP driving the third Ferrari. And Lauda, hyper-protective of his position like all the great champions, could not stand for that.

refused, because Carlos ran the test – and then he won the race. Niki never forgave me for the rest of the season, which dragged on with him being even more suspicious. He was making a major mistake, because he should have understood that to me he was the team's point of reference. It couldn't have been any other way, given that when he was driving a winning car he dominated completely. He never left anything to chance and he had a driving style of implacable effectiveness, without conceding anything to spectacle.

Yet he went as far as reproaching me, saying that during my usual telephone call to the Commendatore to give him the times, I only mentioned tenths of a second and not hundredths.

He was convinced I did so to detract from his performance, while in fact it was a detail of no importance.

On the contrary, Niki always had my help and at times in a quite determinate way. In that famous 1977, Goodyear produced tyres for both us and Lotus, but the production capacity of their factory at Bushbury in Britain was limited (their F1 tyres were later built in Akron, Ohio, Ed) and during the summer months there were always very few absolutely perfect sets. At the Dutch GP, Andretti took the pole but Goodyear only had one single set of competitive tyres for the race and their manager, Denny Chrobak, wanted to give those to Andretti. A little persuasion was needed: so I locked myself in our caravan-office with that gentleman and I started a knives-out discussion. "Those tyres are ours", I shouted, "you can't give them to Lotus, because you've got a contract with Ferrari for testing and original equipment for our road cars. If you prefer, we'll call Enzo Ferrari and talk to him about it...". But, naturally, the call was no longer necessary. Niki dominated the GP and practically won his second world title. After the race, I spoke to the Italian journalists and Nestore Morosini of the Corriere della Sera said to me, "Congratulations, because now Ferrari has a world champion who has just signed for Brabham-Parmalat...". I stood rooted to the spot, because none of us knew anything about it. I chased over to Niki, who had gone to change before catching his

Above: there was a real battle for fourth place in the German Grand Prix at Hockenheim between Reutemann and Andretti (Lotus-Ford), with the Argentinean eventually succeeding. Right: Ferrari's list of adversaries got longer in 1977, but Lauda and the 312 T2 came back big time from the previous year. Niki got his own back and beat Scheckter (Wolf-Ford) in the GP of Germany at Hockenheim and then he scored his 14th victory with Ferrari (right). A first place that enabled him to become the driver with the most F1 wins in a car from Maranello. The previous record belonged to Alberto Ascari with 13 victories. Less than a month later, Lauda also won in Holland and was within a heartbeat of his second world title – and his surprising departure from Ferrari. The Austrian's victory record was not broken until 1999, when Michael Schumacher won the Grand Prix of Monaco for the Prancing Horse.

plane, and asked him to tell me the truth, making it clear that it would remain between us. "Are you joking, Mauro? I haven't signed for anyone", Lauda said.

The next morning, the news was in all the papers. Niki was always a great driver, but he became impudent. Because due to his suspicions and fixations, he no longer trusted Ferrari. So Lauda left, leaving Enzo Ferrari more surprised than furious. He was satisfied with two world championships – the drivers' and constructors' – and everything was going fine during that period. Which doesn't always happen in racing, where a little luck is always necessary – but that alone is not enough. The Commendatore often said, "Luck and bad luck don't exist. Everything

depends on how you work", but in private he didn't think that way. I well remember when he maintained, "It's better to have a driver a little less talented, but who's lucky". He even said it in an even more colourful way in the Modenese dialect, said, *"Lè mei un pilota con un gran cul, putost che un campion sfurtunè..."*.

These witticisms came out of an evening, maybe after 8 pm when Ferrari stopped work and chatted about things like that, maybe gossip without any scorn at all. All mixed in with highly colourful jokes, another of his great passions. And he laughed and enjoyed it all, because he was only tough and rigid at work. For instance, on Saturdays at the traditional meeting-lunch at Fiorano, where the regulars were Sergio Scaglietti the fa-

mous body builder – master of a car's lines, but also of the latest jokes – and Carlo Benzi, the Commendatore's personal financial adviser. To Ferrari, an excellent table companion who waited the entire week for that "feast"; the Saturday meeting was a ritual. I was one of the invitees, but I didn't go very often. With the life I led, I wanted to be with my family on non-race Saturdays. And even if I personally love good cuisine, I had the impression that somewhat spirited atmosphere could have limited my independence at work. I liked all of them, and you'd better believe I enjoyed talking to Ferrari, but being in motor racing is a bit like being on the national football team: everyone wants to drive his own points home. Gilles Villeneuve arrived at the end of the sum-

mer in 1977 and he contributed a great deal towards making Ferrari forget Lauda's departure. It is well-known that the Commendatore liked this young Canadian, who was perhaps his most audacious "bet". They really began to get to know each other on Wednesday 21 September when Gilles came to Maranello (to be precise, the previous evening, Ed) for a test in the 312 T2 with a view to his competing in the Grand Prix of Canada on 9 October. Enzo Ferrari watched the test but we were in a bit of a hurry, because at the time the cars were sent off to GPs across the Atlantic well in advance. And we immediately noted one little matter in particular: after just three laps, the brakes were "destroyed", white hot. Ferrari soon realised that here we had a driver of natural talent,

Left and top: Lauda talking to technician Antonio Tomaini as Reutemann listens with interest. Engineer Forghieri recalls that the Austrian driver's class remained intact after his serious accident, but his character changed so that he became more jealous. He had it fixed in his mind that Enzo Ferrari had assigned the number one driver's role to Reutemann, which was untrue. A week before the 1977 Grand Prix of South Africa, Ferrari had taken part in a collective test at Kyalami with Niki Lauda. All the modifications previously tested at Fiorano and Vallelunga came to light on the T2, including new rear suspension mounts and different air vents to lower the water radiators' temperature. A good test, given that Lauda scored his first victory after his horrendous accident, which conditioned the finale of the 1976 season. Above: Carlos Reutemann in the T2 at the 1977 Japanese GP at Fuji. It was Ferrari's last race on Goodyear tyres for a few years before returning to the American manufacturer in 1982. Opposite page: Reutemann competing in the 1978 GP of Monaco.

Top, left: Gilles Villeneuve in the Ferrari 312 T3 at the 1978 Grand Prix of Monaco; the Canadian's race ended on the 62nd lap after he smashed into the tunnel's guardrail
Below, left: at the beginning of 1978 in South Africa, Ferrari ran a test session with Villeneuve. The car was fitted with Michelin tyres after Maranello had left Goodyear, which had supplied its tyres to all the F1 teams in 1977, except the debutante Renault. It was a crowded situation that created a number of misunderstandings: so Ferrari preferred to hammer out an agreement with the French tyre maker, which had introduced radials to F1 in place of the widely used, older cross ply type of construction. It was a technical matter and Goodyear also moved into radials later. Thanks to Ferrari, Michelin achieved its first Formula 1 victory with Carlos Reutemann at the '78 GP of Brazil. The first contact between Ferrari and Michelin dates back to January 1970 when their steel belted radials, for which the company held a patent, were tested on a 312 B at the Vallelunga circuit. It was significant that the tyres had no tread pattern, an absolute first of the period. But other tyre makers soon cottoned on and slicks, as the patternless tyres are called, began to spread.
Below, right: a 312 T3 turning vane, one of the first of its kind used by a single-seater – and their use has never stopped.

but who had no idea of how to manage his driving. He was fast and determined, but he lacked experience. Then at the Japanese Grand Prix he was at the centre of a bad accident with Ronnie Peterson's Tyrrell, which caused the deaths of two spectators who were in a prohibited area.

It was an accident with relative blame – neither of the drivers lifted his right foot – and that's why Gilles was nicknamed the "aviator".

Between the autumn of 1977 and the end of the following winter, we literally "constructed" Villeneuve as a driver at the Fiorano circuit. He put everything into learning how to drive the T3 as well as possible, and the instrumentation at Fiorano helped him a lot.

There was no modern electronic telemetry in those days, but the Ferrari track did have 45 photo-electric cells installed by Heuer to relay partial times. In addition, there were 10 closed-circuit television cameras as well as a calculator which indicated whether or not a certain trajectory used by the driver was right or that there was a better one, all based on a mathematical formulae.

While Villeneuve was at his "driving school", I went ahead with the new T3 project, which was an evolution of the T2 except that the suspension design was for a car of a lower, squarer lines, developed to better direct the air flow towards the rear wing. The modifications were partially motivated by the need to use Michelin radial tyres in place of the Goodyear cross plies.

We had changed supplier partly due to my previous year's battles with the Americans to obtain valid tyres.

The move to radials brought with it a series of long tests, because the different construction of that tyre type required substantial modifications to the suspension and the drivers had to get used to controlling the car in a different way. So we weren't able to debut the T3 until the third GP of the season in South Africa, but meanwhile Reutemann had dominated the Brazilian GP in a surprising manner. Carlos, who was a fast driver but one who was perennially in doubt, had it fixed in his mind that the "old" car was better than the new one. Villeneuve had even taken on a decidedly critical attitude to the T3,

After his debut as a replacement for Niki Lauda, Gilles Ville-neuve not only confirmed his innate sense of speed, he also matured and had won his first Grand Prix – in Canada – by the end of the 1978 season. But he retired from the British Grand Prix at Brands Hatch (above, left) with a broken drive shaft. Right: Villeneuve takes a close look at the front end of his car at Monza.

because it had no mini-skirts like the Andretti/ Peterson Lotus 49s. The new Lotus made its first appearance at the beginning of the year and their ground effect, which Ferrari had discovered and used for its cars in the early Seventies, was strongly accentuated by lateral devices that ran along the lower edges of the car and slithered across the asphalt. Those "seals" stopped the air exiting laterally and were immediately baptised mini-skirts; they created a stronger negative lift, squashing the car to the ground and so increasing speed through corners.

Naturally, many teams tried to follow the Lotus example, but Enzo Ferrari was of a unique coherence over certain things, especially concerning safety and regulations. Our motor sport director Marco Piccinini, who was very young but had a natural inclination towards sports regulations, made official enquiries at the Federation concerning the legality or otherwise of mini-skirts and the answer was that they were not legal. Then, naturally, with its usual attitude the Federation became uncertain and Lotus was never told to eliminate the devices.

But the Commendatore would not be moved. He thundered, "I'm not interested in what the others do. If we maintain they're illegal, how can we contradict ourselves? I'm for legality, even if the legislators are unable to have their regulations respected – and it certainly isn't the first time that's happened".

However, even without mini-skirts the T3 was

Above: a dramatic picture of the accident that happened right after the start of the 1978 Grand Prix of Italy at Monza, the cause of which could only have been the narrowing of the track at the first variant. A number of cars collided and Ronnie Peterson's Lotus 78 got the worst of it. The Swede's car hit the guardrail and burst into flames; the driver was extracted from the cockpit, but died later in hospital of a seriously fractured foot and the consequent embolism.
Below: Engineer Forghieri talking to Gilles Villeneuve and Jody Scheckter during a test session at the Fiorano track. Scheckter joined the team especially due to Enzo Ferrari, who was impressed with his exuberant driving. But at Maranello, he showed he was fast, but more of a thinker than he had been in the past.

able to bring strong pressure to bear on a team that Ferrari considered technically "illegal". Despite a year I could define as a "running-in" period for Michelin – at the GP of France, Reutemann used qualifiers in the race after the French company had run out of race tyres – Carlos won four GPs against Mario Andretti's six and, if only for the class the American had shown over many years including with Ferrari, Mario deserved the world title. Meanwhile, Villeneuve won the Canadian Grand Prix.

In 1979, Jody Scheckter, who replaced Reutemann, joined Ferrari and brought the drivers' world title back to Maranello, with Gilles Villeneuve second in the championship table. Rumours circulated that we had pushed the title

Scheckter's way, because Jody had a contract of $200,000 a year and, therefore, he was the number one driver. Except that Gilles, who was pampered by the sponsors and Ferrari, couldn't complain; such rumours were of historic stupidity. Scheckter and Villeneuve won three GPs each, but the South African was more consistent, as was Reutemann the year before.

The 1979 was an optimum season in which Ferrari also won the constructors' championship. Yet the mini-skirts problem bounced back worse than ever. Ferrari conceded to reality and authorised us to use them, but those adopted for the T4 were obsolete. What happened was something that often took place in Formula 1: those who follow always stay behind. We copied the Lotus

system with mini-skirts in ceramic resin and a system of springs to keep them on the ground. Frankly, though, they didn't work too well on a rather undulating track. On flat circuits there was no problem: Jody and Gilles were really fast. On tracks with a few humps like Silverstone – our millstone – the mini-skirts inclined slightly and the air leaked out of the back producing serious stability problems. That was because they ensured the pressure on the ground was independent of the behaviour of the car which changed continuously, depending on its speed.

Meanwhile, Williams had improved incredibly and so had the Ligier, where the genial – and sometimes nonchalant – Gerard Ducarouge worked in aerodynamics. Gerard conceived

Above, right: in 1979, Villeneuve (12) and Scheckter dominated qualifying for the Monaco Grand Prix and in the race Jody led from start to finish, but Gilles had to retire with transmission trouble. The Canadian had previously won the Grands Prix of South Africa and USA-West at Long Beach and Scheckter had taken the Belgian GP, confirming the validity of the new Ferrari 312 T4 despite the so-called mini-skirts arriving late, having previously been banned by the regulations, even if they were used by many teams starting with Lotus.

Centre: Giorgio Piola's partial cutaway of the 312 T4; more of the car's details emerge in the picture (centre, right). The car was a further version of the T-series and its aerodynamics were much developed in a wind tunnel. The wide body's lateral channels were prominent and directed air flow towards the rear wing for better ground effect. For the same reason, there was just one fuel tank and that was in the centre of the car, so it was possible to design a really narrow monocoque. When the mini-skirts crested a depression, the sheets pushed them downwards.

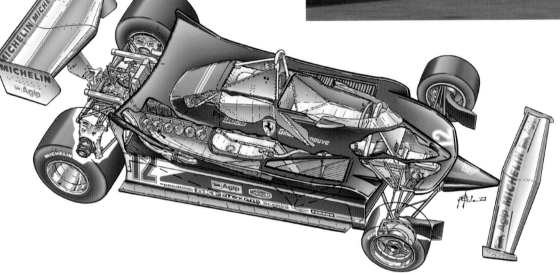

a system that envisaged a sheet fixed to the monocoque and the mini-skirts that slid up on the surface. Without considering that Ligier was a French team for which a number of British mechanics worked; it was rather like a clan from which Ferrari was always excluded (I had known that as far back as 1962 when I went to Silverstone with Ireland...) and it was more than likely that experience was passed from one team to another. It's just a pity that when they banned the mini-skirts (at the end of 1981, Ed) we had finally got them right, but one of our mechanics let something slip so the opposition soon caught on to what we had done.

Apart from the mini-skirt problem, the T4 was still the result of a completely new project, the ump-teenth evolution of the T layout. It was a car conceived in a wind tunnel based on research by engineer Gian Franco Poncini, an exceptional young man of a singular character and personality who excelled in individual work. Poncini carried out the first aerodynamic studies on the mini-skirts in the Pininfarina tunnel. But an annoying internal controversy developed due to a certain provincial attitude that sometimes cropped up at Ferrari. The concept was: Pininfarina is OK, but the British have specialised tunnels, which work much better... I missed the fruitful conflicts I had had for about 15 years with engineer Bussi who, unfortunately, died in October 1978 after an absurd and ferocious kidnapping in Sardinia.

I did not react all that much to the wind tunnel

situation, but studied a "radical" plan. I asked
Ferrari if I could produce a 1:5 model to test it in
all the tunnels used by the British teams. Result:
five wind tunnels and five different answers! So
I asked my colleagues which road we should
take – but I was given no answer.

I was not at all surprised, because we needed
comparative coefficients that we certainly didn't
have. A useless controversy, because the Pininfarina wind tunnel, where we took our 1:1 scale
car, was more than enough at the time.

The T4's win can best be explained by the coherence of the whole team, but this single-seater
was, anyway, of top level.

Using Poncini's calculations, I designed the
large, overhanging front wing and the lateral

pontoons that were kept under pressure – that way, the air never broke away under any circumstances – and which were the result of a mathematical formula.

We were always talking about whether or not the flat 12-cylinder allowed the air to "release itself" at the rear due to its width to create a good ground effect; unlike the narrower Ford-Cosworth, a shape used by most of the teams. But the results proved we were right: there is no real technical explanation for this theory, which was started by the same people who left Ferrari taking the designs for the flat 12 engine with them as a "memento" so that it could be built by another company...

Of the two drivers, Jody was the tester I trust-ed. He was much more expert than Gilles, who still did a good job but in a different way. Ferrari formed a curious opinion of Scheckter right after his first GPs with us. He said, "I took him because he seemed to me like a man with a knife between his teeth, but then I found I had another Lauda on my hands...". Evidently he remembered Jody's first years in Formula 1, when he was a bit of a kamikaze, but later the South African used his head more in racing.

Villeneuve had a special ability: if we improved the yield of the car, it was certain he would go even faster. But with Scheckter, that might not have happened, he would probably have turned in more consistent lap times.

To say we went from the sublime to the ridic-

ulous the following year is, perhaps, not an exaggeration. But we had the same drivers, the same cars that were only partially revised. Some areas of the cars were lightened, including the engine so they weren't only more fragile but the mini-skirts, which sometimes worked in an anomalous way the previous year, were even worse due to the excessive lightness of the car's upper area. And that's without taking into account the fact that the Federation, despite the fact that a "tough guy" like Jean-Marie Balestre had become its president, didn't push the teams that belong to FOCA, in other words the British, at all.

Everyone expected a reaction from Ferrari – but there was none. The division of the income from the Grands Prix was to be decided with Bernie Ecclestone and as the mediator was firmly on the side of the British, it was not the time to quibble. On top of that, the Commendatore had a new turbo engine in mind that would compete in 1981 and I was thinking solely of the new car. I was rather sorry for the drivers. Gilles gave his heart and soul to racing and Jody, a good young man in human terms, said to me, "Sorry Mauro, it's also my fault that we don't get results. I'm going to retire at the end of the year and perhaps I don't have the motivation any more".

But that was not the problem and I told him so, although I did appreciate the thought.

Above, left: Clay Regazzoni in a Ferrari 312 B2 during an exhibition that took place on the morning of the 1979 Grand Prix of Italy at Monza to mark the 50th anniversary of the Grand Prix of Italy: the theme was drivers and cars that were part of the history of the race. At the time Clay was a Williams driver, but he had no problem with climbing into the "old" Ferrari.
Above right and below: Jody Scheckter testing before the 1979 Grand Prix of Italy.
As did Lauda in 1975, Jody Scheckter became Formula 1 World Champion the day he won the Italian Grand Prix on 9 September 1979, with Villeneuve second, a historic day for Ferrari.
Opposite page, above: the two Ferraris after the bridge on the breakaway from the Ascari corner, and their two drivers being cheered by spectators after their usual peaceful invasion of the track. After the Monza success, Villeneuve won the GP USA-East at Watkins Glen, the last victory of a T-series Ferrari and the 12-cylinder engine designed by Mauro Forghieri in 1969: the cars won a remarkable 37 GPs.

1980-1983

The Turbo Arrives
Among triumphs and defeats

A car under my management once went from success to disappointment in a single season. A completely unacceptable situation to Enzo Ferrari: he gave himself no peace, tried to understand and, naturally, he became annoyed with his technicians. In 1980, he was stupefied by the lack of results from the car (the T5, Ed), which had done so well the previous season. Yet he didn't make a tragedy out of it, because he had been seduced by the idea of the turbo and he had ordered me to take on the new technology, and I didn't have the slightest doubt of the correctness of his decision.

The engine continued to be at the centre of a car project to the Commendatore, but it was significant that a man of over 80 years-old had decided to disrupt the technical target of his company with a choice which, at the time, was by no means natural.

Renault opened the F1 engine era with an exhaust gas turbocharger in 1977, but by the end of the 1979 season it had only won once. Yet we clearly understood that was the right road to follow: we couldn't obtain more than 515 hp from a 3000 cc normally aspirated unit – with a rev limiter, due to the ignition distributors of the period - but with the 1500 turbo (the regulations demanded turbocharged engines with half the cubic capacity, Ed) we aimed at a starting point of 550 hp.

It all began in 1979 and by mid-1980 we had presented a prototype of the 126 C, which was to race in 1981. It was no mean feat, because that kind of technology was unknown – except to Renault – not only by Ferrari but by all the other constructors. I was probably one of the few who had some notion of it all, due to my passion for aeronautical piston and turbine engines. Rocchi and Salvarani were not far off retirement, but in the meantime engineers Caruso and Materazzi had arrived, so we designed a V6 engine with 120° cylinder banks, a highly advanced unit in which we poured everything we had learnt with the flat-12, including short exhausts at the centre to avoid high temperature problems under the monocoque.

We tested both the American Garrett and German KKK turbines and opted for the European

version. Our relations with KKK were those of "normal customers" without any technical support, and this turned out to be a problem when the German constructors' turbo engines arrived in Formula 1 with BMW and Porsche, which enjoyed much different relationships with their supplier. But we divided our experience with the Fiat Research Centre, which were preparing to move into the turbo sector with the Uno. The car was unveiled in early 1984, but the buyers ignored the fact that there was a little of Ferrari F1 in their engines.

Electronic systems able to avoid turbo lag had not been developed by that time, so a turbine's approximate 180,000 revs would fall substantially when the accelerator was partially down:

it seemed the engine had no power, which then arrived all at once. So we worked out a system of overboost through which the turbine continued to rotate at very high levels in all situations. It was not an especially intelligent solution to the problem in my view, but it was practical and it worked.

We also tried another route to avoid turbo lag using the Comprex system conceived by the Swiss company Brown Boveri. It was based on a rotor powered by a belt, which in turn was actioned by the engine. The exhaust gas passed through the rotor and determined a resonance that compressed the air feed that then flowed into the engine. With the Comprex, the engine ran like an aspirated unit with the addition of

Previous page: Gilles Villeneuve driving the 1981 126 CK, a duo that remained in the hearts of all the fans. In 1980, Gilles had driven the T5 (see photo on page 197 of him in the pits at Imola) unveiled on 26 November 1979 at Fiorano with engineer Forghieri, Villeneuve, motor sport director Piccinini, Enzo Ferrari (the two are leafing through Italian motor sport weekly Autosprint, which ran a paradoxical comic story on the Commendatore by Eugenio Loi) and the new world champion, Jody Scheckter. *Above:* Villeneuve and Scheckter chatting at Monte Carlo in 1980.

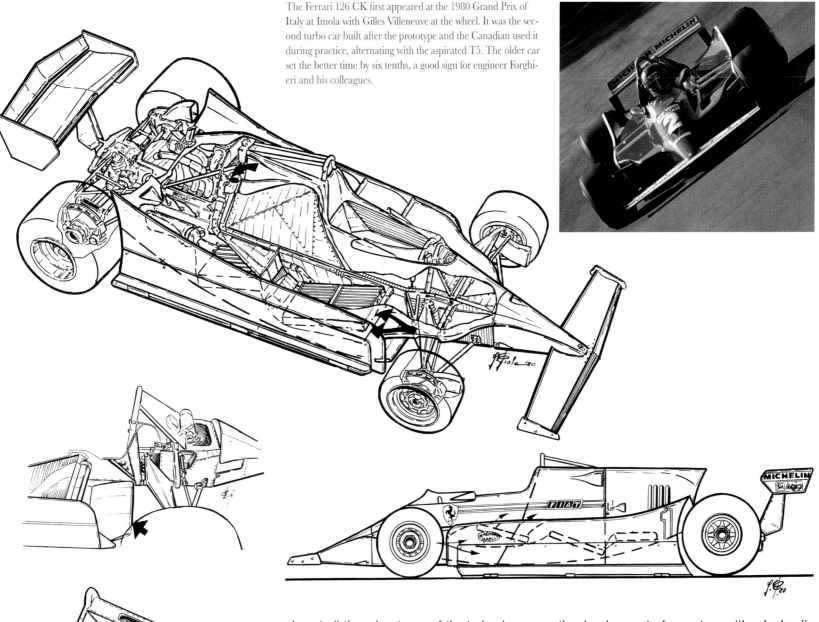

The Ferrari 126 CK first appeared at the 1980 Grand Prix of Italy at Imola with Gilles Villeneuve at the wheel. It was the second turbo car built after the prototype and the Canadian used it during practice, alternating with the aspirated T5. The older car set the better time by six tenths, a good sign for engineer Forghieri and his colleagues.

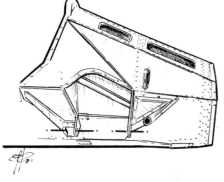

Giorgio Piola's illustrations show the details of the Ferrari 126 CK: the arrows indicate the air flow, which is fundamental to the turbo engine to lower the temperature of the radiators' coolant and oil, as well as the heat exchangers. They are fitted into the sidepods (oil on the left) starting from the front. The 126 CK's chassis was modified from the 1981 British GP: the new developments included an increase in width and a greater overall "drainage".

almost all the advantages of the turbocharger. But it was heavy and raised the car's centre of gravity. It had good qualities, among them the absence of the turbo's high temperature to the point that we used a simple, auto-fed air-to-air radiator. We tested the Comprex for a long time and negotiated an interesting exclusive agreement with the Swiss company.

Then, while practicing for the GP USA-West at Long Beach, it became clear that a system was necessary in which the drive belt stopped breaking. That happened because of the speed variation between one gear change and another, and the subsequent inertia. We didn't come across that problem at Fiorano, a circuit that didn't demand great differences of that kind. I suggested

the development of a system with a hydraulic coupling and spoke to the Brown Boveri technicians about it. They agreed, but the directors requested a contribution of about a billion lire towards the work.

The matter ended there, even though Ferrari often mentioned that Fiat's contribution towards racing from 1969 was an annual 500 million lire, so that in part should have formed the budget through the company annual turnover.

To help drive the turbo car, in 1980 we also looked at a new semi-automatic gearbox. A great deal of power came on stream all of a sudden with the first prototypes, but if we allowed the driver to keep his hands on the steering wheel during the acceleration phases, the

ability to make corrections would be greater compared to a driver who had to use a gear lever. I was sure of this decision, but Ferrari didn't authorise the automatic gearbox so it had no place in the racing budget. So we had to do our best, and I must say the lads in the team were splendid. We needed a series of hydraulic valves, but those that were suitable would have cost a fortune. So we used machine tool valves, which were massive and crude, fitting them to the T-gearbox of a T5 with its aspirated 12-cylinder engine. The basis of the gearbox was traditional, but instead of a gear lever we envisaged hydraulic actuators controlled by an electrical system. There were two buttons next to the steering wheel, one for changing up and

the other for changing down, on which the driver simply had to place his finger: on contact, the clutch disengaged and the gear was selected. We also tried a version with a traditional clutch actioned by the driver's foot, but it was less effective. Being unable to invest in a more refined project the T5 weighed almost an additional 30 kg, but its handling was beyond all expectations. After initial tests, I asked Villeneuve to do a long run at Fiorano: 100 fast laps (300 km, Ed), the distance of a GP. He did so without any problem, with optimum times and consistency. But after he stepped out of the car, Gilles came out with a request that amazed me. "Mauro, this gearbox works well, but do you authorise me to ask the Commendatore if I can possibly con-

tinue with the traditional one? It's just that with the lever in my hand I feel safer". I told him that, developed properly, the new 'box would have favoured driving – but there was nothing I could do. I spoke to Ferrari and he said, "He even told me he would stop racing if we adopted the automatic gearbox! Because driving is a pleasure to him and he can't accept automation that doesn't let him show his talent".

So we stopped the project, but not because Villeneuve made us, even if Ferrari did adore him. It's a historic absurdity: at least we could have prepared a traditional car for Gilles and an automatic for the other driver, who was probably going to be Didier Pironi for 1981. We didn't go ahead, because we had to invest all our time in

Imola, 14 September 1980: the Grand Prix of Italy was run on the Dino Ferrari circuit at Imola for the first time (after that, the GP of San Marino would take over) but by that time Jody Scheckter was planning to retire from Formula 1 and the T5 was also at the end of its career, with little to show for it. Derived from the T4, winner of both the drivers' and constructors' Formula 1 World Championships in 1979, the T5 was not the result of an in-depth development because Ferrari was putting most of its effort into developing its new turbo engined car. Still powered by the flat 12, the T5's aerodynamics and weight were improved.

Wind tunnel work concerned the study of wing planes and the flow of air inside the body to improve negative lift when cornering. All of that was conditioned by the efficiency of the car's mini-skirts, a problem Ferrari had not yet solved due to the uncertainty of the F1 regulations in support of which the Commendatore still called for maximum respect. The central part of the chassis was narrowed to improve air flow in that area and even the engine had a small amount of extra space due to new heads, which enabled the designer to create a few more centimeters of width. It was a decision that was much discussed internally and which was dropped after the Monaco Grand Prix, because it made the well-tested engine fragile. But both Ferrari, who had advocated the evolution of the T4, and engineer Forghieri and all his colleagues had their minds firmly fixed on the future and the turbo car, an enormous undertaking because they were facing completely new technology.

Just how interested and curious Enzo Ferrari was in the new turbo engines was confirmed by the road car he had recently acquired: it was a Renault R5 Turbo. At 82 years-old, he still had the taste for driving a blown utility car, which was the dream of millions of youngsters.

developing the turbo engine, but we did show that the idea worked. The gearbox used by Ferrari in 1989 – with valves costing $5,000 each – was attributed to John Barnard, but in reality it had been developed by engineer De Silvestri, who knew the project and took it up in 1986. What with the Comprex and the turbo, we had no time to devote to the development of a new chassis; that was partially because the Commendatore asked me to debut the 126 C at the Grand Prix of Italy, which was held at Imola for the first time in September 1980 on the circuit named after his son, Dino. So we used the T5 chassis without any major modifications but with mini-skirts once more, although they continued to cause problems. The car made its first

appearance at Imola and Villeneuve set a time that was six tenths quicker than that of the normally aspirated T5 still in use. Ferrari was happy with that, but we preferred not to take risks in the race so Gilles competed in a T5. And due to his desire to emerge, he was at the centre of an accident at the corner that now carries his name from which – and I have to emphasise this – he walked away without a scratch because of the robust chassis, built in line with our habitual technology of aluminium-covered tubes.

The 126 C was not especially modified for the 1981 season, but it was penalised by total anarchy taking place over the eternal question of the mini-skirts. The Federation had banned them and had even imposed the cars' height from the ground of 60 mm. It would have been impossible to use them, but the British teams got around the problem by fitting hydraulic lifts: leaving the pits the car was lowered and when it returned it was raised to avoid a possible technical check. A farce and after the sham of a "clamp down", the Federation authorised mini-skirts from the GP of Belgium. Ferrari never adopted them, because our mini-skirts continued to be ineffective. But due to the turbo engine's extra 40-50 hp and a Villeneuve who was always ready to take advantage of a situation, we won the Grands Prix of Monaco and Spain. Two memorable days, especially at Monte Carlo because we showed our turbo engine was valid even on slow, tortuous circuits while Renault, which

had pioneered the turbo, had won four Grands Prix but always on extremely fast tracks. Even though we had an outdated chassis, the torque and therefore the traction of the engine enabled us to exploit the superior power of aspirated engines due to our overboost effect, even in slow corners.

As with some of our greatest moments, I became enthusiastic again at that GP of Monaco, but I always had my answer to Ferrari in mind when we began our turbo odyssey. I said, "I am happy with the choice we've made, but it will be impossible not to alternate exciting days with disappointing ones in the early stages". The Commendatore didn't react because he knew we were taking on a technology that, in part, had

not been explored and, indeed, we didn't score results in many GPs. I even asked the drivers to limit their enthusiasm to accumulate kilometres, like Villeneuve before the Dutch Grand Prix on 30 August 1981. "Gilles", I said, "I need a favour from you. Don't go over the top, because we have new turbochargers and I need to understand how they perform over a distance. You have no chance of winning, so let's do a test as we're not far away from the GP of Italy". That's what I needed, but from the moment the race started Gilles forgot everything, went on the grass I don't know how many times and went off before the famous Tarzan corner, ending up hitting an advertising hoarding!

During the first season with the 126 C turbo,

we invested a great deal of time in improving every detail: the dimensions of the compressor, the turbocharging values and relative control systems, the dimensions of the exhaust valve. With turbocharging, we started with a value of 2.3 bar that could increase during qualifying to 2.9-3.0 bar. Thanks to laboratory devised petrol, those values reached 4.0-4.2 bar by 1984/5. We achieved a good level of reliability fairly quickly, too, but with the 1982 season just around the corner, we still had to solve the detonation problem (combustion that was too fast and which sometimes occurred with pre-ignition that advanced the spark from the plugs) that could appear causing a lot of trouble, especially to the pistons, and didn't permit the use

of increasingly higher boost pressures. I knew we had to cool the mix as it entered the combustion chamber so I spoke to the Agip technicians, with which we were associated and carried out considerable research into fuels at the time. So I adopted a technology that was used by Messerschmitt fighter aircraft during the Second World War. When needed, the pilots would press a red button, which operated a system that provided greater power for a number of seconds. The system comprised the injection of water that blended in with the fuel mix and improved combustion, cooled the combustion chamber and provided an increased percentage of power. It was a very delicate operation, because excessive cooling made the pistons seize immediately.

I've never fully understood the chemical basis of this phenomenon, but we did study an analogous system for our engine and it worked perfectly. The increase in power in normal conditions was slight, but what counted was that the detonation disappeared. And when the driver needed more power for a few moments, overpressure became available by operating the wastegate valve that controlled it. So the engine was able to generate 10% more power (from 600 to about 660 hp, Ed) without any particular risk.

Engineer Luciano Caruso, head of the Test Department, set up the system together with the Agip technicians. Ferrari subsequently gave a certain amount of time to the role of the fuel

company in studying water injection, but it was a courtesy by a partner more than anything else. A partner that was also a generous sponsor with whom we had collaborated more directly in other sectors, especially petrol and oil. The technique was later called the Emulsystem and was also used by a diesel section of a Fiat division operating in Germany.

At that point we had an excellent engine, but we still had to build the car. In the T5's time (1980, Ed) we did not fully analyse the roadholding problems derived from the not very efficient mini-skirts, even if we had additional problems due to the Michelin tyres, as Enzo Ferrari declared during an official press conference. Renault also complained about problems with its Michelin

Previous page: during the 1981 season, the Ferrari 126 CK was driven by Didier Pironi and Gilles Villeneuve. Newly arrived at Maranello, the 29 year-old Pironi had already won a GP a year earlier and was considered a cold but determined driver, especially on extremely fast circuits. But there was no doubt Villeneuve got the most out of the 126 CK and its already valid turbo engine, although its chassis was developed starting with that of the T5 because there was no time to come up with something new. Yet Gilles set the second fastest time in the T5 at Monte Carlo and was third quickest in Austria and Las Vegas. Most important of all, he won Monaco and Spain, extracting everything his combative spirit demanded from the car. He was also unforgettable in Canada at Montreal, where he took third after a tremendous climb back up through the field despite having lost his front wing after an on-track skirmish.

tyres that year and blamed the manufacturer, at least in part, for not having been able to win the world championship. At the same time, our mini-skirts respected the regulations, but they were conceptually wrong.

The usual, eternal controversy broke out about the validity of our chassis and I realised it was necessary to attempt something new. The first monocoques in composite materials – a honeycomb of aluminium – had just appeared and those in carbon fibre had recently come out (McLaren and Lotus, Ed); it was clear that area was the new frontier. But we had no real chemical engineer, because the technology – typically aeronautical – was not available in Italy. We found one in Harvey Postlethwaite, an en-

gineer who had worked with considerable success with the Austro-Canadian millionaire Walter Wolf's team, who Ferrari liked because he was perhaps the first – but according to others it was Chris Amon – to point out the then unknown Gilles Villeneuve.

Harvey joined Maranello at the end of spring 1981 spring and he immediately integrated well due to his positive character. He was to create the practical achievement of the chassis and the relative organisation rather than design, which was by a working party to which our usual technicians belonged. We would have liked to start with a carbon fibre chassis right away, but we were forced to depend on outside companies – a situation the Commendatore didn't like, as he

Left: Gilles Villeneuve's triumph in the Grand Prix of Monaco on 31 May 1981 was preceded by another exploit just before the race that was highly significant. In practice and on paper the circuit was less favourable to turbo engines at the time, but the Canadian still set the second fastest time in qualifying at 78 hundredths from pole winner Piquet and his Brabham. Then in the race Gilles never gave himself a moment to breathe, especially in the finale when he was glued to Alan Jones and the Williams before winning and being given flag waving congratulations by the finish line marshals.
The race started at 4.10 pm as it was delayed for over an hour due to a fire in the hotel that spans the tunnel; it was 5.56 pm when a roar from the spectators confirmed the Ferrari had passed the Williams. Gilles, who a few days earlier had renewed his contract with Ferrari until the end of 1983, was then presented with his trophy by the Minister of State and not as usual by Prince Rainier and Princess Grace. The royal couple were absent from the Principality's Grand Prix for the first time because their son Prince Albert was graduating from the University of Boston at the time.
Below: a photo souvenir with dedication for a number of Mauro Forghieri's "faithful". From left to right, Carlo Tedeschi, Forghieri, Elio Piazze, Gianni Tagliabue and Giorgio Giovetti.
Opposite page: Villeneuve's victory overshadowed Pironi's well-driven race a little, seen here talking to engineer Forghieri during practice. The Frenchman made his way up from the ninth row of the grid to fourth place.

was always very jealous of his "things" – apart from our long-standing suppliers, who were almost all local. So while waiting for the installation of an autoclave in which to "cook" the fibre monocoque at Maranello, Harvey designed another in aluminium panels glued together honeycomb style, which he had already used for the Wolf chassis. He was sure a chassis like that was as good in terms of rigidity as one in carbon fibre and I personally agreed.

The aerodynamics of the car were defined by the usual excellent work by engineer Poncini at the Pininfarina wind tunnel with the result that, right from the first tests at the ultra-fast Paul Ricard circuit, Villeneuve and Pironi soon realised the 1982 126 C2 had enormous negative lift, which

was an extremely positive influence on grip. But we also discovered something that didn't work: there was deformation at the rear of the chassis where the gearbox and engine joined and that was reinforced with stiffening mounts. I still had my doubts, but overall the car was very good. Even the mini-skirts were among the C2's good points: it didn't seem true after years of attempts. The Federation had abolished the regulation concerning the mini-skirts' height from the ground, but they had to be fixed and were not allowed to slide anymore. So without regulation restrictions, we tried various paths in our search for materials that could run along the asphalt without breaking: we made them in plastic, then ceramic – with the support of

the Tuscan company Bitossi – but they broke. Then, all of a sudden, there was a new idea: we used really hard marine plywood, fixing it to a firm rubber base. It had the advantage of wearing down gradually, taking on the best shape to "seal" the lower area of the monocoque so that the air couldn't escape outside. We tried it during winter testing at Paul Ricard and the mini-skirts made their official debut at the first GP of the season in South Africa. They gave us an enormous advantage over the opposition, and it was also extremely difficult to understand our little secret. But, as I have said, someone on our team talked with his colleagues in other teams and marine plywood became a trend.

However, the start of the season was distorted

by the illegal –and I would say ridiculous – behavior by some British teams that competed with cars many kilos under weight, that became legal again at the end of the race by topping up their enormous fuel tanks, which contained water for brake cooling! A real farce that made me sick and Enzo Ferrari literally flew into a rage. I recommended that we should oppose these farcical developments and their teams with a technical choice that was legal but provocative. I worked on a wing that was asymmetrically "split", which respected the maximum permitted size (110 cm, Ed) but in a spirit that circumvented the regulations. It was a Ferrari challenge to condemn the climate that was being created in Formula 1 by people who, in a col-

loquialism of many years later, we would have called "small time tricksters". The 126 C with its superwing turned out to be competitive and Villeneuve ended up on the podium of the GP at Long Beach. The Federation intervened a long time afterwards and disqualified Villeneuve, but we had achieved our aim of seeing Piquet and Rosberg, who came first and second in Brazil, also "condemned" due to the water trick and then "absolved" despite Ferrari's protest.

Having been boycotted by the majority of the British teams, the subsequent Grand Prix of San Marino at Imola turned out to be a challenge between us and Renault. In fact, it was a challenge between Gilles Villeneuve and Didier Pironi with the Frenchman making the winning overtaking

manoeuvre, which meant for Ferrari the start of a black, not to say tragic period.

I was not at Imola that day as it was one of those rare occasions when I had deserted a race as technical director. But I still had the opportunity of finding out for real whether or not Pironi overtook when he shouldn't have, or whether it was Villeneuve who had not understood that it was an open race right through to the finish line. Certainly there were misunderstandings, and motor sport director Marco Piccinini involuntarily complicated the situation by showing a "slow" pit signal on the last lap when Gilles was leading. But I feel I can safely say there could not have been an agreement to favour Villeneuve at the fourth GP of the season. Ferrari had never

mentioned such a thing and, anyway, his sports policy was never based on favouritism. It was well known that he used to pit one driver against the other to get the best from their competitive spirit, and he would not have made an exception for Villeneuve, even thought he loved the Canadian like a son.

It was the usual opinion Ferrari had expressed dozens of times: "We have never had a number two driver: the number one is the driver who wins on Sunday. I simply appeal to the drivers' sense of responsibility. The 'slow' signal means: remember that you are Ferrari drivers. I would never inflict on one of my drivers the humiliation that I suffered back in 1924, when I was made to allow a team mate to pass".

Left: well known for his incredibly competitive temperament, Gilles Villeneuve alternated memorable days with others that were a really tough "test bed" for Maranello single-seaters. But Enzo Ferrari was fairly indulgent with the little Canadian, knowing that certain characteristics just could not be changed. In 1981, two weeks after his Monaco win, he was the star of the Grand Prix of Spain at Jarama. He was able to keep a long line of cars behind him, whipping the daylights out of the 580 hp of his 126 CK on the straight and exploiting every centimeter of the track in the corners.

Right: it was a different story at the GP of Austria that same year, when Villeneuve set the third fastest time in qualifying, but after a lap in the lead in front of the Prost and Arnoux Renault turbos, he went off at the chicane and smashed into the barrier with the left side of his car.

Opposite page: the early Eighties Ferrari van. Before the arrival of the motorhome, the drivers used to change in the vehicle.

Certainly, we had had officious "team bosses", but only because they won their spurs in the field, as it were. Surtees was a leader as were Lauda and Scheckter, but in a different way. However, nobody was ever told "don't worry; your team mate won't be a nuisance". And I would add that Didier Pironi, a very correct but temperamental young man, would never have accepted a "pact" to come second and nobody ever criticised him for having taken that success away from his team mate.

Only Enzo Ferrari would have been able to make this single exception but that didn't happen, which was confirmed by his subsequent behavior during the days that followed: Villeneuve would have expected special recognition from

him for his "stolen" victory. But he didn't get it because, apart from affection, Ferrari didn't have to explain a single thing.

Probably, someone who was at Imola that day should have clarified the situation that was created, but that didn't happen.

Accompanied by Jody Scheckter, Gilles came to me to try and understand whether or not I thought he was right. I was clear with him, because he did have the right to an explanation.

Two weeks after Imola, Villeneuve arrived at Zolder in a black mood for the GP of Belgium. It was clear that his only enemy by that time was his team mate: he only took to the track to beat Pironi. He was agitated and a few minutes from the end of qualifying I personally gave the

order to show a signal telling him to return to the pits (radio contact between drivers and the pits would not begin until 1985, Ed) because with worn tyres it was impossible for him to beat Pironi's time of 1 minute 16.501 seconds against Villeneuve's 1 minute 16.616 seconds. I had the feeling that he was coming in but at qualifying speed, which was useless because there was no time for further attempts: he drove nervously and when he came across Jochen Mass' March proceeding slowly, he probably tried to overtake on the right, exactly the area chosen by the much slower German to let him pass. Gilles's 126 C2 hit the rear right wheel of the March at a speed estimated at between 100 kph and 150 kph. Contact between the wheels

Opposite page: Gilles Villeneuve and Didier Pironi, one against the other at the 1981 Monza Grand Prix. On 25 April 1982, at San Marino Grand Prix, the Canadian's drama began on the last lap, when he was certain he had been betrayed by his team mate who overtook him, and also by Enzo Ferrari, who did not subsequently defend him. Engineer Forghieri (above with Gilles) for once was not at Imola on race day as he knew the 126 C2 was now delivering maximum performance. But he excludes the possibility that there was an internal agreement in Villeneuve's favour that was not kept by Pironi. Enzo Ferrari was completely against this kind of "sports" policy, especially at the beginning of a season. Certainly, there was a major lack of clarity by whoever was there to look after the drivers before the race, so a sense of bitterness accompanied Gilles through to the subsequent Grand Prix of Belgium at Zolder. Forghieri recalls that Villeneuve's resentment swamped his serenity and the excessive speed of his driving on his re-entry lap at the end of qualifying turned out to be fatal.

then caused an exceptionally dangerous take-off effect, although the matter remains unclear even today. Villeneuve's car flew about 20 metres up in the air and came down against the trackside embankment. He did not die immediately, but it was clear there was nothing that could be done. It was a terribly painful experience and I couldn't wait to return home as quickly as possible. We realised that the safety belts had come away from the seat and the driver just flew away. The subsequent report of the doctors said the driver would still not have survived the terrible deceleration, but it didn't make us feel any less responsible. Ferrari was deeply saddened by for the death of a driver he loved, but he had no doubts when he gave me carte blanche to car-

ry out a full inquest. I invited Harvey Postlethwaite, who was also most upset by Gilles' death, to technically analyse what had happened. He was the expert in that area and I involved him on purpose, even though I was responsible together with him. In fact, we discovered that the ringlets of the safety belts had come away from the seat because the adhesion system had given way. That's why a large border in carbon fibre was later inserted in the area above the chassis so that the seat became a single unit with the chassis. But we badly needed definitive answers and to obtain them we created a comparison in parallel at the Fiat Research Centre between our chassis and a carbon fibre monocoque. We had no such monocoque but we did use a "testing"

system, small separate pieces that altogether constituted a chassis. A painstaking initiative, but a very useful one. We discovered that the two types of monocoque were similar in rigidity, but there was no comparison in terms of energy absorption. That was the road to take.

Among a thousand thoughts and anxieties, we realised that the 126 C2 had achieved an excellent level in comparison with its opposition. We changed tyre supplier and returned to Goodyear, which had immediately impressed me. Their organisation had become more professional than it was in the Seventies, especially due to the work of a person of the calibre of Leo Mehl, who had been promoted to become absolute boss of the racing sector. However, ours

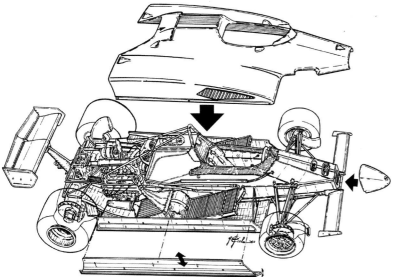

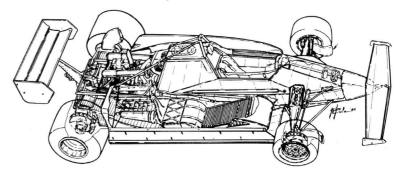

Below: Giorgio Piola's cutaways show a comparison between the Ferrari 126 C2 that kicked off the 1982 season (below) and the version presented at the Italian Grand Prix, with its chassis strengthened in the whole front area and its front suspension with a wide based wishbone. The C2 had a chassis in honeycomb aluminium panels without the need for reinforcement rivets.

was an uphill battle because we were forced to compete in three Grands Prix with just Pironi, who was involuntarily involved in an umpteenth tragic accident. He was in pole position, but he had a problem at the start and his immobile 126 C2 was hit in the back by the unfortunate Riccardo Paletti, who had come up from the second last row of the grid and was killed in the accident. A terrible year!

From the GP of Holland at Zandvoort, Didier was teamed with Patrick Tambay, no champion but he was a good competitor as well as a quality tester. Pironi won convincingly on a tough circuit for the cars to confirm the excellence of the C2, its power and good drivability. With his subsequent placings, Didier had gone to the top of

the drivers' world championship by the time the circus arrived at the fast Hockenheim circuit for the German Grand Prix, in which we were the favourites. After Friday practice, Pironi was in pole and on the Saturday it poured with rain, but Didier went out anyway to test the rain tyres. He did not see Alain Prost's much slower Renault and, perhaps while braking, he hit the French car in the back at almost 300 kph. He was not killed but he was taken to hospital with seriously fractured legs. The following day, Tambay won the race in his lone Ferrari.

It really was a terrible year for Ferrari, but it was also a generally strange one. The points were more thinly spread than almost ever before, and the season started with eight of the 16

Didier Pironi celebrates his victory in the 1982 GP of San Marino, while Villeneuve (above, in action in the same event) appears in visible disagreement. Pironi would also go on to win the Dutch GP and went into the lead of the drivers' world championship, but he would later be involved in an accident practicing at Hockenheim that forced him to retire from racing. He tried to channel his competitive spirit into off-shore powerboat racing, but he died in an accident at sea in August 1987.

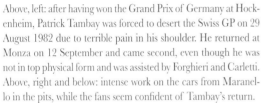

Above, left: after having won the Grand Prix of Germany at Hockenheim, Patrick Tambay was forced to desert the Swiss GP on 29 August 1982 due to terrible pain in his shoulder. He returned at Monza on 12 September and came second, even though he was not in top physical form and was assisted by Forghieri and Carletti. Above, right and below: intense work on the cars from Maranello in the pits, while the fans seem confident of Tambay's return.

races less in which Tambay could aim for the title. But there was nothing we could do; destiny was just not with us. Patrick was able to drive the 126 C2 to victory but he was not sufficiently well prepared physically and there was a reason. Despite FISA president Jean-Marie Balestre being a champion of safety, he committed a serious mistake by abolishing the cars' need for a certain height from the ground and allowing mini-skirts. But the aerodynamic load of the cars increased enormously as a result, and drivers had to absorb a lateral acceleration of over 4g when cornering: torture for the arms, neck and back and in fact the cars were drastically changed for the following year.

After the Grand Prix of Austria on 15 August,

Tambay began to suffer from severe inflammation of the shoulders and arms and it was motor sport director Marco Piccinini who suggested he sought a remedy by admitting himself to a Swiss clinic. Ferrari had never influenced a driver's choice of how to resolve his health problems; we never had our own consultants in the area because the Commendatore said, "You can't impose a doctor on someone, it's the patient who chooses". Chosen or not, Tambay's doctors treated him with cortisone and the result was much worse pain than previously. Evidently, he was unable to tolerate the cure, because when he arrived at the Dijon circuit for the GP of Switzerland on 29 August he was worn out. He didn't even have a clear idea of the circuit. After

a few practice laps, I telephoned Ferrari to let him know and we retired the car. It was no coincidence that the Commendatore had changed his doctor theory a couple of months later and sent Tambay to Professor Rowland, the director of the Columbia University in the United States, for a special examination.

There is no doubt in my mind that 1982 was the absolutely definitive motor racing season, one that completely defied any logic, in which we should have won with our eyes closed. Incredibly, we were still able to win the Formula 1 World Championship for constructors, while the drivers' title went to Keke Rosberg with 44 points to Pironi's 39; in my opinion Rosberg didn't deserve it and cannot be considered on the same

level as other world champions. Fortunately, in 1983 there were no black days that had so tragically overshadowed the previous year. René Arnoux joined Ferrari from Renault, a Frenchman like Tambay. He was a pleasant, simple young man and was a good "speedster", yet there was something not quite right with the team atmosphere. There was not the serenity typical of other periods, although we were still recovering from that black 1982. As I will explain, the car was extremely competitive but there was not the cohesion of the Lauda-Regazzoni seasons and especially not that of Scheckter-Villeneuve in 1979, when we all worked for each other.

In my opinion, Enzo Ferrari involuntarily contributed to worsening the atmosphere with one

of his rare mistakes. He had already declared quite openly in September 1982 that once his contract with Tyrrell had ended, Michele Alboreto would be coming to Maranello. But as the Italian's contract lasted until the end of 1983, it was clear more than a year in advance that one of our drivers would have to go. Was he trying to keep both of them in suspense? That's perfectly possible; but before the '82 season had even ended Tambay, a wide-awake, intelligent young man, had understood from the attitude of motor sport director Marco Piccinini that the finger pointed at him. Although he had won the GP of San Marino, he was not told he would have to go until September.

The title was within our reach, even if we were

Above and opposite page: once again, the validity of the 126 C2 proved itself, this time in the hands of Mario Andretti seen here taking the chequered flag and sitting in the cockpit of his Ferrari. The American set the fastest time in practice after having only driven the car for a few laps earlier at Fiorano. He came third in a GP of San Marino at Imola, where his team mates Arnoux and Tambay came first and second respectively. Meanwhile, Patrick is shown in the cockpit of the 126 C2 B at the GP of San Marino at Imola early in the 1983 season and with Arnoux in Canada. The C3 was unveiled at the end of June and was soon to win the Grands Prix of Germany and Holland driven by Arnoux, who could certainly have aimed for the world title. But the last part of the season was conditioned by Piquet's Brabham using fuel that did not conform to the regulations. A suspicion that was confirmed by a Federation technical analysis, but nothing was done about it.

unable to use the new 126 C3 with its carbon fibre chassis until the Grand Prix of Great Britain on 16 July.

Instead, we entered the 126C2B, a considerably updated version of its predecessor, for the first eight GPs. The new regulations dictated that the lower part of the single-seater between its front and rear wheels should be flat and without mini-skirts, so aerodynamic load was drastically reduced to the physical advantage of the drivers. To make up for the loss of the mini-skirts, we had to considerably increase the front and back wings' dimensions. And we achieved the unthinkable with the turbo engine: over 1000 hp in testing with a boost of more than 4 bar. Power that had to be handled by the wings in corners

and due to which the tyres would not last more than one lap in qualifying. Goodyear reacted with professionalism to this sudden power increase, but they made us suffer in at least six GPs.

When we started to use the new 126 C3 that season we were even more competitive against the best of our opposition, Renault and especially Brabham with their BMW engine. To create the 126 C3, we equipped a department at Maranello for the construction of monocoques in carbon fibre and installed an autoclave in which to "cook" the chassis by a constant temperature increase system. Of course, Postlethwaite was determinate, but some of our people quickly learnt the technique, including engineer Menicucci, who later followed me to Lamborghini Engineering.

Anyway, we had experience with carbon fibre moulds because for many years we built our car bodies in-house in fibre.

The C3 went well from the start, which was just as well as we would not have any opportunity of modifying it. The aerodynamic shape, established as usual by Poncini, did not include a real body. The monocoque was part of the bodywork and we were the first, together with Germany's ATS, to debut this technology which later became universal.

We could possibly have won the world title with the atmosphere that pervaded the team, but from mid-season the engine started to make us doubt it. We competed in GPs with turbo pressures of 3 to 3.3 bar, about 650-700 hp. And all

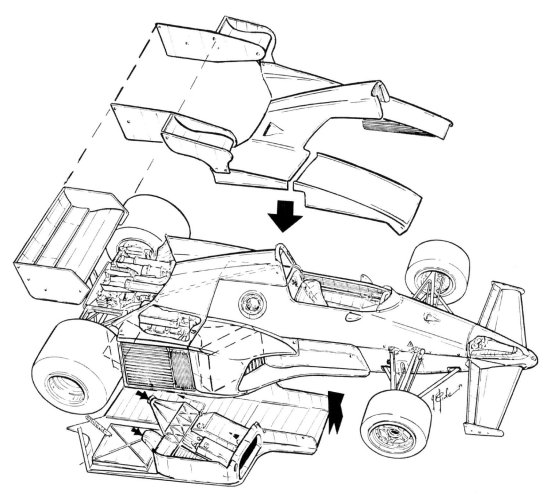

of a sudden that wasn't enough to stand up to the Brabham-BMWs. To go as fast as the Brabham on the straights, we had to use wings with little aerodynamic load, so we suffered in corners. But we did discover that the term "commercial petrol" had disappeared from the Federation's regulations, although it had been F1's basic fuel for years. We used special fuels, but they always respected commercial parameters. The new regulation, about which there was no official communication, envisaged other very free parameters. I am sure Bernie Ecclestone had a hand in them as he was the owner of the Brabham team at the time and their BMW engines had given particular problems until the previous year. Besides, Bernie managed the fi-

nancial power of Grand Prix racing and was in close contact with Jean-Marie Balestre, even if they did pretend they were at war.
We found out that the fuel used by Brabham, which was created in a laboratory, produced more horse power with higher boost and made the engine less fragile. So if we wanted to match their speed, we had to use higher turbine pressures and that took us back to the detonation problem of the early turbo engines. Agip reacted but they needed time, so much time that they didn't come up with a new fuel until the following year for the 1984 Dutch GP. But at the subsequent Grand Prix of Italy at Monza, we were able to raise the boost pressure to 4.4 bar to produce power peaks of over 1000 hp in prac-

tice. But during the 1983 season the validity of the 126 C3 still gave us eight pole positions and Arnoux three victories. After the GP of Holland, we were really on our way.
Instead, after the first practice session at Monza Arnoux told me "We're at the beginning again. The Brabham passes me on the straight and it seems like I'm standing still. I can't even slipstream the car". Unfortunately, he was right and there was nothing we could do in the race: first Piquet, second Arnoux. But we all suspected that Brabham had gone beyond the limit of the new regulation and, fortunately, a sample of the car's fuel was taken for analysis. That happened on 11 September, but the results of the investigation weren't

Above: of pleasant character, René Arnoux was very decisive in his driving and had a good "feeling" for engineer Forghieri. When he was really young he was a mechanic with Conrero tuners and as part of his future as a driver he "trained" every weekend on the road between Grenoble, where he lived, and Turin.
Right: the 1984 Ferrari drivers, the newly arrived Michele Alboreto and René Arnoux.

even given at the subsequent GP of Europe at Brands Hatch on 25 September, which Piquet won. The problem was becoming increasingly tangled, because then it was said the Brabham fuel was many points higher in octane than was permitted. Theirs was a formidable car as far as power and avoiding detonation were concerned. There was enough evidence on the basis of which to disqualify Piquet but, incredibly, nothing of the kind happened. People began to maintain that fuel analysis could be open to a thousand interpretations and that the regulations were unclear, but more than anything else nobody wanted to punish a driver for "a petrol supply mistake" after risking in the race. Naturally, many were absolutely stupefied by

Enzo Ferrari's lack of reaction, especially as one of our drivers was directly involved. It's true that we couldn't react because the sample taken at Monza was taken officially and not due to our protest, but we expected him to at least take a position on the matter, partly because we had talked about it a long time and the Commendatore knew the situation well. The explanation is multi-faceted in that we had won the constructors' championship and to Ferrari that was a matter of pride. In addition, he had a sense of victory and sport that led him to consider it an injustice to disqualify Piquet for a question of fuel, which he perhaps felt was secondary. That was a mistake in my opinion, because the other drivers risked more to try to match the perfor-

mance of the new world champion.
To be clear Ferrari never ever permitted sharp practice, but he had a respect that was, I would say, almost mystical for champions and their victories. And all this despite the fact that he didn't like Piquet much, because a year earlier the Brazilian had talked about "fragility", referring to our cars. It was senseless, typical of Piquet, a much more respectable person when he was driving. And importantly, the Commendatore was privy to the exchange of letters between Bernie Ecclestone, himself and the Renault team manager Gérard Larousse. But by that time, Bernie carried enormous weight in the division of Grands Prix income and had an extremely high opinion of Ferrari.

200...

1984-1987

Ferrari Epilogue
My last Formula 1 seasons

During my long time at Ferrari I fought many battles but always with the Commendatore's support, even during the most difficult moments. There was a special rapport between us, one that mixed both the professional and human aspects of our lives. We clashed violently at times, even if that was not as frequent as one often hears. Each shouted louder than the other, but it was a simple outburst, because underneath it all was a deep reciprocal respect motivated by the certainty that we both pursued the same objectives: success in racing and the good of the factory. I resigned more than once, but Ferrari always intervened to find a solution to the problem. In a word, without the Commendatore I would never have become Forghieri, so I owe him a lot.

Unfortunately, men aren't eternal and in February 1984 Ferrari turned 86. Towards the end of that year, I decided that the situation in the Racing Department, of which I was still the head, had changed definitively. Ferrari no longer had the energy to dominate with his previous energy, even if he did sense perfectly well that things weren't working. My rapport with him hadn't changed but the organisational system of the Fiat Group was permeating the company, with many of its executives there to command but nobody was taking decisions. And they were executives who were not racing men, people from production and had taken on responsibilities they couldn't really handle. It was like promoting me to become the manager of a bank: I would have ruined it!

The 1984 season was fairly busy, in my opinion not because of presumed defects of the new 126 C4's chassis as maintained by those who – more or less openly – opposed me. The car was substantially an evolution of the C3 and the problems that had to be solved were twofold. The set-up of the new electronic fuel injection system designed by Weber-Marelli – fundamental because the fuel available for each GP was limited to 220 litres – and the fuel itself, which was supplied by Agip. All of our competitors' suppliers fell in line with the new F1 regulations, so they respected the 102 octane limit and had worked out how to obtain fuel additives with chemical compositions essential to extracting more power from turbo engines, so limiting consumption and avoiding detonation.

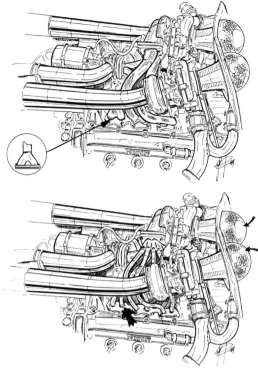

Previous page: Michele Alboreto in the Ferrari 126 C4 passing the Hotel de Paris during practice for the 1984 Grand Prix of Monaco. Previous page: Michele Alboreto's 156/85B smokes at the 1985 Italian GP and his dream of becoming world champion fades. Left, above: René Arnoux has his hands full at Monza in car number 28. Below: in the harbor area. Above: details of the C4's V6 turbo engine with two different kinds of exhaust, the traditional (above) and "the spaghetti system" (below). Right: Ayrton Senna with a Ferrari 288 GTO. Highly thought of by Mauro Forghieri from the moment he first competed in Formula 1, the Brazilian met Enzo Ferrari at Maranello in early June 1986. A possible contract was mentioned, but the driver was with Lotus and would not have been free until 1988. Cesare Fiorio tried to negotiate a contract with Ayrton five years later, but that also came to nothing.

At the time, Agip was a little behind the rest and although I pushed, I had the impression that we should not "disturb" our fuel partner too much as it was also an important sponsor. In the good old days, Enzo Ferrari would have hammered the table with his fist and obtained that fuel that we needed so badly.

But it was electronic injection that worried us more than anything else. An advanced type was spreading and we had been testing it for some time, having previously always used the fairly simple Lucas mechanical method. We had used injection-ignition as early as 1983, which not only took account of the mixture in relation to the number of revolutions, but also the position of the butterfly, the advance, temperature and oth-

er details. It was engineer Caruso, head of that section, who was being subjected to an incessant evolution and he carried out an enormous number of tests. A situation that condemned us to see-saw competitiveness, the reason being complaints from Michele Alboreto, our new driver, whose team mate was René Arnoux. Michele was correct, but the reasons were technical. Weber-Marelli had achieved miracles and later became the sector's leader in electronic fuel injection, but it was beginning from a blank sheet of paper with Ferrari. It was no coincidence that the 1984/5/6 world championships were dominated by the TAG-Porsche engine, which enjoyed the much greater experience of Bosch in that area. We were still exploring electronics and were

among the first, together with Brabham, to develop telemetry – a system that enables technicians to obtain data from a moving car, which is fundamental to modern F1, Ed – with the help of the Fiat Research Centre. And it was thanks to the cooperation with Fiat in early 1984 that we reached an acceptable level. Then, just before the Grand Prix of Belgium on 29 April, we tested it at Imola with Alboreto and we came away as if we were out of our minds. We continued making use of telemetry at Fiorano and could not understand why the ignition tension dropped so frighteningly and we didn't know why. We were so furious that we even continued the tests after dark and at that point a miracle happened. Passing the pits, the car's monocoque seemed like a televi-

1984 Grand Prix of Italy: top, right, Michele Alboreto in the Ferrari 126 C4 talking to Antonio Tomaini and Maurizio Nardon. It was one of the GPs not attended by Mauro Forghieri, whose work as head technician had been hampered for months. Below: Tomaini has a few words with Stefan Johansson, who joined Ferrari in 1985 after the sudden departure of René Arnoux following the Grand Prix of Brazil, the first round in the world championship.

The illustration shows the C4 at the start of its career. Among the new developments were slimmer lines than those of the C3, the advancement of the driving position to improve weight distribution and the rear wing complex. The engine-gearbox was also lightened by a considerable 18 kg. Competitive at the start of the season, in Forghieri's opinion the C4 later suffered from a lack of fuel that could match the opposition's petrol. But at Maranello a current of dissent formed during the year, which led to a technical revolution that was extremely difficult to manage. So after various intermediate solutions, a highly modified C4 appeared at the end of the season.

sion screen: the cables supplied by Marelli downloaded the current on the carbon fibre chassis to the point that the technicians could see a trail of sparks that were invisible to the naked eye. We replaced the cables and Alboreto won in Belgium! But we would not have won at Zolder without a valid chassis and aerodynamics. In 1983, we were among the first to add aerodynamic winglets to the classic wing and that was the first step that led to the myriad of flaps of more recent F1 seasons. Yet I was once again the object of the usual criticisms – almost always indirect – which became accentuated from the three GPs on the other side of the Atlantic in June, where Arnoux took second place at Dallas. I knew we weren't competitive but the problem wasn't roadholding,

we simply couldn't use the wings' maximum aerodynamic load in corners to increase top speed on the straights. At the time, we didn't have the kind of fuel able to produce high enough turbocharger pressures and Agip needed time to react to the opposition's competitive level. It became an engine championship: Brabham-BMW did well in qualifying with nine pole positions and it seemed they had over 1200 hp: but in racing, an equilibrium between fuel consumption and power favoured McLaren's V6 Porsche unit.

Once again a current of technical dissent built up within the Ferrari team, but those responsible didn't limit themselves to just criticism. They took advantage of the fact that they were at the race circuits to work out modifications to the car with-

out me knowing. A matter that was as intolerable as it was negative for our F1 programme. Unfortunately, some of my men who had won with me and whom I put in certain positions, didn't defend me. Among them was Harvey Postlethwaite, who I respected and wanted at Ferrari in 1981 for his competence in the field of chemistry. But most of all there was Marco Piccinini, who had gone from simple motor sport director to a confidante of Enzo Ferrari's and had joined the company's board. Previously, he had executed his specific responsibilities and had never been a nuisance. I realised too late that behind him was an intrigue that led to an unacceptable division of the team. I also noticed that Piero, the Commendatore's son, was progressively assuming control of the

Above: in 1985, Michele Alboreto made all of Italy dream a little by showing he was worthy of the world championship, which he lost in the season's finale due to the technical woes of the 156/85. He lapped his team mate Stefan Johansson in the pouring rain in at the Portuguese Grand Prix, the Swede having just taken over from René Arnoux. After an unhappy qualifying session due to his low speed on the straight, Alboreto was the only driver not to have been lapped by Ayrton Senna, the star of this historic race who scored his first victory in Formula 1 that day.

Racing Department. An expected succession, but nobody had the courage to tell me about it to my face. And I couldn't tolerate having to run a team with someone who worked against me. I personally continued to have an excellent friendly relationship with Piero. There was no doubt, though, that in 1984 the diminished control of the Commendatore, who was tired and not in the best of health, was being replaced by anarchy: I would return from a GP and, instead of solving the problems that arose during the race weekend, I had to become involved in what had been done back at the factory in my absence. As a matter of principle, I never unreasonably opposed modifications to "my" cars. They had often been made in the past, but all out in the open. And to these

new "critics" I offered the simplest solution: to go to the track to see whether or not your modifications work.

The whole affair began in June: we tested these modifications and the cars didn't improve at all. It wasn't a chassis problem and that became obvious on 5 August at the GP of Germany on the superfast Hockenheim circuit. In the mixed section – the famous Motodrome – there was a lack of grip because our wings were unable to "load" like those of the McLaren-Porsche and Brabham-BMW, our main opposition. But if we did "load" the wings we would lose 10-15 kph: and without the kind of fuel our opposition used, our V6 didn't develop the necessary power to use the correct aerodynamic load. The difference was

enormous: 630-650 hp of the Ferrari against the 750-780 hp of the others.

I spoke to Ferrari about it many times, but he was not the commander of years gone by and was also having to deal with new general management problems in the factory, as always due to the ever greater commitment of Fiat at Maranello. By that time, the drivers were also less motivated. In particular, I no longer felt the support of Michele Alboreto after his initial defeats. The victory in Belgium made him feel he would have an optimum season, but then he saw me as the person who had taken a possible success away from him because I was against the current that wanted to devastate the 126 C4. Michele was a great driver who was always very dear to me, and

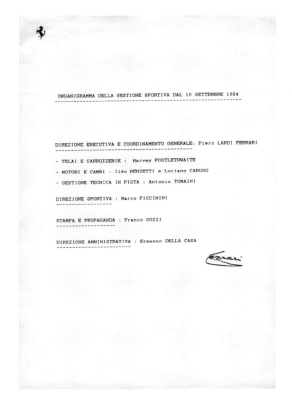

ORGANIGRAMMA DELLA GESTIONE SPORTIVA DAL 10 SETTEMBRE 1984

DIREZIONE ESECUTIVA E COORDINAMENTO GENERALE: Piero LARDI FERRARI

- TELAI E CARROZZERIE : Harvey POSTLETHWAITE
- MOTORI E CAMBI : Ildo RENZETTI e Luciano CARUSO
- GESTIONE TECNICA IN PISTA : Antonio TOMAINI

DIREZIONE SPORTIVA : Marco PICCININI

STAMPA E PROPAGANDA : Franco GOZZI

DIREZIONE AMMINISTRATIVA : Ermanno DELLA CASA

Above: a historic document. On 9 September 1984, the day after the GP of Italy, Enzo Ferrari circulated this note containing a new organisation chart that appointed his son Piero as executive director and Antonio Tomaini as track technical manager. Right: just before the 1985 Italian Grand Prix, Gianni Agnelli landed at Monza in his helicopter. He visited all the pits accompanied by engineer Ghidella, managing director of Fiat and president of Ferrari at the time. Then he watched the Ferraris practice, chatted to Michele Alboreto who had risen to second in the drivers' world championship at three points from Prost; but the youngster could only manage seventh fastest time, partially due to difficulty in setting up the car after certain modifications.

I was deeply saddened when he was killed in that accident with the sports car in 2001. In reality, I had tried to pull off miracles to give Michele the best possible car and he almost always did better than Arnoux. Certainly not because I wanted to humiliate René, but I really did give everything I had for Michele in certain situations.

Finally, Agip came up with something positive, so that from the Grand Prix of Holland on 26 August Arnoux set the race's fastest time without having to work on turbo pressure too much: it was our first quickest lap since the Belgian GP. From that moment on, we began a season's finale that really was positive, most of all because we were able to take the turbo pressure to 4.4 bar. Alboreto ended 1984 with two second places at Monza and the Nürburgring respectively and a fourth in Portugal.

At Monza, Michele drove a car in practice with a rear aerodynamic modification I didn't believe in. He didn't record a significant time but in the race with classic aerodynamics he was exceptional, which confirmed my theory.

I enjoyed the satisfaction from long distance, knowing I was right. After Holland, I couldn't put up with it anymore and literally disappeared. I took refuge in a friends' house at Portofino and didn't go to Monza. I had taken a few days' holiday – I had years owing to me! – and I didn't leave any contact address. But Ferrari was extremely agitated and wanted to talk to me at all costs, to have my comments on the Monza result. Never before had he been unable to reach me in one way or another and he went as far as having the police search for me. He found me on the Sunday night and shouted down the telephone, "Where are you, Maurooo?" And that confirmed how much I still counted for him.

But I was tired of the whole thing because, despite the habitual tension and the recurring periods of dissent, I was at the centre of an unclear situation for the first time. This had never happened at Ferrari before and I couldn't accept that the Racing Department was run with a sub-division of decision-making roles. So in November 1984, with great displeasure, I resigned again. And this time, I really wanted to go, partly because I had received some great offers. I had an

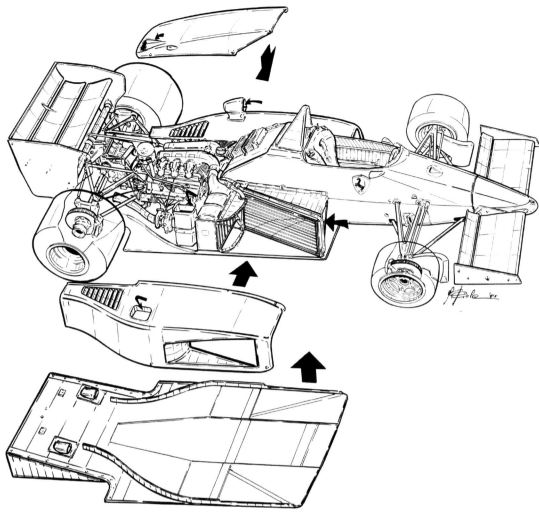

Left: the Ferrari 156/85 being tested at Monza by Alboreto, assisted by technician Nardon. The car had its water radiators in a fan-like position and the heat exchangers just behind them in a "front march" position, as shown in the illustration. Later, exchanger radiators at the sides of the sidepods (left) were also tried, as seen in the initial version of the C4.

unforgettably bitter conversation with the Commendatore from a human standpoint. I explained to him that my team management ideas were different from those of the people with whom I worked; that I couldn't be involved in a situation I didn't believe in and which would mean untold problems for the company. Unfortunately, it was confirmed to me that he was no longer the Ferrari who could change a situation by giving a simple order. He didn't react as energetically as he used to and I noticed he was very sad. But he did use the strength he had left to firmly oppose my decision to go. However, I had made up my mind and I said, "Commendatore, I have worked very well with you, but we're not exactly married". He arranged a meeting with Ghidella and Sguazzini,

respectively the managing directors of Fiat and Ferrari. We discussed, we shouted and in the end Ghidella found the answer: "Change department, design whatever you want and with men selected by you, but don't resign". Proof of confidence I was pleased with, but it wouldn't have been enough to make me stay. I did so for Enzo Ferrari and no-one else.

And that's how I moved to Ferrari Engineering. I was happy there, because I was a long way from racing, although I have always adored the sport. I worked at the Fiorano circuit in the building opposite the famous Casa Rossa, where Enzo Ferrari loved to take refuge in his final years.

So I saw him often and, inevitably, he asked for my opinion on the F1 programme. "What do you

think"? he would inevitably ask, convinced that my exile was just temporary and that – as on other occasions – I would go back to running the Racing Department in the end.

I continued to have many friendly and completely private conversations with the Commendatore, who didn't seem at all sure that the new organisation of the Racing Department had much of a future. It didn't envisage a proper boss any more, a technical expert able to coordinate the whole project and assume all responsibilities. Piero Ferrari was the executive director in charge of general coordination, an enthusiast but not a specialised technician. The others responsible for the sections of the department, all from my period, had become bosses in line with the new

Stefan Johansson came seventh in the 1985 drivers' world championship. The Ferrari 156/85 had a crisis in the second part of the season in which the two drivers retired seven times in eight races. There followed a frenzy of changes, with modifications – some of them radical – to the original car project during the season. For example, modified monocoques were taken to the French GP on 7 July at Le Castellet with two large holes in the front suspension's tie-rod mount area. That did not work and after Saturday practice two standard monocoques were hastily taken to the French track. The Racing Department had had no real boss since the end of the previous year, one who assumed responsibility for making decisions, the custom at Ferrari since the mid-Fifties. For this reason, engineer Forghieri resigned – his resignation was rejected by the Commendatore – in September 1984, certain that without a pyramid distribution of key posts it would not be possible to be successful in F1. Besides, from the earliest days of the company's management, Enzo Ferrari decided to promote some of his collaborators to the status of executives to stimulate them, but also to make them face their responsibilities. Inevitably at the start Ferrari, who was technical and highly expert, lacked the culture necessary to manage a factory. So he assigned that responsibility to a board of friends, like Cavalier Pelloni, managing director of the company that ran the "Il Resto del Carlino" daily newspaper and "Stadio", who explained to him the secrets of politics; industrialist Pietro Barilla, a friend and enthusiastic client, who advised him on the management of the factory. In fact, Barilla criticised the completely absolutist conduct of Ferrari, which had no executives at all. He added that without a sub-division of responsibilities, the factory would find it difficult to grow. The Commendatore became convinced and introduced the first promotions in line with that rapport of confidence that could cost a great deal in the case of the smallest mistake. As happened on that notorious October of 1961 when "the eight" were fired.

methodology, so everyone gave their opinion. So overlapping of competence was inevitable between Harvey Postlethwaite (chassis and bodies), engineers Renzetti (he came from Fiat, Ed) and Caruso (engines and gearboxes) and Antonio Tomaini (track management). In his sector, Harvey was a good technician, but he knew nothing about engines and gearboxes so he had no overall vision of the car.

The desire to progressively make radical changes to the C4 to show they knew better is a conclusion that could be drawn from the 156/85 project. Especially using modifications that were already on other F1 cars that were popular, in particular moving the turbine and exhausts down low and the aspiration in the upper area of the V6;

they would probably have been better as part of a new project.

Early in the 1985 season, the updated C4 was still a positive car. Alboreto won the Grands Prix of Canada and Germany in it and it really seemed he could become world champion. But the second part of the season was a disaster, with a laboured adoption of modifications, all decisions that I don't want to judge and, perhaps, ones that had basic technical logic.

But around mid-season a worried Enzo Ferrari called me once more for my opinion. He said, "Mauro, they're revising the whole car. Have you seen it? Is it right to change it in your view? We weren't doing too badly". What could I say? "Commendatore", I replied, "perhaps they did a good

job; how can I tell? It was you who taught me that, at this point in the season, you don't change a winning car. There's nothing else I can add".

With those hurriedly conceived modifications, especially of the engine and its accessories, Alboreto was no longer a potential winner. And when I met him at the end of the season, Ferrari came out with a quip, "You've got it right this time, too". I got no satisfaction out of it, which I did on other occasions, because unfortunately that was the start of a period of failure from which Ferrari was unable to extract itself for many years.

Beyond Formula 1
Ferrari Engineering

In my two years at Ferrari without being involved in Formula 1, I never deceived myself about being able to return to the previous situation, even if I did continue to work on the evolution of the turbo at the Fiat Research Centre in Turin for the upcoming regulation of having to use no more than 4-cylinder engines. This was until the end of autumn 1986, when the Federation went back on everything and banned turbo engines from Formula 1. Pushed by Ecclestone most of the teams believed normally aspirated power units would lower costs, but it was easy to see that precisely the opposite would be the case.

Personally, I felt bitter because I fought a battle that I considered unjust after having sacrificed my whole life for Ferrari. I believe they should have treated me with more respect, but instead only the Commendatore and engineer Ghidella, whom I never doubted, were really loyal. By this time, I no longer had the motivation that gave me the courage over many previous years to completely shake up a whole Racing Department. In the Ferrari of the Seventies and early Eighties, there was an incomparable team spirit and cohesion between the technical office and all the mechanics. In Salvarani, Rocchi, Maioli, Merchetti, Zambelli, Panini – if I carried on I would have to list about 20 of them – I found people who were not just colleagues, but brothers. Each made his own contribution to building a great Ferrari and now it was being taken away.

They betrayed my trust, which had always been 100% in the Prancing Horse. Among other things, I had never asked questions of a financial nature. I had just accepted the salaries they offered me, which were always in line with those of any other company. Formula 1 didn't make me rich, as it did many engineers who came after me. It was John Barnard, technical director of the Racing Department in 1986, who changed many habits at Maranello. A Commendatore in form had asked Barnard whether or not he had gone mad when he asked if he could work in England. And probably, despite his tiredness, he had a few doubts himself. "What do you think, Mauro, did we do the right thing in employing Barnard?" he asked me one day on one of those

not infrequent chats at Fiorano. And I must add that I came out with something that had been sticking in my craw for some time. "Commendatore", I said, "there's no way I can know whether or not you did right. He's certainly a valid technician, but he has also to be a good businessman, given that he has done so well for himself out of this deal".

He didn't react as he would have years earlier, and I noticed once more that he was no longer the one in command. More accurately, he was trying to manage the situation in his old style, because he wanted to be informed about everything, but he allowed himself to be easily convinced and at one time that would never have happened.

But deep in my heart I continued to be attached to Ferrari and still considered it my home in some ways. I certainly had no feeling of revenge when it took Ferrari so many years to return to the top of Formula 1, even if they tried to get rid of me at a certain time. I was a nuisance. I was amazed, because I believe I conducted myself in the best possible way with the company. I always defended it in interviews, even when it was perfectly obvious mistakes had been made. I believe Ferrari should not only have been judged on the conduct of its executives. It wasn't right that everyone, from those in the technical offices to the last mechanic, should be crucified because the team didn't win world championships.

I certainly didn't hide my satisfaction when Luca Montezemolo became president of Ferrari in 1991 and he restructured the company – the factory and the Racing Department – vertically, the methodology I had always defended and which forced me to resign. And I was delighted for them when they scored that incredible series of world titles from the 2000 season on.

Life was not all sweetness and light before leaving Maranello completely, but once I began my work at Ferrari Engineering I was satisfied. Research has always been my world and I rediscovered the stimulus of innovative projects. On top of which, I had a cohesive and competent team that included an outstanding Claudio Scaglietti, one of the two sons of the celebrated body builder Sergio. After I discussed the matter with engineer Ghidella I took on the problem of Ferrari road car chassis, which were made of pressed steel and tubes at the time and that was not an adequate technology for the level of the brand. That's how I conceived the 408/4RM (in fact, there were two prototypes, Ed) with a chassis inspired by F1 technology that was simple and inexpensive to produce in quantity. One of the car's chassis was made using the riveted sheet metal technology and glued with material prepared by Alcan using a layer of epoxy resin on one side. The sheets were subsequently bent – just like in a child's game – into a

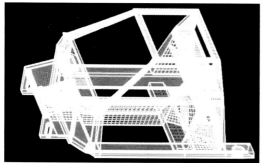

pre-ordained layout. Then they were fixed with special rivets and after quick cooking the adhesion was completed. They didn't use expensive tooling, which is always one of the most significant problems with "niche" cars. The body was built of a series of low cost composite material panels and a cavity wall filled with expanding material to improve rigidity. It had a simple and resistant crash proof chassis, which enabled Ferrari to register many patents. Another solution involved laser welding, a field in which the Fiat Research Centre has become the leader today.

The car, powered by a 4-litre V8 that put out 299 hp, had four-wheel drive with a central hydraulic coupling for which I was inspired by studying the 1969 F1 4x4 that was eventually prohibited by the regulations. Anyway, to Maranello 4WD was a new development, but it wasn't used until 24 years later with the introduction of the FF in 2011.

The 408/4RM took into account the expectations of clients who had never liked a Ferrari that was too docile, meaning the anti-slip system did not take away the handling and sensitivity qualities from the driver. Among the car's interesting characteristics was a CX of 0.274, really low for the period, which contributed to a top speed of 310 kph.

The 408/4RM was unveiled at the 1987 Detroit Motor Show and generated a great deal of interest. But when the project was finished I clashed with Maranello's director of production who was cold towards the car, saying it embodied too much advanced technology for Ferrari. The 348 sports coupé was introduced right after that, a "Ferrari" built in line to Fiat traditions suitable for vehicles of limited power output and was the lowest point in the history of the cars from the Prancing Horse. Among its many defects, was a chassis that deformed to the point where the metal sunroof wouldn't even return to its housing.

It was a period of transition: engineer Ghidella had too many problems in Turin to be able to also devote himself to Ferrari and the executives at Maranello were not up to the job, as they showed in the years that followed.

RGHINI

1988-2011

From Lamborghini to Oral Engineering
After Ferrari

In early 1987 after the 4x4 408 experience, it was clear to me once and for all that I had to leave Ferrari. Then, quite by chance at the Geneva Motor Show in early March I met Daniele Audetto, who had been motor racing director of Ferrari 11 years earlier and was the PRO of Lamborghini at the time. Without mincing his words, which was his style, he told me that the big boss of Chrysler, Lee Iacocca who had just acquired Lamborghini, wanted to offer me a job. I wasn't all that sure and told Iacocca that I would have preferred to continue in racing.

The Lamborghini programme was still rather vague, but on my way back to Bologna as a guest aboard the American manager's Gulfstream, I signed a letter of intent – not a re-al contract – after I had been assured that the company's plans included the construction of a Formula 1 engine. The new regulations coming into force in 1988 allowed aspirated engines again, so that was in line with the traditions of the Sant'Agata company. According to an internal statute, Chrysler was not permitted to take part in racing itself, but the programme did envisage engine supply to teams.

I was a little doubtful, but having spoken about the offer with my family and friends I made my decision: in May, after 27 years and five months, I left Ferrari. I had no room for nostalgia; there was not much time in which to create a new F1 engine, a 3500 cc aspirated V12. I started work on the project at Lamborghini's Sant'Agata headquarters, where Audetto was based, and he later became the head of the whole operation. Engineer Marmiroli, who was with me at Ferrari over 10 years earlier, was also there but he worked on production and anyway my stay at Sant'Agata was a short one: the office was very small, the whole factory was a long way from the result of a recent restoration that took place later and, in practice, lacked the necessary isolation typical of all racing departments. So with a number of newly employed designers, I transferred to an apartment in Viale Corassori on the outskirts of Modena and after a year to the offices of Lamborghini Engineering in Viale delle Nazioni.

There was tremendous enthusiasm in the air,

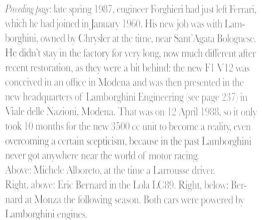

Preceding page: late spring 1987, engineer Forghieri had just left Ferrari, which he had joined in January 1960. His new job was with Lamborghini, owned by Chrysler at the time, near Sant'Agata Bolognese. He didn't stay in the factory for very long, now much different after recent restoration, as they were a bit behind: the new F1 V12 was conceived in an office in Modena and was then presented in the new headquarters of Lamborghini Engineering (see page 237) in Viale delle Nazioni, Modena. That was on 12 April 1988, so it only took 10 months for the new 3500 cc unit to become a reality, even overcoming a certain scepticism, because in the past Lamborghini never got anywhere near the world of motor racing.
Above: Michele Alboreto, at the time a Larrousse driver.
Right, above: Eric Bernard in the Lola LC89. Right, below: Bernard at Monza the following season. Both cars were powered by Lamborghini engines.

so much so that in August 1988 we were able to try out the first engine on the test bench at Sant'Agata. It was entirely conceived, designed and built in cooperation with those excellent suppliers that gravitate around Modena and installed at Lamborghini Engineering by a team coordinated by Franco Antoniazzi, who still works with me at ORAL Engineering.

I was pleased with the result, even if Chrysler was going through a crisis and we had to revise the programme, so we could no longer even think about competing against the top teams. But our 3495 cc 80° V12 didn't just stand out for its good level of power and decidedly favourable torque, it was also economical, simple to assemble and advantageous to the teams

that adopted it. An optimum engine for teams just below the top contenders. And that despite the fact that we could not use the compressed air system of valve spring return, new technology at the time that enabled engines to turn at extremely high revolutions. We were even forced to be content with an injection-ignition system, which was basically to reduce fuel consumption.

I asked Weber-Marelli for the same kind of system adopted by Ferrari, but engineer Sandro Colombo – the man who took my place at Maranello in 1972/3 while I investigated the future of F1 with the T-gearbox and who later moved to Marelli – said we could only reach an agreement on a system that was slightly inferior. An

As well as the 80° V12 engine – on the right, installed in a Lola-Larousse – Lamborghini Engineering also supplied its customer teams with a transverse gearbox, part of engineer Forghieri's technical philosophy which he had introduced at Ferrari many years earlier. The need to guarantee the best operational conditions for the chassis led the Lamborghini technicians to working closely with their colleagues belonging to the teams. Below: among them was Gérard Ducarouge, who Forghieri knew well as the boss of the Ligier and Lotus teams.

The Frenchman started working for Gérard Larrousse, ex-driver and motor sport director of Renault and Ligier, in September 1988 as he had founded a new team linked to Britain's Lola, which would simply supply the chassis as Larousse would run the team independently. As a new team, Lola-Larousse had to be successful in pre-qualifying for every Grand Prix due to the large number of entries, but in 1990 the expert Ducarouge best exploited the power and reliability of the Lamborghini V12, the second year in which he used it. As a result of the 11 points taken by drivers Bernard and Suzuki, the team came sixth in the 1991 Formula 1 World Championship for constructors and competed for the championship in 1991 without having to pre-qualify. Right: the Lotus 102 Lamborghini being driven by Derek Warwick; even though it was a long way off its best, in 1990 the British team did well and scored championship points.

answer I didn't like, partly because we were talking about a system that was an evolution of the one I had contributed to the development of years earlier for Ferrari. An irritating situation because it showed useless jealousy, so I turned to Bosch who supplied a good system along with the DARAB method of data acquisition, which was decidedly modern.

In early 1989, I was distracted from my development job due to an offer that came from Alejandro De Tomaso. I knew and had always admired him somewhat for his ability to navigate his way through a thousand financial and industrial problems. At the time, De Tomaso spoke to engineer Ghidella, who had left Fiat three months earlier due to a clash with Ce-

sare Romiti, the then president of the Turin group. In practice, they asked me to acquire Lamborghini Engineering through the classic system of "leverage buyout": a takeover of a share package with finance from Ghidella (of whose presence I was completely in the dark), that was to remain under cover. A completely legitimate operation that would have been to my financial advantage, even if my position had much improved compared to when I was at Ferrari. But, quite frankly, I didn't think I was up to such a substantial financial operation; more than anything else, though, I wouldn't have liked to spring this surprise on Chrysler and the president of Lamborghini Emile Novaro, with whom I worked well. All those in-

volved were conducting themselves correctly and honoured their financial commitments despite the difficulties of the parent company. On top of that, the company of about 60 people worked well, and we had concluded our first deal to supply our engine and transverse gearbox – completely designed and built by us – to Lola for the 1989 season. We scored one point that year, in the GP of Spain. We continued to supply our engines until 1993, committing ourselves to Lola-Larrousse and Lotus in '90 and they scored seven and three points respectively; direct supply to Team Modena in '91; Larrouse and Minardi in '92 (one point each); and Larrousse in '93 (one point). They were minor teams, so with continuous payment problems

except for Lotus, where I found my friend Tony Rudd again, an engineer of automobile culture. These contracts of a fairly low financial level prohibited any development, which was also further held back by the drivers who were certainly not top level. We pulled off miracles to keep within our budget, even welding used crankcases of the V12 together to use for testing.

But I had the satisfaction of the flattering judgement of Ayrton Senna, who tested a McLaren powered by our Lamborghini engine in 1993. Helped along by the test Ron Dennis, manager of the British team, signed a pre-contract to equip his cars with our engine but then he called it off, wooed by a financial offer from Peugeot. We didn't burn the midnight oil just for the en-

Eighteen teams competed for the 1991 Formula 1 World Championship, a considerable number which required a serious commitment, especially for debut drivers in qualifying. Among them was the Modena Team, which was unveiled at the end of February at the famous Restaurant Fini in the heart of Italy's Motown.
Left: engineer Forghieri, the team's technical director, with Nicola Larini, who drove one of the Lambo 291s. The other driver was Eric Van de Poele.
Above: Larini during a technical briefing in the pits at the GP USA on 10 March, when the car made its debut. The Lambo was designed by Mario Tolentino, starting with the Lamborghini engine-gearbox group, in close collaboration with Mauro Forghieri, who was also head of Lamborghini Engineering at the time. After a promising beginning, the team was affected by financial problems. In 1991 the Lamborghini V12 was also supplied to Ligier, a famous team that was going through a technically negative period. Financial problems conditioned Gérard Larrousse's team, which went back to the Lamborghini engines in 1992. Opposite page: Gachot at Monte Carlo in the LC92, in which he took a good sixth place.

gines, either; in early 1990 Lamborghini Engineering also received a request to create and manage its own F1 car.

A fabulous business from some points of view that started from an apparently solid base. We were contacted by an Italian who lived in Mexico because a wealthy businessman in that country, Fernando Gonzales Luna, wanted to create a Formula 1 team that was to make its debut during the 1991 season. But he asked if he could introduce the car at the 1990 Grand Prix of Mexico, set for 24 June that year. It was a political and image operation aimed at the country and, in fact, half the team's mechanics would be Mexican. We had our doubts, but the information on Mr. Luna, which came from Chrysler,

was completely positive. Luna rented a building next to Lamborghini Engineering and brought about 10 mechanics to Italy, and I must say they were good at their work.

We also signed a contract with technician Mario Tolentino, who immediately began to design the car in which I was much involved as a consultant. But I must admit that I let the technical decisions become too ambitious for such a small team. I also spoke to Gordon Murray, who designed the winning Brabhams of the early Eighties, and I was sure touch control radiators used by fighter planes would have been ideal to dramatically improve the car's aerodynamics. Radiators in the "forward march" position had always been a big headache in terms of air flow direction.

The Lambo should have had radiators in contact with the sidepods, so creating a perfectly clean air flow. But the speeds of fighter planes and F1 cars are totally different: the aircraft travels at between 300 kph and 800 kph and the single-seaters from 80 kph – sometimes even less – to about 300 kph. We unfortunately realised that to achieve a positive result we would have to invest several billion lire in wind tunnel development, which was unthinkable so that the technicians of the various teams soon came to a halt despite the undoubted advantages.

But then, just before the Mexican Grand Prix a mystery emerged, certain aspects of which still haven't been cleared up. The Lambo van was seen close to Paris and it was from there that

Left: the 1992 Geneva Motor Show, engineer Forghieri on the Bugatti stand talking to Romano Artioli, president of the company that had its headquarters at Campogalliano, and Clay Regazzoni. The toast is in honour of the Bugatti EB110 Supersport, which made its debut at the show. Unveiled in September 1991, the EB110 still had to be industrialised and sorted, which became Mauro Forghieri's responsibility. The engineer was contacted by Artioli, who had previously been a Ferrari distributor and had acquired the French marque. Extremely sophisticated and expensive – 550 million lire for the basic version – 126 Bugatti EB110s were built before the factory closed having been unable to get beyond its start-up period. One of the cars was acquired by Michael Schumacher. Above: an EB110 next to a veteran Bugatti T35, with the Campogalliano factory in the background.

the F1 car was to leave for Mexico City – and that was when we were told that Mr. Luna had disappeared. We stopped the dispatch of the car just in time and we were later told vaguely of a political upset in Mexico; but there was no trace of Luna, although we received the agreed payments in the normal way 20-25 days in arrears. Our morale was extremely low at that point, because it seemed we would have to just throw away all the work we had done. Then, quite suddenly, we received finance from Carlo Patrucco, vice-president of the Italian manufacturers' association Confindustria at the time, to whom I had been introduced by Gianni Agnelli and Beppe Lucchini, son of the ex-president of Confindustria and owner of Scuderia Italia. So

we continued to develop the car for the new team, initially on the track even if there were not many tests, driven by Mauro Baldi, whose great professionalism I well remember. Unfortunately, the car's design was partially conditioned by the impossibility of using touch controlled radiators, so that had its effect on aerodynamics. Carlo Patrucco's Modena Team entered the 1991 Formula 1 World Championship with drivers Larini and Van de Poele. His motor sport director was Gianfranco Silecchia, who had previously been with Lancia and whose efficiency and professionalism I respected. Given the level of the team, in my view it would have been better to enter just one driver but the decision to make it two was fallout from initial "financial exuber-

ance" of Patrucco: trappings included a large motorhome like Ferrari's, special uniforms for everyone, catering and other "embellishments" of that kind. And when the personal financial affairs of our owner, who knew little about Formula 1, ended up on the front pages of the daily newspapers during the second part of the season, the team's collapse ended that adventure. Yet if Van de Poele had come fifth at the GP of San Marino, it was certain the team would have escaped the guillotine of pre-qualifying, would have received prize money and matters would probably have taken a different direction. Instead, due to the fault of the chief mechanic, who had been unprofessional when "refilling" the fuel tank – a very long operation due

During the 1992 Formula 1 season, the Lamborghini V12 was supplied to Larrousse and Minardi of Faenza, whose drivers were Gianni Morbidelli and Christian Fittipaldi, Wilson's son and ex-world champion Emerson's nephew. Christian was very tall and the team had to develop a special cockpit for his M192, above being driven by the Brazilian in the Imola pit lane. At the end of the season, Fittipaldi came sixth in the Grand Prix of Japan at Suzuka.

to the various connections – the Belgian driver stopped on the last lap a few hundred metres from the finish line! Between 1993 and 1994, I worked at Bugatti at Bugatti at Campogalliano for about 20 months. I sorted and industrialised the EB110 sports coupé project, a really ambitious car designed by other colleagues, and developed the EB112 saloon. And it was not easy to speak with the marque's owner Romano Artioli, definitely a man of character and an optimum commercial manager, but impossible to convince, especially concerning industrial technology.

Then in 1995 I was asked to start Oral Engineering, a prototype design and construction company that belongs to the Oral Group under the presidency of Sergio Lugli. Together with Franco Antoniazzi, who had worked with me at both Ferrari and Lamborghini, I explored all fields of mechanics, from engines to gearboxes for offshore boats and F1. Together with an effective group of technicians, I worked for the most diverse companies, from BMW – 11 years of collaboration for which we created their first F1 engine (1996-2000) as well as others for Grand Prix motorcycles (800 cc – 900 cc) – to roll-hoop inlets for offshore boats, which are now so fashionable. We even accepted a commission to set up direct injection vintage Mercedes-Benz engines and competed in rallying, although with rather unflattering results. And we're still battling away for anyone who believes in us.

F1 1986-2011

From Prost to Alonso via Schumacher
The 1986 – 2011 F1 seasons

Between 1986 and 1996, Ferrari won 17 Grands Prix out of a possible 177. An extremely low percentage that clearly illustrates the surprising period of crisis the team experienced, interrupted briefly by a good 1990 season. Lean years in return for the investments made and the technicians' efforts, almost all of them top men in their fields.

At the end of 1991, Luca Cordero di Montezemolo returned to Maranello, this time as president and managing director of Ferrari. Pragmatic and energetic as always, he was the man who guided the Prancing Horse towards its rebirth, but it was not a brief or simple task, partly because he had to first devote most of his time to the re-launch of the road car sector, as that had been devalued by models that were not in line with the company's traditions.

The president only achieved his objective when he was able to reorganise the motor sport management according to the traditions of Enzo Ferrari, traditions that had worked so well until the early Eighties. His prescription was an absolute boss, able to assume all responsibilities and, below him, men with roles that were crystal clear. That absolute boss was Jean Todt, a racing expert and an undoubtedly strong personality, whose prime objective was to take Ferrari back to the top. He had to live with John Barnard, who was protected by a four-year contract that allowed him to work in England, where Ferrari had opened the GTO Centre in Guilford near London in 1987 and subsequently the FDD, neither of which enabled him to enter into the spirit of Maranello. From 1986 there was an incredible alternation of peo-

ple with vague roles – technicians and others – in motor sport management and that certainly had a negative effect on attempts to emerge from the crisis. Many commanded but nobody was in command; there is a long list of the people involved to which no other team has ever come close. They include Piero Ferrari, Harvey Postlethwaite, engineers Cappelli, Castelli, Renzetti, Lombardi, motor sport director Piccinini, who was also on the Ferrari board and, of course, John Barnard, who entered and exited twice – and he's not the only person who did so. Of no less importance was the presence of Cesare Fiorio, Gustav Brunner, George Ryton, Steve Nichols, Enrique Scalabroni, Jean Jacques His, Jean Claude Migeot and Osamu Goto. All with the right credentials, but F1 has always rewarded the continuity of programmes, not continuous technical restarts.

1986 F1: much technology but few results

The F1 86 project was completely new in relation to previous turbos. The car was designed by Harvey Postlethwaite (chassis) and engineer Renzetti (engine). The Englishman was "general manager" of the team, but did not possess the characteristics of a real boss. Harvey, a highly respectable person, was a good chassis designer but he was unable to recreate the kind of harmony in the team that was the basis of its success in better times. There was no win for Alboreto or Johansson, while the chassis bosses argued with those of the engine over their lack of success and vice-versa. A classic case of no real coordinator. There were many small problems that often stopped the cars even during practice, sometimes caused by the engine, which had been profoundly changed. It was still a V6 with 120° cylinder banks with the location of the aspiration in the upper area of the engine as it should be, but the turbine and exhausts were down low. And that affected the rear aerodynamics, which should have been much less "cluttered" to ensure the discharge of air and, therefore, the wing load. It was the Coca-Cola bottle shape introduced by McLaren, which had not brought the F1 86 the expected results.

Quite the opposite, the new turbine location and exhausts created cooling and therefore reliability problems. There were doubts about the KKK turbine so they opted for the American Garrett unit, which was probably an avoidable decision (the German turbine worked perfectly well on McLaren's Porsche engine) and complicated to manage when the season started. The search for power initially led to an increase of the compression ratio from 7:1 to 7.5:1; that was also favoured by the use of non-commercial petrol as had been the case until 1982, and the higher turbocharging pressure of up to 4.6 bar in practice for one single lap. Power output was increased from the 780 hp of 1985 to 850 hp, but the revs also went from 11,000 rpm to 11,500 rpm. That's how the previous car lost its reliability, so much so that the transverse gearbox, which was always a safe bet, started to vibrate. And there were problems with the smaller clutch with a much reduced polar inertia to the point of engaging dangerous frequencies.

Previous page: the dance of the mechanics around Michael Schumacher's F310 seems like a liberating rite; after a decade of difficulties, president Montezemolo (page 246 with Gerhard Berger) selected the right people with whom to find once more the right road to the world championship. Previously, not even John Barnard (photograph on page 247 with Piero Ferrari, Berger and motor sport director Piccinini) had been able to do so. Above: Michele Alboreto and Stefan Johansson. Below: the F1 86's engine with its injection system between the V of its cylinder banks.

Above: Stefan Johansson taking the famous La Source corner during the 1986 Grand Prix of Belgium at Spa. Right: working on the F1 86 at Spa, where the cars made their debut with Garrett turbochargers having used the German KKK units in practice. Ferraris retired from the previous four GPs six times, mainly due to engine problems. The F1 86 revived at the Belgian GP, where Alboreto took third and Johansson behind the uncatchable Nigel Mansell in the Williams-Honda and Senna's Lotus-Renault. The two Ferrari drivers raced in close order, so much so that the pits held out the "slow" signal, identical to the one that created the celebrated Pironi-Villeneuve misunderstanding at Imola in 1982. This time, too, the drivers decided they knew best: Johansson had started with soft compound tyres and had no problem in overtaking his team mate, who was penalised by the hard Goodyear "C" rubber. But, unlike at Imola, there was no post-race controversy. Far right: Alboreto in the Monza pit lane.

The disappointing results forced Harvey Postlethwaite to design a new car. At Maranello, they were convinced their lack of past success was mainly due to inefficient rear aerodynamics because of the engine's 120° cylinder banks and the T-gearbox, which didn't favour air flow down low. That was a concept I didn't share and it led to the creation of a new engine with 90° cylinder banks, despite it having been known for some time that, with new regulations in the offing, the new turbo unit would only have two years of life. The transverse gearbox also made way for a longitudinal unit that went from five to six speeds. With these changes, Ferrari lost advantages that had always worked well in the past, without an apparent improvement in the car's efficiency. As well as engineer Renzetti, Jean Jacques His, ex-Renault, was operating at Maranello, but internally the V6 was not substantially modified, apart from the drive shaft, of course. Postlethwaite was already feeling under pressure due to the Ferrari-John Barnard agreement and the

addition of Gustav Brunner, who in 1986 had been given the task of creating the F Indy car, which never raced, as well as aerodynamics specialist Jean Claude Migeot. So the Briton paid for the partial lack of success. In reality, though, the revised aerodynamics of the chassis, with its lower sidepods and reduced air intakes, were reasonably positive. But still the Alboreto and Berger cars retired a record 19 times due to mechanical problems. In the hunt for power – about 880 hp in racing – the compression ratio was taken to 8:1, a high value for a turbocharged engine. Then, towards the end of the season, a surprise: Berger scored three pole positions and two victories, in part because of the optimum exploitation of the turbine overboost. That year regulations demanded pop-off valves, which stopped the pressure exceeding 4 bar. It was a mechanical system supplied by the Federation and had a certain inertia. So for a few seconds, the pressure could reach 4.3 bar producing an increase of about a 50 hp, especially in practice.

In his fourth season with Ferrari, Michele Alboreto was paired with Gerhard Berger. It was a rather disappointing year for Maranello due to the many problems with the F1 87s, which retired 21 times with mechanical problems 11 of them caused by the engine. But surprisingly, Berger won the two final GPs of the season in Japan and Australia due to the perfect calibration of the turbine pressure regulation valve, which the Federation fixed at 4 bar that year. Below: John Barnard checking the front end of the car so that he could see the pull rod suspension with its double wishbones and tie rod, in this case only fixed at the base of the spring-damper group, all of which working in traction.

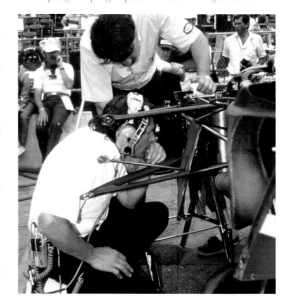

Above: John Barnard, the famous technician who designed the winning McLarens of 1984/5 and seen here talking to Michele Alboreto, signed a contract with Ferrari in the autumn of 1986. Not often at Maranello or the circuits, Barnard managed the Ferrari Racing Department from his GTO offices in Guilford, England. He only worked on a few details of Harvey Postlethwaite's F1 87 project, as did two well-established technicians Gustav Brunner and Jean Claude Migeot. With no real boss, the overlapping of roles – in the engine sector, engineer Ildo Renzetti and Jean Jacques His worked at the same level – certainly did not help the growth and set-up of the car, which only overcame its mechanical fragility towards the end of the season.
Below: an F1 87 covered by a red sheet and on its narrow rims and tyres for ease of transport in the truck.

Many believed that John Barnard, who had been with Ferrari since 1986, would have presented his own F1 design. Instead, the F1 87-88 C was strictly related to the previous year's car, because they maintained that the radical new regulations envisaged for 1989 with the move to 3500 cc aspirated engines would have dissuaded all the teams from introducing new models. But McLaren chose the new car route and they could count on the formidable Senna-Prost duo. So the British team completely dominated the sport and made the last months of Enzo Ferrari's life truly bitter: he died on 14 August. The Commendatore could not understand why his drivers Berger and Alboreto found it impossible to at least stay close to the McLaren duo, let alone beat them; and he was disappointed at Barnard's slowness in presenting a really new development. On top of that, there were the complaints of his technicians, who were unable to go ahead with anything without having to continually seek Barnard's approval, with obvious complications of all kinds. Fortunately, a chance accident between Ayrton Senna and a lapped Jean-Louis Schlesser enabled Berger to win the Italian Grand Prix, so honouring the memory of Enzo Ferrari. A success about which Fiat Group and Ferrari managing director Vittorio Ghidella said from the Monza podium, "From this moment, a new era has begun at Maranello". He was referring to a restructuring he intended to complete quickly, but after a few months it was he who had to resign, beaten in a power struggle with the president of the Turin group, Cesare Romiti. That was the beginning of an even more troubled period, which continued until the successes of 1990.

For Ferrari, which had confirmed Gerhard Berger (above) and Michele Alboreto (below), the 1988 season was conditioned by a revolution in the roles of command, which took place at the end of June. Postlethwaite was moved to F40 production and the top job in the Racing Department went to Dr. Pier Giorgio Cappelli, a physics graduate, and engineer Pier Guido Castelli, both with experience of the Fiat Research Centre. And, naturally, there was John Barnard.

Enzo Ferrari died on 14 August 1988. Everyone at Maranello would have liked to honour him with victory in a Grand Prix, but doing so proved really difficult given the absolute domination of McLaren-Honda. Theirs' was the only really car with an engine developed to meet the new regulation that limited turbine pressure to 2.5 bar and fuel for each race to150 litres. Berger only set the fastest lap in the Belgian Grand Prix on 28 August, but the miracle happened at the GP of Italy on 11 September. The Prost and Senna McLarens were undisturbed in the lead as usual, but Prost's engine broke mid-race and he retired: it was the first time such a thing had happened all season. So that left Senna in first place with Berger and Alboreto at a safe distance, but two laps from the end the Brazilian was about to lap Schlesser's Williams – the Frenchman had replaced an indisposed Nigel Mansell – for the second time when there was high drama. Senna probably put too much pressure on Schlesser, anyway half way through the first chicane the McLaren went off line but became enmeshed with the spinning Williams. So Berger took the lead and won, while Alboreto crossed the finish line a little more than five tenths from his team mate (above): an opportunity that did not crop up again during the subsequent four GPs. Eddie Cheever was also on the podium with the ecstatic Ferrari duo, having come third in his Arrows-Megatron.

The turnaround happened with the arrival of John Barnard's long-awaited 640 or the F1 89, derived from the 639 prototype that was tested during the second half of 1988. It was undoubtedly a valid project, even if it was complicated by the distance between Guilford and Maranello. But I must emphasise that Barnard not only designed a car able to win a GP. I believe his main achievement was to have brought a new means of designing to Ferrari, and especially of analysing each individual detail. According to the comments of many technicians who had already worked with me, close examination of the smallest details was his strongpoint, even though he lost his overall view of the whole project on some occasions. But it was a very useful lesson.

In addition, Barnard showed great skill at exploiting the good things about Maranello, and the electro-hydraulic gearbox with paddles on the steering wheel for changing gear was the best demonstration of that fact. Just such a system was successfully tested as far back as 1980, but only the development of electronics and a substantial financial investment that had been unthinkable in the past permitted its definitive creation 10 years later. It was a major turnaround that set a trend in F1, because gear changing was faster – after its arrival, the clutch was no longer used – and driving a Grand Prix car was less tiring. It was not an easy system to set up, because engineer De Silvestri and his colleagues took most of the 1989 season to do it. Nigel Mansell, the new Ferrari driver, won the season's opening GP in Brazil in the car and that was an incredible surprise, because during practice the F1 89 was only able to cover a few laps before stopping with a seized gearbox. Mansell also won in Hungary and Berger in Portugal: one of only three GPs in which the Austrian crossed the finish line. This string of retirements considerably influenced development of the new 65° 3497 cc V12. It had a head with

five valves per cylinder, three aspiration and two exhaust, a choice I would never have made because although it produced a few more horsepower at high revs, it didn't favour torque and, therefore, drivability. On the power front, there was a declared 600 hp at 12,000 rpm, not really earth-shaking data and similar to that of the V12 Lamborghini of the same period, which had been conceived and built with a much smaller budget. The 12,000 rpm are especially surprising and the same as those of the 312 flat engine of 11 years earlier, which could run up to 14,000 revs. I remember that I wasn't exactly surprised when my ex-colleagues told me that the 312 was brought back so that its components could be

examined, normal practice in the company. The cylinder block was in cast iron with thin walls, like the V10 Honda of the same year. It was undoubtedly a major technological commitment by Fiat and its subsidiary Teksid.

Anyway, during the first years of aspirated engines Ferrari didn't show the supremacy that some had predicted, which was considered a tradition at Maranello. But it was not just the power and torque. The F1 89's V12 was sufficiently competitive; during the same period the Honda and Renault engines stood out for the miniaturisation of their components (crankcase and head in particular) to reduce weight, which Ferrari only achieved – but with optimum results – many years later.

Previous page: the Brazilian Grand Prix podium, the surprise winner Nigel Mansell in his debut with the 640, for which it was also the first race. With the Briton are Alain Prost (McLaren-Honda) and Mauricio Gugelmin (March-Judd).

The only car to be created by John Barnard in almost three years of working for Ferrari was the F1 89, also known by its project number 640. It was a revolutionary car, particularly due to the adoption of a seven speed, longitudinal, semi-automatic gearbox with small paddles behind the steering wheel with which to change gear. The British technician drew from previous experience with Ferrari, but he has to be given credit for having believed in a choice that was courageous for the period and that set a trend, with its optimum technology that was fairly traditional in its general concepts. Aerodynamic research at the rear recalled the now classic "bottle of Coca-Cola" shape to improve air escape, while the suspension was push rod. The monocoque had two small lateral tanks that were added to the central unit, which was eliminated in the 1990 version as it was banned by the Federation after Berger's fiery accident at Imola in 1989. The F1 89 initially had two small air intakes behind the driver's helmet (bottom, right with Nigel Mansell in the cockpit and Berger ... observing). But the intakes turned out to be inadequate for the V12 (below, left), so they were replaced by a more traditional central one.

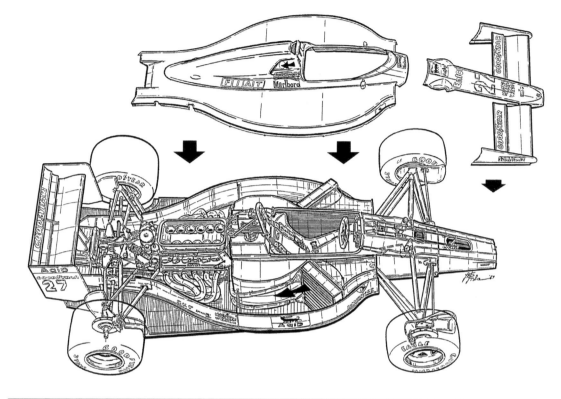

The chassis, for which Barnard had kept everyone waiting for so long, was certainly well executed although there was nothing new about it, apart from the initial absence of the air scoop, which reduced aerodynamic efficiency fairly substantially. At Ferrari, we discovered that fact back in 1976, when we moved the engine's air intakes to the front of the body. But with subsequent ground effect cars that was no longer logical, so Barnard opted for two "ears" just behind the driver's head. But it was inevitable that the air flow from the front wing dispersed in precisely that zone, so much so that the two small intakes had a lot of trouble "breathing". There was a reaction from the engine specialists, so Barnard had to quickly go back to the normal air scoop which, if it is designed well and integrated into the roll bar, improves power output by 5-6%. The F1 89, nicknamed the duckling due to the particular shape of its nose, was aerodynamically efficient, with large sidepods that hid two lateral fuel tanks, which improved weight distribution; but the car was right on 500 kg weight. limit.

Barnard also took torsion bar suspension technology to Ferrari as a replacement for coil springs, plus the "fashionable" push rod layout. That meant the connection bracket between the wheel hub and the damper functioned under pressure, not traction as was the case with the pull rod system, which had been used at Ferrari since 1982. I must say the importance that has always surrounded these two opposing systems made me smile a little. It seems a car can be more or less competitive with one choice or the other, which I don't believe is so fundamental, at least as far as the front suspension is concerned.

The very high nose fashion made the use of the pull rod layout more complicated up front, yet it appeared again in 2012. It's different with the rear suspension, for which there have been countless switches between push and pull rod, especially when Adrian Newey brought back the latter on the 2009 Red Bull RB5.

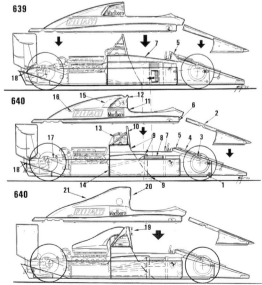

With Gerhard Berger at the wheel, two versions of the 640: above with ear-like air intakes and an air scoop (page 257). Right: Nigel Mansell and Alain Prost just before the announcement confirming the Frenchman would be joining Ferrari for 1990. Below: a comparison in profile between the 639 prototype, the 640 on its debut and the definitive version: 1. Stepped bottom. 2. Lower frontal area. 3. Spring control. 4. Damper without coil spring. 5. Separate mount. 6-7. Lowered zone. 8. Bigger radiator. 9. Fuel tank dimensions. 10. Low roll bar. 11. New body. 12. Narrow engine cover. 13. Vertical management system. 14. Water channels. 15. Air intakes. 16. Engine cover. 17. Gearbox. 18. Internal sensors. 19-20-21. Roll bar with air intake and new engine cover.

F1 641: Prost "almost" world champion

Judgment of John Barnard's first Formula 1 Ferrari must inevitably be accompanied by one of its evolution, the F1 641, even if the British technician did resign before the end of the '89 season and move to Benetton. In substance, the 1990 car was an evolution of its predecessor without major modifications, but updated by a more practically minded technician, Argentinean Enrique Scalabroni. The South American had never previously designed a whole Formula 1 car, but he had trained in the down-to-earth Gian Paolo Dallara school, before moving to Williams. That's why many members of Ferrari said at the time, "Barnard has gone at last. At least weeks won't elapse any more before decisions are taken". The kind of comment that was, perhaps, based on truth but which I find unjust, because much of the 1990 project was still Barnard's. But Scala-

broni improved the aerodynamics by slimming down the car's flanks with intelligent decisions that influenced cooling the mechanical components, one of the main problems of 1989. Then came the development of a new seven speed gearbox that was much more reliable, and had programming that enabled the driver to skip gears when changing up; its automatic use was seen as the first step towards such gearboxes that became so widespread years later. Besides, Scalabroni had already dealt the F1 sequential 'box at Williams.

Engine weight reduction was also important to the 641, but power was especially so, increased as it was to 680 hp at 12,750 rpm. So the gap between the Honda and Renault engines narrowed but, strangely, Ferrari continued to follow the opposition.

Yet the season was packed with success: Alain

Prost, the 1989 world champion, was his eventual successor Ayrton Senna's toughest opposition. Prost, an extremely sensitive test driver and tyre selector, won five GPs, while his team mate Mansell managed one. Unfortunately, reliability was not the Ferrari's strongest point, but Senna was also able to take advantage of five top three placings on his way to the championship.

And that world championship, which ended with the famous collision between Prost and Senna at Suzuka, created an internal rivalry between Prost and Mansell that certainly didn't help Ferrari. There was a great deal of controversy, which also involved Racing Department director Cesare Fiorio, but in my view criticism of him was totally unwarranted.

The story of Ferrari's 1990 Formula 1 World Championship in photographs: Mansell (2) and Prost (1) at the GP of Great Britain at Silverstone, won by the Frenchman while Nigel, feeling bitter about having to drop out of the race, announced his retirement from racing. Prost had already won the Grand Prix of Brazil (above, right) and went on to take Mexico, France and Spain (below) with Mansell the winner of a controversial Portuguese Grand Prix. Prost's expression (above, left) confirms that result. Below, left: Jean Alesi, a 1991 Ferrari works driver, lowers himself into the cockpit of the F 641 during one of his first tests at the team's Fiorano track.

The latest evolution of the Barnard car was fielded for the 1991 season. Scalabroni had left Ferrari by the end of '90, but the arrival of celebrated American technician Steve Nichols in late 1989 had compensated for that and Nichols continued with Maranello until December 1991. The American had designed the unbeatable 1988 McLaren MP4-4, but unfortunately his attempts to update the Ferrari 641 were a lot less successful. Neither Alain Prost nor new arrival Jean Alesi won a single GP in 1991, the 642 being outclassed by the McLaren- Hondas and Williams-Renaults. As often happens in F1, a single season was all that was needed to change technical direction. The brilliant Tyrrell 019 had already set the trend in 1990, created as it was by two ex-Ferrari technicians Harvey Postlethwaite and Jean Claude Migeot. The 019 had a very high

nose with angled wings and the lower area of the chassis was conceived to exploit air flow towards the flat bottom. So it produced tremendous benefits in terms of aerodynamic load and reduced drag.

The 642 was updated with a slightly longer wheelbase and that permitted an increase in the size of the sidepods with a more linear progression than those of 1990. The front suspension changes were notable, with the return of coil springs in place of torsion bars, which appeared again in definitive form on the mid-season's 643 that was mainly different in its front aerodynamics. The car had no high nose, but it was clear Ferrari was following Tyrrell, partly because Alesi had moved from the British team to Maranello and did little else but laud the new concept.

The monocoque was also tapered to increase

the car's height from the ground in the area under the driver's legs to increase air flow from the bottom to the rear extractor plane. But it was a sort of draft project, probably with a view to building a definitive version for 1992. Meanwhile, progress was being made with the engine, which would be credited with 725 hp at 14,500 rpm due to variable geometry aspiration trumpets.

In November 1991, Luca Cordero di Montezemolo became president and managing director of Ferrari, so the prospect of a major turnaround in road car and F1 production was on the cards. Besides, two ex-*Ferraristi* returned to Maranello after setting the trend with the Tyrrell 019: Postlethwaite and Migeot. So who wouldn't have bet on a positive result coming from all this?

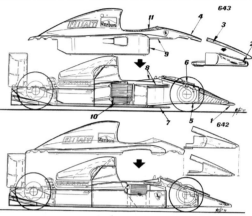

The 1991 642 driven by Prost and Alesi was derived from the 641 with just a few modifications. The nose was squarer, the sidepods slimmer and the rear of the chassis was wider. The 643 turned up mid-season, so here is a comparison between the two. 1. Integrated front wing. 2. End plates. 3. Divided nose. 4. Lower lines. 5. Raised chassis. 6. New front suspension. 7. Knife-edge splitter. 8. Strengthened chassis. 9. Short sides. 10. Low windshield.

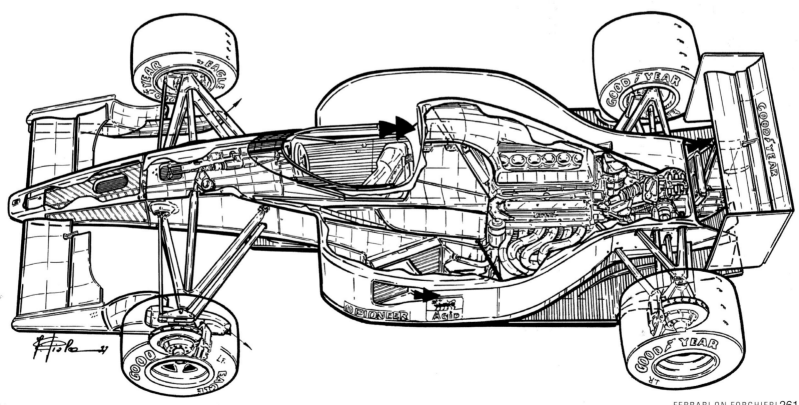

The 22 months of Cesare Fiorio at Ferrari: jealousy and spite

Ferrari did not enjoy much success between 1986 – 1995; 14 wins, nine of them in 1989/90 when the Racing Department director was Cesare Fiorio. One certainly can't talk of fortuitousness, partly because the Turin executive was in charge of Ferrari racing for just two seasons. He was forced to leave due to the pressure exerted on him by the company's president, Piero Fusaro, an episode typical of the period in which there was not much serenity or planning.

Under Fiorio Alain Prost came close to winning the world championship, yet it was the motor sport director became the "accused". To hark back this period and bring in comments by engineer Forghieri, we asked Cesare Fiorio to recall his 26 months at Maranello.

"It gives me great pleasure to provide my recollections for a book by engineer Forghieri", said the manager who won 18 world rally and racing championships with Lancia. "I have always had the highest regard for him and it would have given me tremendous pleasure to have been able to work with him, adding my organisational competence to his outstanding technical ability. Unfortunately, this never happened and certainly not because Enzo Ferrari didn't want me at Maranello. To nip that rumour in the bud, just remember that it was the Commendatore who asked that I run the team that won the Targa Florio in 1972, when we entered Ferrari 312 PB for Sandro Munari and Arturo Marzario. And earlier than that, I personally suggested to Lancia that we ask Ferrari if we could use the Dino engine for the construction of the Lancia Stratos. An operation that went really well and which led engineer Forghieri to devoting a little of his time to setting up the Stratos in the mid-Seventies, a quick version of which was tested at the Fiorano circuit".

Even so, Cesare Fiorio wasn't called to Maranello until in early March 1989.

"I was at the Rally of Portugal and I had to return to Milan quickly at the request of Cesare Romiti, managing director of Fiat at the time. I met him on Sunday 5 March and the day afterwards I was already in my office at Maranello. The first GP of the season was only 20 days away in Brazil, and the drivers were Gerhard Berger and Nigel Mansell. We made our debut with the revolutionary 640 with its semi-automatic gearbox, still a long way from reliable, yet the British driver surprised us all by winning the race. My first major task was to look again at the production process and quality control, which weren't up to Ferrari traditions during that period. At the same time, I also started to get to know the personalities of the two drivers in depth and I realised that Mansell had talent and sensitivity in driving, even if with some emotional instability problems, while Berger, a man of great courage, had performance troughs due to insufficient physical preparation. Obviously Ferrari had to have two top drivers, so I got to work a long way in advance in an effort to attract the best of the period, Alain Prost and Ayrton Senna, to the team. I reached agreement with Alain for the 1990 and 1991 seasons during the German Grand Prix weekend at the end of July.

"And I approached Ayrton in secret in the spring at the GP of Monaco. He was not available for 1990, but we decided to stay in touch to reach agreement for 1991.

"Meanwhile, the technical level of the team had improved considerably and the 641 enabled Prost to stake a claim to the world championship early in his first year at Ferrari. Despite Mansell's major psychological crisis, he was no less talented than Prost, although the Frenchman had a stronger personality. But I was satisfied with the results and even more so because I reached preliminary agreement with Senna – I still have the document concerned – on Monday 9 July. In 1991, Ferrari would have had the dream team of Senna and Prost, the maximum imaginable. It was, of course, agreed that the matter would remain secret between him and me until the end of the season. But, incredibly, the managing director of Ferrari, Piero Fusaro, started an open war against me and put me in a bad light with Fiat Group executives. An incomprehensible fact and one for which I could only find a single explanation: jealousy had broken out because the press recognised the success of my work after Ferrari had been through years of bitter defeat. I had become troublesome to him. And while I personally tried to keep things on an even keel, the inevitable clash happened

between the highly strung and suspicious Mansell and the egocentric Prost, so engineer Fusaro found nothing better to do than to send for Prost and tell him that his motor sport director was pulling the rug from under his feet by bringing Senna to Maranello, but that Alain shouldn't worry because Senna would never join Ferrari. I was astonished: I had been able to engage the best driver in the

world and Fusaro did everything he could to slam the door in Senna's face!"

Confirmation of Enzo Ferrari's gradual withdrawal from the management of his scuderia and his subsequent death didn't help the cohesion of the team.

"The last act in this show of spite", Fiorio continued, "came to an end in the spring of 1991. I had found in the active suspension technology (electronically controlled, Ed) a sure-fire winner. To develop it, I created a separate team with engineer Baldisserri and Andrea Montermini as the test driver, and by the spring the results were all positive. We had been several months ahead of Williams on a similar project, which then enabled the British team to dominate two consecutive world championships, but instead someone literally threw a spanner in the works. It was mainly Alain Prost who influenced the decision, as he was certain the new technical development would detract from his enormous driving finesse. But the last word came, as usual, from engineer Fusaro, who proved once again that he was more "a civil servant" than a commander.

"In that environment, I resigned from Ferrari in mid-May. But I was left with the satisfaction of the results we had achieved: three victories in 1989 and six in 1990. Ferrari would wait another seven years to beat its '90 score – by one win".

F92 A: innovative and unlucky

Left: Jean Alesi flying over the Monte Carlo kerbs in 1992, but his fighting spirit was not enough to win with the complicated F92 A, designed by Steve Nichols and expert aerodynamicist Jean Claude Migeot. Right: Alessandro Nannini in the cockpit of the F92 A with which he tested at Fiorano after he had left F1 due to being injured in a helicopter accident in 1990. The Siena driver made a brilliant return to motor racing with the Alfa Romeo 155 in the German DTM championship.

Unfortunately, the car conceived for 1992 was a complete disappointment and way below expectations; it even compromised the career of Ivan Capelli, who had inherited Prost's place in the team. The technical reasons can be blamed on the usual lack of a real team boss to coordinate the project (Nichols had contributed to the new car's chassis, but he left Maranello in 1991). And it was possible that Migeot decided to "overdo" his aerodynamic studies to showcase his ability, not a rare situation among returning technicians after an initial departure. The F92 A had a high nose over the front wing mount with sidepods from which stood out air intakes detached from the body, like those on a fighter aircraft. The true originality of the car was its double bottom, the purpose of which was to favour negative lift without increasing drag. In practice, the lateral air channels – the sidepods – were raised 15 cm in relation to the flat bottom, as demanded by the regulations.

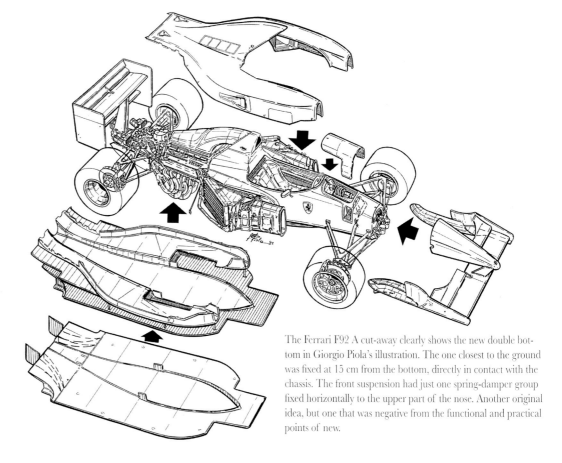

The Ferrari F92 A cut-away clearly shows the new double bottom in Giorgio Piola's illustration. The one closest to the ground was fixed at 15 cm from the bottom, directly in contact with the chassis. The front suspension had just one spring-damper group fixed horizontally to the upper part of the nose. Another original idea, but one that was negative from the functional and practical points of new.

So the bottom was detached from the monocoque to create channels for the passage of air along each side as far as the rear extractor plane, which would have experienced a notable ground effect. The system meant the centre of gravity had to be raised slightly – always a negative factor on a racing car – but that would have been compensated for if the aerodynamics really worked. Unfortunately, the results obtained with models in the wind tunnel had to be carefully interpreted, because the car's behaviour on the track inevitably changes depending on various parameters such as the track's surface, which is never flat like those of the tunnel; competitors' cars and their slipstreams; air flow that changes near the stands or other buildings. It's a well-known situation to people who work in wind tunnels, but evidently this project had its limits, even if Migeot, who was later involved in successful projects, was an optimum expert in aerodynamics. Not even the engine could make

up for the chassis problems, because the new short stroke V12 (88x47.9 mm compared to the previous 86x50.2 mm) was taken to 735 hp at 14,800 rpm, but then along came reliability problems. Some were caused by revolutions that were too high and would have required pneumatic valve gear in place of springs, a system that had already been adopted by Renault for its latest V6 turbos.

Among the many modifications conceived during the season, the new F92 AT six speed, transverse gearbox stood out and was a return to the recent past. The T-gearbox was set aside with the appearance of the F1 87 in favour of a traditional longitudinal unit because it was thought the rear aerodynamic extractor plane with its Coca-Cola bottle shape would have less downforce. A technique about which I wasn't convinced and which cancelled out the advantages of the T-box lowering the polar moment of inertia and weight.

Above: the Alesi and Capelli F92 As at the first Monza chicane. Below: Alesi talking to engineer Claudio Lombardi, Racing Department director. He was previously in charge of engines, a task that was handed to engineer Massai in 1992 Lombardi became motor sport director in 1991 before passing that role on to Sante Ghedini the following year. Niki Lauda had returned to Maranello as an "expert observer" at the invitation of president Luca di Montezemolo. So the reappearance of Ghedini did not surprise anyone, as he was always close to Lauda in the Seventies. Harvey Postlethwaite also returned to the Ferrari fold at the end of 1991, but by that time Nichols had already designed the F92 A's chassis.

D isillusioned by a lack of results, at the end of 1992 Montezemolo surprised everyone by recalling John Barnard to Maranello under a four-year contract. Doubts emerged once again, certainly not concerning the ability of the British technician but about his "long arm" way of working, which manifested itself this time by the opening of a new Ferrari centre in the UK called the FDD.

Given the time it took to create, the 1993 F93 A should really be considered a transition car. Apart from dropping Migeot's double bottom, the most significant modifications were only made to the lateral air channels and the dimensions of the air scoop. But major progress had been made in electronics, so Williams, McLaren and Benetton had no rivals.

Without traction and differential control or active suspension, it was impossible to make a mark in F1 and the supremacy of the Williams-Renault in 1992/3 was a result of this technology. Despite having set a trend with the automatic gearbox – immediately taken up by almost everybody else – it was only later that Ferrari developed effective electronic systems, while in Britain Lotus and Williams had already got into active suspension as early as the second half of the Eighties. The F93 A did effectively have electronically controlled suspension, but the cars retired many times because of it, ending with Alesi taking sixth place in the drivers' world championship with 16 points and Berger eighth with 12.

A basic new development for the future made its debut at the Grand Prix of Germany in July. Engineer Lombardi, who had been responsible for the V12 engine over the years, considered the use of 4-valves per cylinder heads and pneumatic valve gear. Engine torque would improve with "just" four valves and revolutions would increase up to 15,000 rpm for a declared 745 hp. The previous power variations were cancelled out between the start and the end of the GP. Tappet wear was also resolved and in general the percentage of breakdowns diminished. Meanwhile, Jean Todt arrived at Maranello on 1 July to take up the not-so-simple job of motor sport director. Although not a technician, Todt became the new head of the Racing Department – a task he always carried out with decided firmness, as he had at Peugeot.

Developed under the technical direction of Harvey Postleth-waite, who was also sole boss of the Racing Department at the time, the Ferrari F93 A driven by Jean Alesi and a returning Gerhard Berger, respected the Federation's maximum width and front wing height regulations. Apart from the late introduction of active suspension compared to other top teams, the F93 A did not shine for any special new development. Maranello knew that John Barnard would be coming back in 1993, and he was already at work on the following year's car. In such cases, it is difficult for a boss on his way out to act positively. Above, left: Niki Lauda, who continued as a consultant until Michael Schumacher's arrival. Lauda was, of course, an outstanding driver, but it did not seem that his contribution outside the cockpit was especially brilliant, typical of many greats. Above, right: but Jean Todt was a different case altogether. He joined Maranello on 1 July 1993 and his reorganisation of the Racing Department was of fundamental importance to the Prancing Horse.
Below: Jean Alesi parades a Ferrari flag around the Monza circuit after taking an excellent second place in the 1993 Grand Prix of Italy.

The first car of John Barnard's second period with Ferrari was unveiled in January 1994 and was called the 412 T1 to capture the flavour of the four valves per cylinder technology and transverse gearbox, which was accepted by the British technician this time. Unfortunately, the car did not take Maranello back to the top of the sport, but it was still important due to its longevity: even though heavily modified, it was raced by the team until the 1997 season.

Meanwhile, the Federation gave Barnard and Ferrari a helping hand by banning active suspension. So all the teams started on equal terms again and Barnard took advantage of that by introducing a major new development for the front suspension mounts: plates (also called flexures) instead of the traditional uniball. Small titanium blades were fixed to the ends of the carbon fibre suspension arms that bent, following the arms' minimum movement. As far as the ball joints were concerned, the flexible plates ensured just minor friction and were lighter but, in particular, distributed tension inside the chassis in a uniform manner. Naturally, the move to plates was helped along by the much reduced suspension travel that had become a characteristic of Formula 1 from which the technicians never looked back. It was the ingenious Adrian Newey who kicked off with the rigid F1 car like a go-kart syndrome of the end of the Eighties. To tell the truth, for years F1 suspension travel didn't exceed 15 mm, but Newey drastically lowered that value with the March-Leyton House of 1989/90.

In the beginning, the plates created a few problems and forced technicians into a momentary return to the uniball, which had made the development of the car rather laboured from the harmonics point of view and fairly slim but without especially interesting elements of chassis and aerodynamics. Its wheelbase was long at 2950 mm, a concept sometimes used by technicians to protect them from possible grip problems and adopted by Barnard

Designed by John Barnard, the Ferrari 412 T1 was packed with innovations, among them boxed gears and a front suspension mount and torsion bars, but its aerodynamics were wrong. The pointed air intakes on the sidepods (photograph above and illustration below) were radically revised by Gustav Brunner, who added airflow changers as shown below.

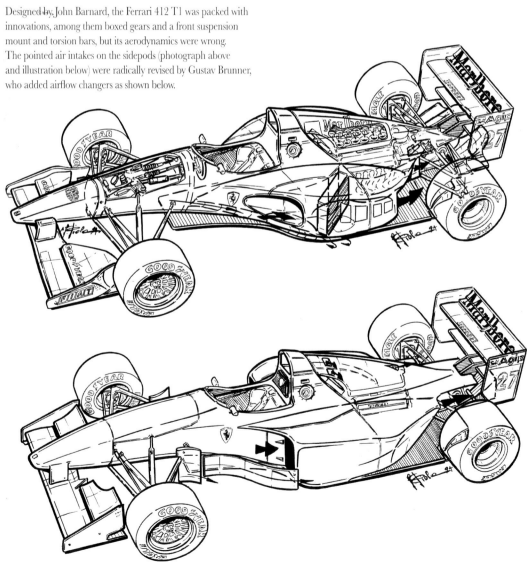

several times, as well as a smaller fuel tank with the Federation's return to refuelling during the race. The 412 T1 was not an easy car to set up and it was rather nervous to drive, despite the better torque of the new engine. Because the distribution of aerodynamic load was not completely correct the car lacked traction, especially on tortuous circuits. It was more at home on fast tracks, so much so that Berger and Alesi were on the front row of the Hockenheim grid for the Grand Prix of Germany. The Austrian won, and by the end of the season he had come third in a drivers' Formula 1 World Championship monopolised by Michael Schumacher and his Benetton and Damon Hill in the Williams after the tragic death of Ayrton Senna at Imola during the same weekend in which Roland Ratzenberger also died.

In the beginning the 412 T1 also suffered from cooling problems, solved with the T1 B version to which Gustav Brunner made a substantial contribution, having returned to Maranello at the end of 1993. The B's sidepods and air intakes were revised as well as the turning vanes, which were becoming fashionable in F1. It was evidently an effective job, because at the GP of Canada at the end of June the Federation imposed a drastic reduction on the effectiveness of the cars' air boxes as well as various aerodynamic limitations which the technicians – as always – had soon overcome by further wind tunnel studies! Yet with the right kin of "breathing" the engine, updated by Claudio Lombardi with consultancy by Osamu Goto (ex-Honda), it was, perhaps, the most powerful unit of the season, putting out 750 hp at 15,300 rpm.

Above: two shots of Jean Alesi driving hard. For the 1994 GPs of the Pacific and San Marino, the injured Jean Alesi's place was taken by Nicola Larini, who was Maranello's test driver at the time. Larini took a fine second place at Imola (the podium on the left with winner Michael Schumacher and third placed Mika Hakkinen), but the day was overshadowed by the terrible accident that cost Ayrton Senna his life.

Above: Jean Alesi finally won a Grand Prix in Canada in 1995 driving a 412 T2, derived from the B version of the car that first appeared at the French Grand Prix the previous year. It was not a revolutionary project, but Barnard simplified the car's constructional layout by rationalising the work of the mechanics and enabling them to take action themselves if small modifications were needed, without having to reconstruct entire sections.

The T2 wasn't much different from the T1 B, yet the British technician began to criticise the 12-cylinder engine, which he said was equally guilty of the car's lack of success due to the unit's greater bulk compared to that of the Renault V10 used by Benetton and Williams. A specious controversy in my opinion, because Ferrari had already shown it could design and build compact, light V12 engines, while the division certainly favoured power. Then there was Michael Schumacher's historic judgement after he had joined Ferrari in 1995: during his first test drive – in the 412 T2 – he asked why we went to the V10, because he had never driven an F1 car with a more potent engine.

Concentrating on the design and development of the V10, Barnard limited himself to shortening the wheelbase and reducing the sidepods' dimensions. Strangely, the nose had returned to its low position and incorporated a wing mount: a completely different approach to those of the super-victorious Benetton and Williams, which stood out for their extremely high noses and separate wings. As with the previous year, the drivers continued to ask for more traction, a sign that the aerodynamic distribution was not at its best.

In 1995, an engine shone in a Ferrari again. The Federation dropped the cubic capacity to 3-litres and Maranello came up with a new version of its V12, with its crankcase in precision-cast iron that brought together robustness and lightness. It was an avant garde technology that particularly impressed me at the time, developed with the support of the Fiat Research Centre and its subsidiary Teksid, which meant a drastic reduction in the thickness of the walls and about 10 kg in weight compared to traditionally cast units. These advanced castings were made by the French company Microcast with a special vacuum procedure that was certainly very expensive and even then not free of criticism. Cast iron has a capacity for absorbing heat and a lower conductibility factor that is clearly inferior to aluminium, a metal of which the heads were made. In fact, in 1996 no solution could be found to the problem of the temperature difference between the various points of the engine, so Ferrari went back to aluminium crankcases. Developed during the season by engineer Paolo Martinelli – using various bore and stroke measurements, starting from 86x43 mm – the 2997.34 cc V12 could rev to 17,000 rpm, at which it put out 690 hp.

There were not many new developments from Barnard on the chassis and aerodynamics fronts.

From the historic point of view, the 412 T2 will be remembered as the car in which Jean Alesi achieved the only world championship GP win of his career in Canada – and Ferrari's only win that season.

But an interesting technical footnote concerns the transverse gearbox, made of welded sheet metal for the 1994 412 and titanium for the 412 T2. Twenty-four panels of titanium were used for the latter, which were welded together to form the box. An example of the great traditional operational capability of the men from Maranello, which meant the weight of the 'box was reduced by 40%.

Alesi (below, left) departed at the end of 1995, so the new team for the following year was presented to the press, comprising reigning world champion Michael Schumacher and Eddie Irvine (below, right) with Racing Department boss, Jean Todt. Above: in November, Schumacher tested a 412 T2 at Fiorano and was surprised by the power output of the V12, but the 1996 10-cylinder required by Barnard was ready at Maranello.

The 1996 F310 created a certain astonishment. With the V10 engine that John Barnard had yearned for, it didn't seem much different from the previous year's car at the press presentation, especially in the front, the area that had been the focus of so much of the other aerodynamicists' attention. The nose was particularly low and, naturally, the wing was fixed under it. A completely unconventional layout, but one that had evidently been suggested by the wind tunnel as part of the car's aerodynamics. Michael Schumacher won the Grand Prix of Spain with this configuration, but the use of the safety car had not been developed to the full by that time and the German had been able to show his undoubted

class in the pouring rain. After that, though, the F310 raced in a markedly different configuration: the nose was really high and the front wing was fixed with a large bridge. Almost a return to the 1994 412 T1, if not certainly clear recognition of the Williams school, as their FW18 was taking Damon Hill, a driver who certainly wasn't the greatest, to the world championship. It is possible that was the real configuration of the F310 and that a delay in data analysis from the wind tunnel had made them postpone the debut. Whatever, Barnard is remembered even today by his colleagues not only for his ability, but also for the long time he took to achieve his objectives. On top of that, he had a mania for personally keep-

ing track of the smallest details, which made it more difficult to have an overall view of the project. The F310 was a typical example, called an "easy chair" by the British technician's collaborators due to the extremely large amount of protection at the sides of the driver, conceived by detaching it from the general project except, of course, the measurements. The protection was made obligatory by the Federation but the teams – Williams in particular – were able to encase it with elegance in the cockpit. But after the modifications the F310 was a fairly valid car, even if its lack of reliability continued to torture Ferrari for a few years and forced Schumacher and Irvine to retire too many times.

The turnaround sought with such determination by president Montezemolo finally happened with the F310. Opposite page, left to right: Eddie Irvine, Nicola Larini and Michael Schumacher pose with president Montezemolo at the new car's presentation. Larini (above) took 11th place in the world championship, but Schumacher won the GPs of Spain, Belgium (left, celebrating with Jean Todt) and Italy. Illustration: when it made its debut the F310 seemed to hark back to the 1995 T2, but from the GP of Canada the aerodynamics were much modified with a high nose and turning vanes on the flanks of the sidepods. The practice of substantially modifying the car during the season to adapt it to the various circuits had also begun. In 1996, Ferrari used nine different rear wings, five extractor planes, six types of noses and six different layouts for the rear ramp. Then there were four types of gearbox, seven aspiration manifolds, three versions of the exhaust and 15 different radiator layouts. The small illustration shows the rear end with the seven speed boxed gears used from the Grand Prix of Belgium.

Nobody had ever been successful in Formula 1 without an equilibrated organisation and a precise distribution of individual roles. That became clear to Michael Schumacher during his first year at Ferrari, and his insistence on bringing Rory Byrne and Ross Brawn to Maranello made that point. All of which was accentuated by the isolation of John Barnard, who rarely made an appearance at the circuits. Bringing in the two technicians to work with Schumacher turned out to be an extremely positive move: the three understood each other instinctively from their time together at Benetton. Brawn had the qualities of a fine technical director and was a great track strategist, while Byrne, sophisticated and even tempered, opened up a dialogue with everyone.

That is how the team that finally took Ferrari back to the top was born; and its tally was a rich one, winning six Formula 1 World Championships for constructors and five drivers' titles between 1999 and 2004.

Barnard left Ferrari in January 1997 but had already designed a car for that season. It didn't beat the previous year's F310 hands down, but the car looked svelte with reduced bulk: the sidepods were modified, as were the rear aerodynamics. Byrne and Brawn inherited a car with improved reliability and they did their best with it with their gifted track management. The F310 B didn't really create set-up problems, so the time saved was spent developing strategies. The quite effective set-up could be radically changed at a circuit at the last moment due to the right horizontal position of the torsion bars and the front suspension dampers.

Towards the end of the year, the V10 046 generated 750 hp at almost 17,000 rpm, data similar to its great rival that season, the 10-cylinder Renault which powered the Williams FW19.

The fact that Ferrari was back was confirmed by Schumacher's five wins, although he ruined everything at the GP of Jerez finale, where the championship was to be won.

Previous page, above: Schumacher leading the Monaco Grand Prix in an F310 B on his way to the first of his five 1997 victories. Previous page, below: Schumacher, Todt and Irvine at the F310 B's presentation. The last Ferrari designed by John Barnard was the F310 B, an evolution of the 1996 single-seater with numerous modifications; some of the more important changes, like the higher nose and rear wing end plates extending forward. In particular, Barnard simplified the project for ease of management at the circuits, and that was perfected by new arrivals Rory Byrne and Ross Brawn. Rear torsion bar suspension made its return, and had been on the front end since the 1989 640.

Illustration above: note the engine air box (2) that first appeared at the GP of Canada; it is slightly inclined and has a small support down low, different from the previous version (1). Above: the new, lighter chassis introduced at the Grand Prix of Hungary:
1. Deformable structure. 2. Fuel tank with small lateral extensions. 3. Engine mounts for the chassis. 4. Fuel tank filler neck.
Right: Gianni Agnelli talking to Michael Schumacher in the pits. When he won his first world championship in a Ferrari, Mr. Agnelli said the driver was "…on an equal footing with greats like Fangio and Pelè. And if Del Piero can be compared with Pinturicchio, Schumacher is an Andy Warhol".

The F300 was the first car entirely designed by Rory Byrne. It was important to Maranello, even if it was beaten by the McLaren-Mercedes MP4-13 penned by Adrian Newey and in which Mika Hakkinen became world champion driver. Michael Schumacher won six Grands Prix in 1998 and the F300 revealed itself to be an excellent basis for the evolution of subsequent cars. Among the new elements, was a V10 engine with 80° cylinder banks instead of the previous 70°. I don't believe they wanted to lower the centre of gravity, as a 5° difference is resolved in an trice in the global evaluation of the car. Anyway, McLaren won with a 72° V10, the angulation selected by BMW for its first F1 engine. But an 80° V10 is the best combination between the need to lower weight and to balance it.

In 1998, the Federation imposed new rules that concerned, among other things, tyres with three grooves in the tread and no more slicks, plus a reduction in the cars' width from 200 cm to 180 cm. Track was reduced and traditional concepts associated with the distribution of weight changed. That's why wheelbase dimensions increased, ranging from 2953 mm for the basic version to 3083 mm for fast circuits. New regulations that had their influence on the cars' aerodynamics, conditioned by the wheels moving closer to the chassis with a reduction in air channels front and rear. And that brought a rash of different aerodynamic solutions. Ferrari was linked to Goodyear, while Bridgestone equipped McLaren and had technicians at Woking, all of whom posed the problem of less contact of the grooved tyres with the track's surface. That's where the idea for wider front tyres came from, increasing the tread width. A problem Ferrari and Goodyear had to overcome, but always as followers. Bridgestone came out with a 265 mm tread to then move on to 270 mm and 282 mm, while Goodyear had to settle for 241 mm and 254 mm.

Below: the F300 with tall asymmetric aerodynamic devices being tested at Imola, but which were banned by the Federation for safety reasons. Following page: the colour cutaways show the version of the car that competed in the Japanese Grand Prix, so already with lengthened wheelbase using a spacer between the engine and gearbox. The car first appeared at the GP of Belgium and aimed at improving weight distribution. The engine cover and stepped bottom (in brown in the illustration more to the right) changed with the lengthened wheelbase.
Below: exhausts that exited the upper part of the car made their debut on the F300 (also the photograph above), designed to improve engine yield and to avoid contact with hot gasses, with elements of the suspension in carbon fibre. Rory Byrne's idea set a trend in F1. Above, left: Ross Brawn, technician and GP strategist.

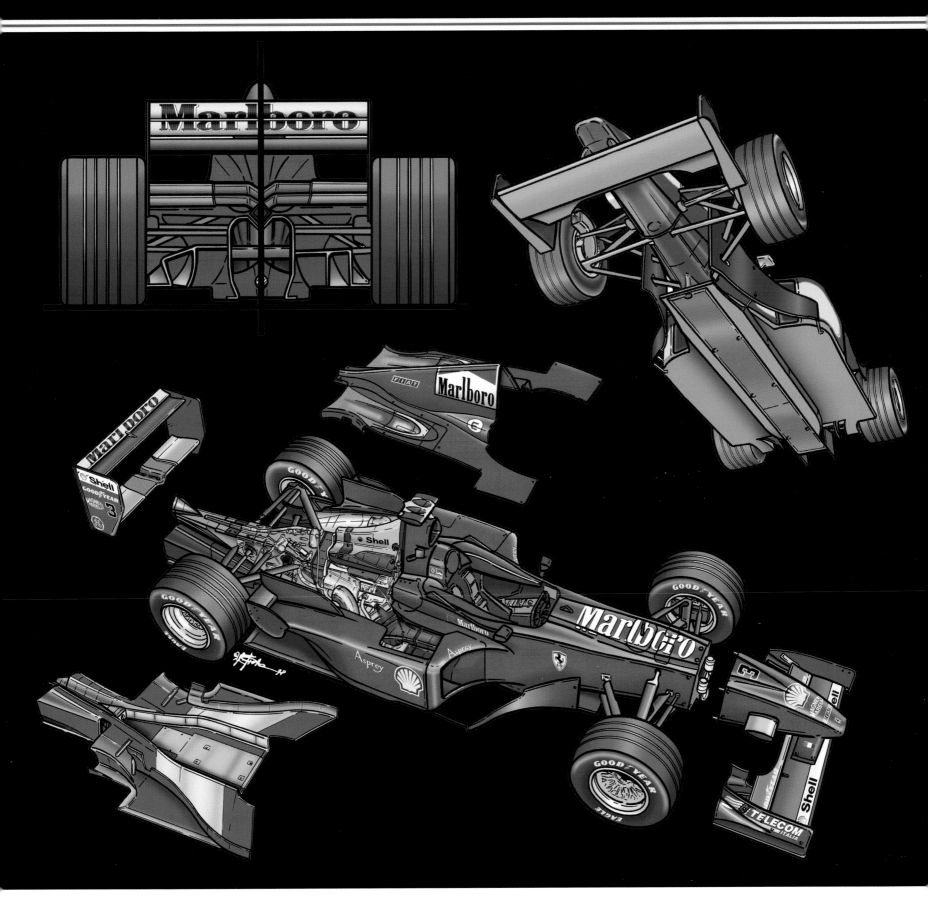

The 048C engine with its new design head and valve gear brought a containment of bulk and lowered the centre of gravity, as can be seen in the illustrations on the opposite page next to the 1998 engine design. Once again the evolution of the previous car, the F399 had a longer wheelbase than the basic F300 and was extremely reliable. In the illustration on the right, the cleanliness of the underbody and the stepped bottom stand out, separated as they were from the monocoque at the front – an area later called the "knife edge" – and destined to hold ballast, which had been concentrated in the centre of the bottom with thin plates until the Grand Prix of Spain. The main illustration with the side details shows the configurations fielded at each GP. Note that an arrow shaped rear wing made its debut at the German race weekend with a shape similar to those used by Ferrari during the second half of the Seventies, when they were completely new. Michael Schumacher had an accident during the 1999 Grand Prix of Great Britain at Silverstone and that meant he had to miss six races. His place was taken by Mika Salo (left) but Eddie Irvine (below) briefly became the number one driver from the Austrian GP onwards and won that race. Second and third were Ferrari's eternal rivals, McLaren's David Coulthard and Mika Hakkinen, shown below on the podium with the Northern Irishman, who fought for the world championship right through to the last round.

Goodyear's retirement from Formula 1 in 1999 was the end of an era. The American manufacturer had been a regular contributor to the sport since 1965, and I have excellent recollections of them from my years with Ferrari. But the presence of Bridgestone as the sole tyre supplier certainly simplified life for all the teams. With the same tyres for everyone – with four grooves on the fronts instead of only three from 1998 – the Japanese manufacturer's role was reduced somewhat excessively due to a lack of opposition. Bridgestone didn't stop its research but conducted itself with greater firmness towards the teams, only changing typology in the case of real need.

Ferrari had a brilliant season, because it won the Formula 1 World Championship for constructors. It last won a world title with Arnoux-Tambay driving a 126 C3 in 1983, when I was still director of the Racing Department, and it took them 16 years to bring a world championship back to Maranello again. During this period of rediscovered success, someone even tried to put in the poison saying my "record"

had been broken. I objected simply because I was very, very pleased for Ferrari and all those people who had worked with such intensity to achieve this result. If Schumacher hadn't been involved in that famous accident at the GB GP, it is also likely that the drivers' title battle would have been between the German and Mika Hakkinen.

It was an interesting season that confirmed the validity of the Byrne-Brawn way of working, a world away from radically changing the car of the previous year, and even further from changing it completely, a habit that was too well established at Maranello before they arrived. Instead, the two newcomers put their money on continuity, optimising elements that had been effective. But before the start of the 1999 season there was still a revolution at Ferrari, and it was an important one. It concerned the management of the GES (the Racing Department) and the improvement of quality control, which was already good but it became even more demanding: a move that would prove to be decisive in the coming seasons.

Ferrari's fortunes changed very much for the better with the start of the new millennium, but the car hadn't changed. A sensational period in Maranello's history began in 2000 with nine victories by Michael Schumacher, who also became world champion driver, and Ferrari carried off the world constructors' title. The pragmatism of Byrne and Brawn also triumphed as they improved the 1999 car without changing the concepts on which it was based. Many new developments stood out on the F1 2000, all of them evolutions of those of the F399. There was the new V10 engine with 90° instead of 80° cylinder banks; the car was extremely light at 100 kg and equally reliable, advantages acquired with strict quality control. The car was made much lighter to be able to exploit ballast to meet the 600 kg minimum weight regulation. The way of using its ballast – from 60 kg to 100 kg per unit – to balance the car's behaviour was first tried the previous year, it having been launched by Adrian Newey on the McLaren. With technology, modern materials and finance, it was not all that difficult to create an "underweight" car, especially being able to position the ballast at the points the technicians considered most suitable, even though it was contrary to the spirit of the Federation's regulations. From the designers' point of view, the use of ballast was the simplest way to set the car up without wasting energy on studies and tests. But lightening a car like that could only be afforded by the top teams; the ballast itself cost about 140,000 euros in the early part of the 2000s for just one of the two or three expected components. They used the tungsten, a rare material with a weight of precisely 19.1 kg per dm, 2.5 times more than steel. So it was easy to make blocks to take their places at key points of the chassis, and move them forward as far as possible in the lower area. Ross Brawn also came up with the successful strategy of sub-dividing every GP into brief stints, each to be run on a limited quantity of fuel and with fresh tyres.

Above: double world champion Michael Schumacher, who brought the drivers' title back to Maranello after a 21-year absence. Here, he acknowledges the cheers of the spectators after one of his victories in 2000. Below: Michael raises his trophy to the skies after having won the Grand Prix of Japan on 8 October, the race in which he also became the 2000 world champion driver. The first Byrne-Brawn car that exploited the regulations on minimum weight to the full, including the use of ballast to reach 600 kg with the driver aboard, chassis dimensions and a reduced centre of gravity with 90° cylinder banks for the 049 engine. Protection either side of the driver respected the regulations, but it was inside of the monocoque so as not to interfere with air flow to the rear, as shown by the blue arrows on the opposite page.

Among the F2001's new developments was the split position of the water and oil radiators in the sidepods, which appeared narrower than those of 2000. The oil tank (opposite page, central illustration) was increased in size and its definitive position was between the engine's cylinder banks in the area directed towards the monocoque. Ferrari was the first to introduce drum brake air intakes to screen the inside of the rims and reduce turbulence between the front wheels and the chassis. A highly equilibrated car, the F2001 took Michael Schumacher (below) to yet another world title with nine victories, while Rubens Barrichello (above) made 10 podium appearances.

To limit performance electronic control systems were prohibited in 1994, but it was suspected that some sensors that controlled various F1 cars' parameters – especially the engine and wheels – were able to hide some illegal functions of the kind. So despite new restrictions on the wings, cars still had traction control to minimise wheel spin, the automatic start system launch control, and a gearbox with pre-designated gear changes. Ferrari was ready for such new developments due to the excellent cooperation between the optimum technicians who had grown up inside Maranello and those of Marelli, a brand of excellence. In this area – but not that one alone – Ferrari was superior to McLaren.

But once again there were few new elements for the F2001, developed to be robust and easy to set up, even if there were many high level refinements. The car's front aerodynamics were changed, mainly to channel air and increase the flow towards the car's bottom. The nose was no longer high and the wing was fitted to it with long vertical supports, but it was moved lower. For years, high noses were considered a more practical proposition for the development of aerodynamic load, but by 2000 McLaren had already shown that similar results could be obtained without sacrificing the height of the centre of gravity.

An important happening was the return of Michelin to F1, even if Ferrari and McLaren continued with Bridgestone. With competition from the French, it was logical that Bridgestone would commit itself to a more intense development of tyres and compounds, ending up by choosing Ferrari as its team of reference. And that was for many reasons: the methodology, structure and financial resources of the team and the presence of Schumacher as well as being able to supply tyres for the company's road cars. Bridgestone's was a political decision, because Ferrari had a superior image. Maranello made a well-considered choice as tyres had assumed a fundamental role in F1 again.

It was a record year! Michael Schumacher became world champion driver with 144 points and 11 victories; his team mate Rubens Barrichello came second with 77 points and four wins. Records that would later be beaten by both of them, but which still pay homage to the intelligent technical conduct of Rory Byrne, Ross Brawn and Martinelli, the engine expert. The F2002, which enabled Schumacher to equal Juan Manuel Fangio's record of winning five F1 world championships, may be considered the extreme evolution of the car that made its debut in 1998. The basic layout was unchanged, even if the aerodynamics were of ever greater finesse. As in the case of the exhausts that were encased in two small fairings, there was also a slight lowering of the back end of the engine cover. The power unit, called 051, side-stepped the regulations at over 18,000 rpm, at least with the qualifying version that put out more than 850 hp while in racing it generated a "normal" 840 hp at 17,900 rpm.

These are engines which, by this time, habitually performed with extremely high oil and water temperatures of around 120°C. That was the result of a Ferrari study following a decision taken in 1998. Byrne asked the engine developers to use smaller radiators for oil and water as they are usually in the sidepods and their dimensions influence air resistance and weight. But the risk was excessive heat building up in all the engine components, with an inevitable loss of yield. Studies to achieve a result were long and involved technicians of partner Shell for lubricants and fuel. And significant help also came from the use of special materials, like a particular titanium alloy with which the aerospace industry had already conducted experiments.

By 2001, Ferrari had already distinguished itself for a technological choice of notable significance: its gearbox made in cast titanium and no longer of 24 welded sheets of that material.

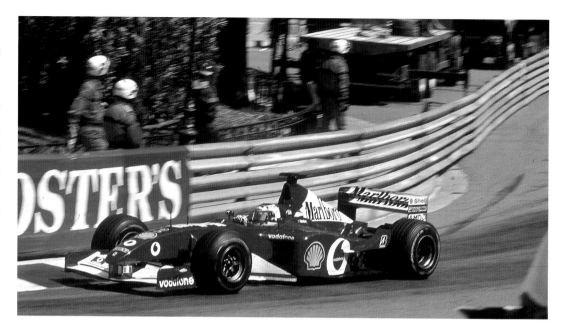

Above: Michael Schumacher won the drivers' world championship way before the end of the season with an outstanding victory in the Grand Prix of France at Magny-Cours on 21 July. Below, the Ferrari team celebrating their conquest of both world titles with president Luca Cordero di Montezemolo. Victorious in 15 out of 17 Grands Prix, the F2002 had many fundamental components of reduced dimensions for better aero-dynamics, like the water and oil radiators of double forward and transverse inclination, as shown in the central illustration on the opposite page. Also note the chimney for the expulsion of hot air, indicated with red arrows. The roundel shows the previous position of the radiators. The rims had three studs instead of five and the gearbox, a version of which had already been installed in the F2001, was visibly slimmed down.

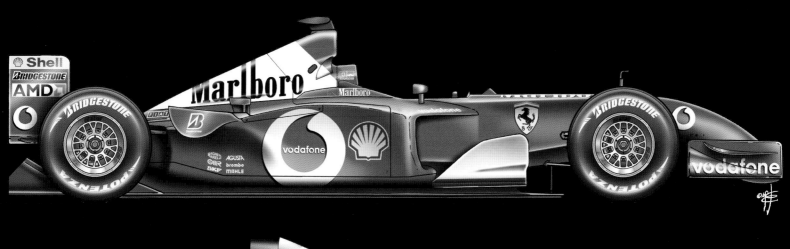

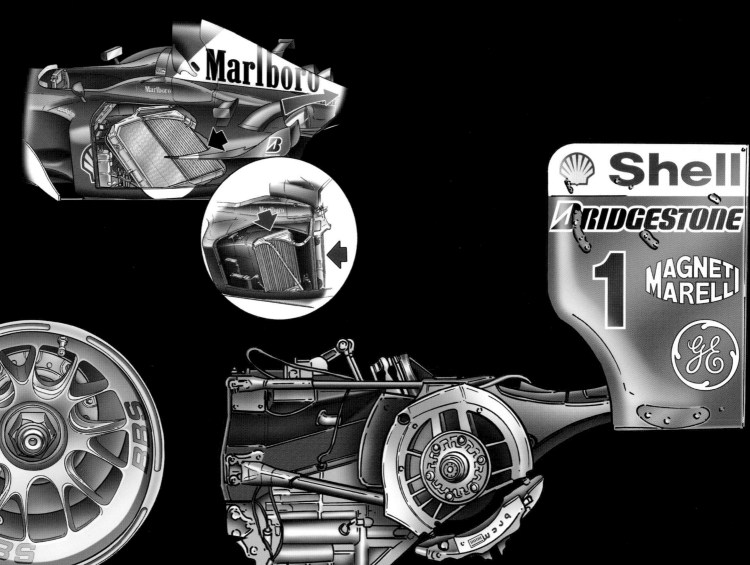

F2003 GA: the unstoppable Schumacher

The 2003 was a lively season with eight different winners of the 16 Grands Prix. Ferrari won eight – six went to Schumacher – and the German won his sixth world title. After having driven perfectly set up cars for years, Schumacher and Barrichello found the F2003 GA (the car dedicated to Gianni Agnelli, who died in January) hard going. The need to keep the advantage over the opposition suggested an innovative project in the areas of lower weight, aerodynamics and chassis. The difficult choice of tyres and set-up complicated the situation even further, because after practice the cars had to go into parc fermé and couldn't be further modified. The regulations also demanded the use of a single engine for both qualifying and the race, but investments enabled teams to achieve a high degree of reliability and under the new qualifying format, drivers ran just one lap. The BMW 90° V10 put out over 900 hp at 18,600 rpm and was a light unit that weighed only 90 kg with a much reduced stroke (97 mm 40.5 mm) to allow the use of bigger valves to rev that high,

which was fundamental to power: at Monza, for instance, the Williams set a record of more than 360 kph. But the BMW engine's torque generation was rather high and driving the car was not easy. Ferrari also took the same direction and it seems that the dimensions of the 052 power unit were the same as those of the V10 BMW: its power output varied from an initial 845 hp at 18,300 rpm up to 870 hp at 18,500 rpm. But it wasn't until the end of the season that the car from Maranello was able to find its usual reliability without having to redesign anything so that it could get a little closer to the official weight, limiting the use of ballast. But ballast was one of the few chances all the teams had of preparing the car, conditioned as they were by wheelbase dimensions that were once unthinkable and which, for some, exceeded the 3,100 mm of the GA. Ferrari continued its association with Bridgestone with a priority plan, but the more aggressive behaviour of Michelin in proposing typologies and compounds was having its effect.

Above: a series of tyres heated by thermal covers: with the new 2003 regulations, after a single warm-up lap, the cars had to remain in parc fermé until two hours before the start of the race, but the teams were not allowed to change tyres and other work was cut to a minimum. Opposite page: among the many new developments brought in on the F2003 GA were a long wheelbase that enabled the designers to increase the fuel tank size, double turning vanes behind the front wheels and side pods set back from the front end which had a water radiator on the left and a split water-oil unit on the right. Behind were the louvers baptised shark's gills for the expulsion of heat. The rear suspension was notable for its arm, anchored inside the lower wishbone and no longer on the gearbox, the case of which was in cast titanium with the engine. A decision made due to the need to lighten the 'box as much as possible and limit stress. For the first time, the rear suspension had rotating dampers, developed together with Sachs to further lighten the gearbox, given that the previous telescopic dampers were inside the casting.

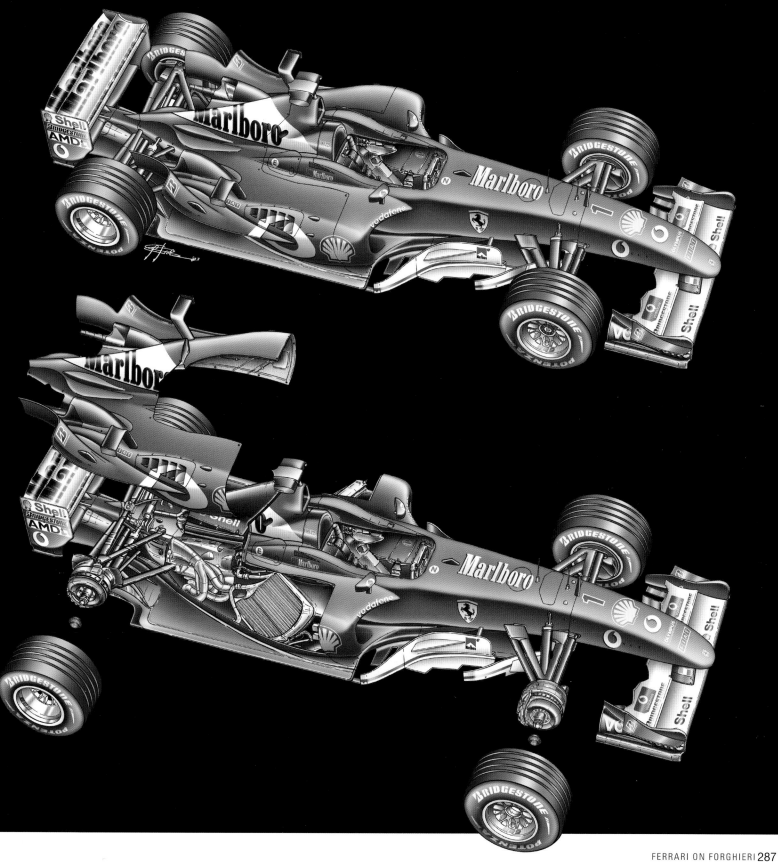

Having been faced with the difficulty of setting up the F2003 GA, we could have expected a radically new car for 2004. Instead, Byrne and Brawn went their own way without any deviation, even if the previous year's car was completely revised, especially with greater ease of setting up. The return to a shorter wheelbase was fundamental and, therefore, more conventional: it was reduced from the F2003 GA's 3100 mm to 3050 mm.

Ferrari was supported by Bridgestone once again, the Japanese manufacturer having more or less worked exclusively for the Schumacher and Barrichello cars. Naturally, Michelin put just as much effort into its work for its own teams, in part to make its way back from the humiliating defeat of 2003, so there was obviously a clash between the tyre makers. There was only one precedent to Bridgestone's substantial commitment to Ferrari: that of Michelin from 1978. An extraordinary job which led to the tremendous stability of the tyres' behaviour as they were less sensitive to variations in temperature and tread wear.

The reduction in the tyres' weight was also interesting as part of the trend of generally lightening F1 cars. This development led to a saving of just over one kilo per tyre and that was significant, because due to the effect of ballast the weight increased to over 4 kg. Credit has to be given to the tyres for lowering lap times rather than the limited evolution of the car or regulations that demanded the use of a single engine per race, even if the V10 053's power output increased – although by less than in the past. It began with 865 hp at 18,300 rpm and rose to 900 hp at 18,800 rpm.

With a perfect car, Ferrari used clever race strategy which, for Schumacher, envisaged the usual brief stints with the car always in optimum condition. With 13 victories – two for Barrichello – it almost seemed as if the world title had become a formality for the German driver.

Above: in 2004, Michael Schumacher won his seventh Formula 1 World Championship for drivers and Ferrari, whose fleet of artics is shown below, became world champion constructor again with 262 points to second placed BAR-Honda's 119.

Opposite page: top, the configuration of the F2004 at the start of the season. Later, modifications involved the engine cover (centre page, in detail) that was more tapered towards the rear and lengthened to just above the gearbox; there were large chimneys for the expulsion of hot air (on the sidepods above the Vodafone logo) that replaced the gills. The detailed designs show a number of the F2004's "peculiarities": like the shark's fin outlets inherited from the F2003 GA in the five outlet version used to dissipate heat at Sepang; and the twin barge boards behind the front wheels with a different inclination, dependent on the track. On the left is an overall view of the gearbox, still without its carbon fibre skin which, once applied, only left a number of suspension components uncovered. The car's overall profile below shows the position of all the F2004's main components.

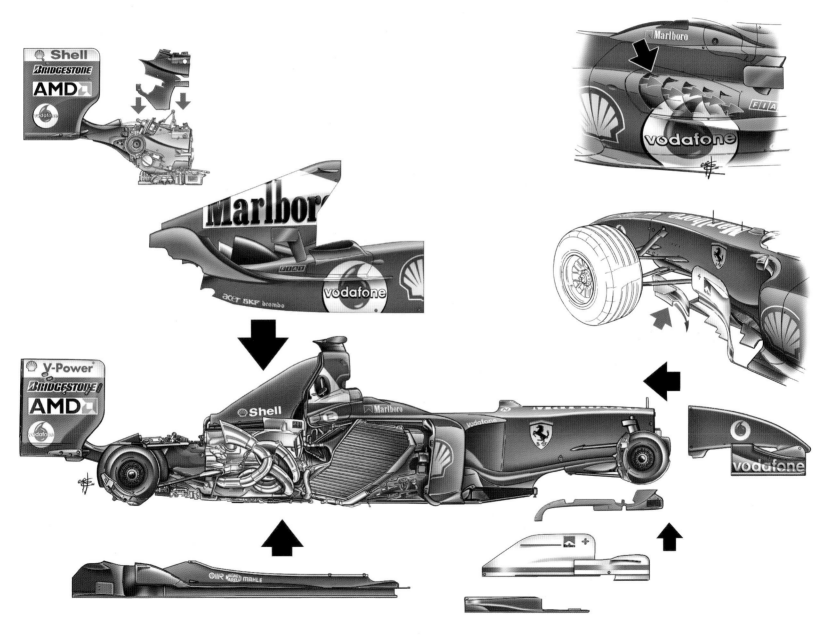

s it possible that a winning car could become inadequate a year later? Well, yes, because that's exactly what happened with the Ferrari F2005 – and for more than one reason. First of all because of the regulation that imposed the use of just one set of tyres per qualifying session – one lap of the track – and for an entire race. All part of a cost cutting drive that started from the right concept, because by that time a top team's tyre budget for a season was not far off a million euros. But between the need to stop some teams using over 100 engines per season and making sure they didn't change tyres during a GP there were many intermediate stages. Maximum incoherence came six years later, when we saw GPs with 3-4 tyre change pit stops!

Anyway, in 2005 Bridgestone were not able to come up with a tyre that could stand up against the yield of the Michelins, which ran a whole GP without worrying degradation. This lack of success was also because of the extremely late development of the F2005, which didn't make its first appearance until the third race of the season, so for the first two GPs out came an M (modified) version of the F2004. In line with a decision taken some time earlier, Rory Byrne became an external consultant to Ferrari, which meant engineer Aldo Costa became the project boss.

The F2005 was yet another evolution of its predecessor, but the aerodynamics had been quite profoundly changed due to the new regulation on wing dimensions and the need to increase air flow to cool the engine. The large spooned front wing was re-dimensioned, so to find load once more a mini-wing was added under the front of the nose. But that didn't work too well and nor did the chimneys at the sides of the engine cover to extract more hot air, because they disrupted the aerodynamics.

The drivers' world championship was won by Fernando Alonso in the effective Renault R25, but Kimi Raikkonen in the McLaren-Mercedes MP4-20 still won 10 GPs.

Apart from a win in the Grand Prix of Indianapolis, helped along by the absence of the teams on Michelin tyres, there was not much to write home about for Schumacher and Barrichello (above) in the F2005s. Unlike Michelin, Bridgestone was unable to react to the new regulations that banned tyre changing during the race. Ferrari got off on the wrong foot after a long series of winning cars based on tyre change strategy. In aerodynamics, the F2005 brandished a new front wing with a central "step" 50 cm wide, the maximum possible because the sides had to respect minimum height from the ground rule.

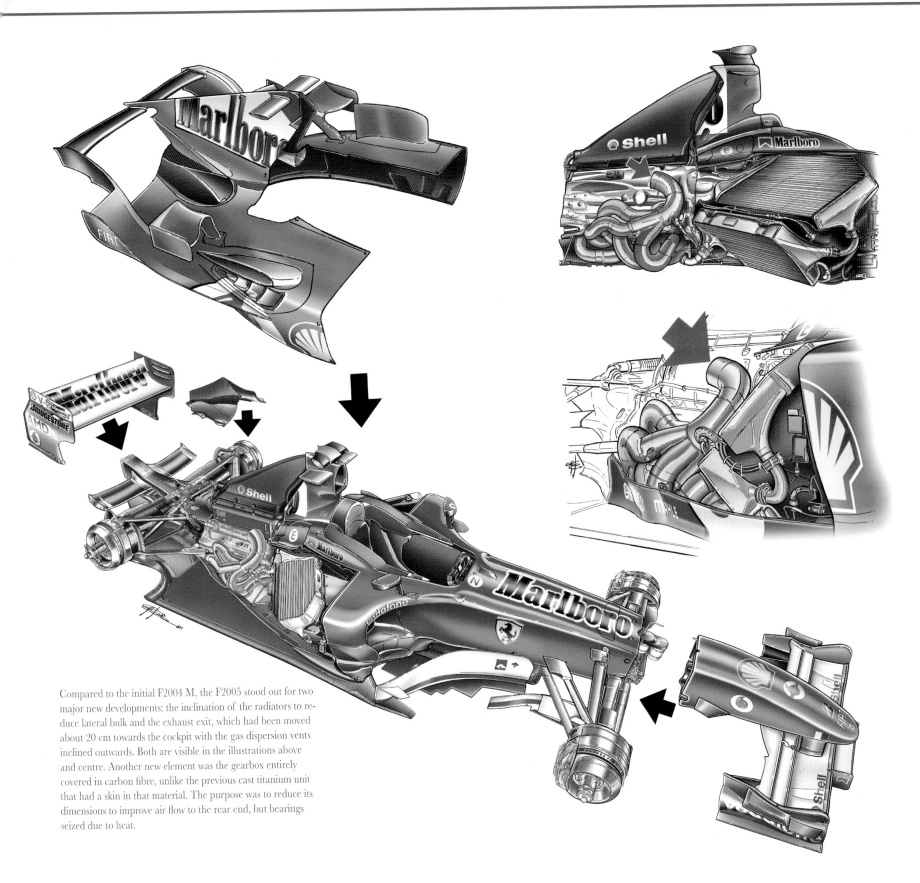

Compared to the initial F2004 M, the F2005 stood out for two major new developments: the inclination of the radiators to reduce lateral bulk and the exhaust exit, which had been moved about 20 cm towards the cockpit with the gas dispersion vents inclined outwards. Both are visible in the illustrations above and centre. Another new element was the gearbox entirely covered in carbon fibre, unlike the previous cast titanium unit that had a skin in that material. The purpose was to reduce its dimensions to improve air flow to the rear end, but bearings seized due to heat.

A number of concepts of the fantastically successful F1 2004 were brought back for the new 248 F1, adapting them to 2006 regulations. After years of aerodynamic limitations that were circumvented by technical development, the Federation dictated that 90° V8 engines of no more than 2400 cc were to be used and that their weight shouldn't exceed 95 kg. An intelligent evaluation: it was sufficient to drop two cylinders from the V10 without having to start again from zero, so "saving" chassis technology created for other engines. Other financial reasons changed the role of the designer and the importance of the engine diminished, placing the accent on aerodynamics. The teams had to present details of their unchanged engines to FIA during a pre-established period. An excessive hold up, which limited interest in a component fundamental to F1, conditioning new ideas. Despite the fact that they were not officially circulated, it was discovered that the bore and stroke measurements were the same for everyone: 98mm x 37.9 mm. That also went for the regulation on power output set at 750 hp at 19,000 rpm, which was then taken to 18,000 rpm. With the new, shorter engine Ferrari kept the F2005's wheelbase of 3050 mm, a length that was not over the top but simplified weight distribution on the axles, also in relation to ballast. Now, without having to last a whole GP, tyres came back as some of the most important variables. The "war" continued between Bridgestone and Michelin, although they announced their retirement from the sport in 2007. But they wanted to leave as winners, so the Frenchmen put in a maximum effort, practically changing the traditional values of F1 tyres: lesser or greater adaptation to the type of asphalt, reactions to heat and cold, higher or lower consumption and so on. Accentuating a change signalled in earlier years, both Michelin and Bridgestone never had a dramatic failure on any track, even if the former shod a Renault R26 with outstanding aerodynamics driven by the ultra-talented Fernando Alonso.

For 2006, Ferrari went back to the super-successful F2004 with a new 8-cylinder engine and Michael Schumacher (above) fought hard right through to the season's last GP in an effort to win an eighth F1 world championship. Note the more accentuated aerodynamic development of the car starting from the front wing, without its step but with a raised flap along its entire width right through to the rear vision mirrors that acted as turning vanes. Like the other aerodynamic devices, their job was to direct air flow towards the rear.

As a result of its tremendous rationality, the engine components and accessories of the 248 F1 (illustration right) could be changed faster. Note the water and oil radiators inclined forward and not installed in V formation: the three designs that follow are a comparison between the units as installed in the F2004, F2005 (see circle) and the 248 F1. The small illustration (centre, left) shows the air flow deflected by the rear view mirrors to the winglets in front of the wheels. For the first time, externally faired rear wheels appeared on the 248 F1; they were first objected to and then copied by all teams. Also note the winglets fixed to the brake air intakes.

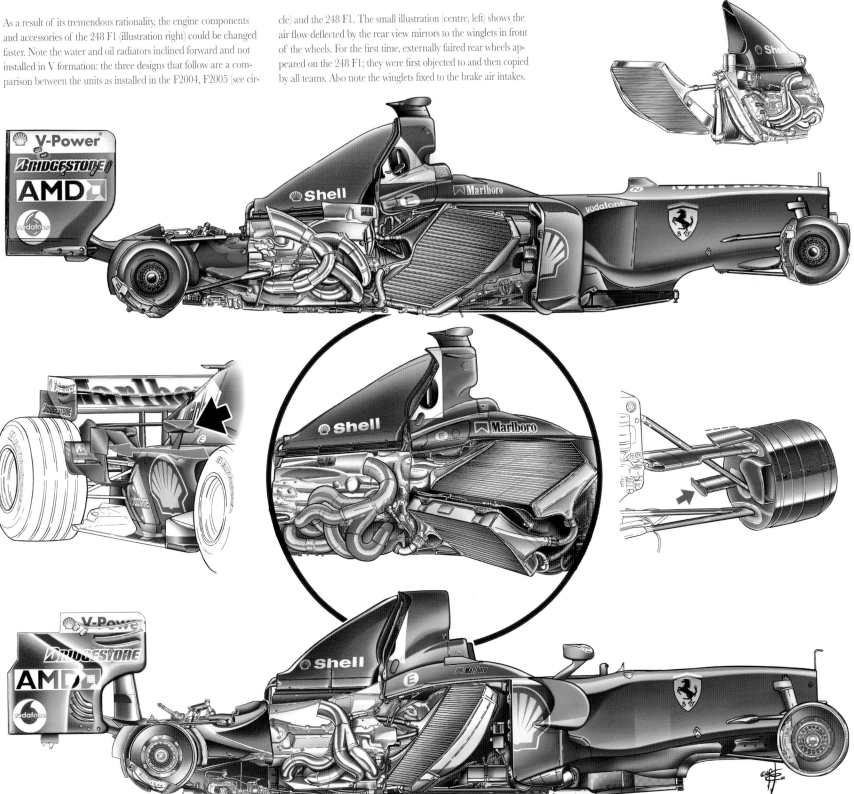

onfirmation that Ferrari was also a great team in terms of cohesion and equilibrium came with the 2007 F1 season, the first without the three architects of its previous successes, Rory Byrne, Ross Brawn and Michael Schumacher. The German was not only an exceptional driver, he had contributed to the development of the cars by the sheer force of his personality. His successor, Kimi Raikkonen, was just the opposite; he was certainly fast, but he had a closed character and that didn't help dialogue at Maranello at all. The departure of Brawn was significant as he wasn't only the technical director but also a great tactician, coordinator and organiser. But Ferrari overcame this upheaval well, taking Raikkonen to the world championship and winning the constructors' world title to boot. A display of strength partially helped by Michelin's retirement, which left Bridgestone as the exclusive tyre supplier to the sport. With the same tyres for all teams, there were fewer tests and not so many doubts at every GP about the various tyres' characteristics. That helped development work, with one fundamental variant less. And it's probable that Schumacher's departure had less influence than expected for this reason.

The first Ferrari designed by engineer Aldo Costa was the F2007, conceived taking Schumacher's complaints into account on the behaviour of the 248 in fast corners, which aerodynamic evolution hadn't yet solved. Believing that one of the explanations was associated with the 248's "short" 3050 mm wheelbase, Maranello chose the easiest way out and increased the F2007's to 3135 mm, changing the area between the driving position and the front axle. The new car was the first Ferrari to adopt a high nose and was without a keel for the lower suspension mounts, which were fixed to the chassis. So the nose was slightly higher, increasing negative lift up front with the advantage of reducing the huge suspension arms for a better use of the tyres.

There was an excellent start to the season for Kimi Raikkonen and Ferrari at the Australian Grand Prix: the Finn (left during a Monza pit stop and above at the first chicane) was able to win his debut race with the Rosse. He is on the podium (below) with Fernando Alonso and Lewis Hamilton, being congratulated by Jean Todt. Opposite page: all the key views of the F2007: in the eternal quest to free the sidepods of harmful air flow generated by the front wheels the car's wheelbase was lengthened, pushing the front axle 8.5 cm further forward.

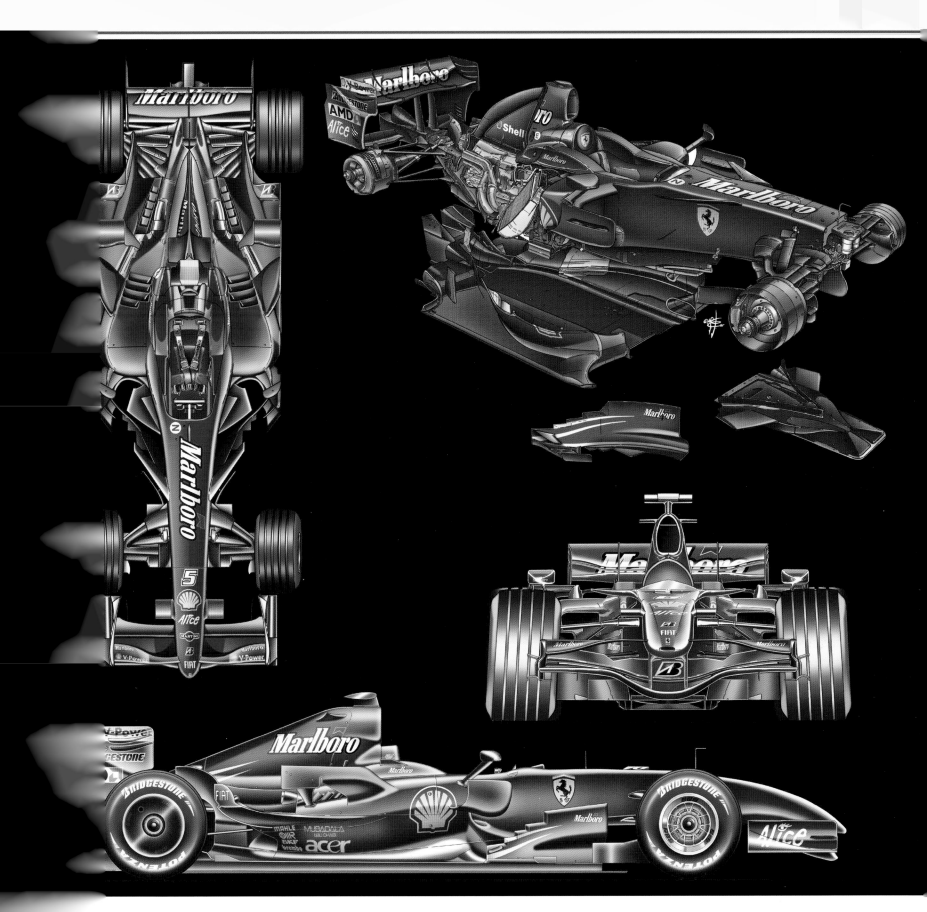

Victory in the Formula 1 World Championship for constructors and Filipe Massa's loss of the drivers title to a comeback by Lewis Hamilton on the last lap of the season's last GP in Brazil were still positive performances by the F2008. There was a certain equilibrium between the Maranello car and the McLaren-Mercedes MP4-23, but one or two unfortunate episodes got in the way of Massa becoming world champion driver. After years of perfection, the men in the Ferrari pits made a few mistakes even in strategy, so that their ability was not 100% as it had been when they were on top. The team suffered a double retirement due to engine problems in the GP of Australia – the first in 14 years – but it was strange that connecting rods were defective in both situations, especially given Maranello's quality control system.

The 2008 car aimed at maintaining previous supremacy on fast tracks and improving its performance on slow circuits where Ferrari was hard put to bring its tyres up to the right temperature in 2007. Costa and Tombazis went to work on the wheelbase, shortening it by 6 cm against the F2007's to 3129 mm. New technical regulations eliminated various electronic aids like traction control, engine torque and braking management. Without traction control, the use of the rear tyres would have posed a few temperature and wear problems and shortening of the wheelbase was an attempt to head that off. As the season progressed, it was clear that the car did well on fast circuits but on slow ones the McLarens delivered more traction and were able to "jump" onto the kerbs at tracks where aerodynamics were less influential and there was a prevalence of suspension behaviour. On fast circuits, especially where there were high atmospheric temperatures, the F2008 exploited its tyres well, particularly the hard compound Bridgestones. But in slower going the 2007 problem and the mono-tyre raised its head again, even stripping the technicians of many variables which didn't help: the manufacturer couldn't supply tyres that were better suited to the needs of an individual team and not others.

Above: Felipe Massa and Kimi Raikkonen driving Ferrari F2008s in a rain-soaked GP of Italy: note the nose just before the cockpit with an air extractor that arrived from the NACA intake in the lower part of the car near the axles. A new idea that favoured aerodynamic load, but which was abolished by the 2009 regulations. With Massa's six victories and Raikkonen's two, Ferrari won its 16th F1 World Championship for constructors. Opposite page: details of the F2008 among which stand out the front of the body with an elegant integration of the flap, the nose and the air extractor visible in the zone next to the driver's number. Its purpose was to improve front wing's efficiency.

Sometimes, complications come from representing a company of great traditions, and that's what happened to Ferrari in 2009, when it felt it was its duty to use the Kenetic Energy Recovery System (KERS) to recoup heat generated under braking and transform it into electrical energy to bolster traditional engine power output. Together with other new developments, KERS was introduced by the Federation to encourage overtaking. The system was optional, but Ferrari just had to adopt it, but it was an additional complication that blocked other sectors including aerodynamics, while some teams just dropped it. The weight of the F60 wasn't a worry: everyone used ballast but that could be deployed at strategic points, while the 40 kg KERS was connected to mechanical components. With the new regulations, the value of aerodynamic load was lowered considerably due to a change in the size of the rear wing and the rules limiting diffusers, which were interpreted by everyone in an extremely restrictive way. But not by Ross Brawn, who had doubts and consulted the Federation's technical working party, which gave him an explanation that didn't alarm him. Why is it that the working party didn't send an informative note to all the other teams if the regulation was in doubt? The fact is that the cars had one flat rear diffuser in the upper area, while the Brawn GP unit was a two level affair with air vents and gills that allowed a high degree of aerodynamic load.

Ferrari was seriously affected by this situation: the F60 often lacked straight line speed because the search for load weighed on the rear wing. To Ross Brawn, it was revenge on his ex-team that – like all of them – updated their car but still Maranello was unable to avoid a poor season with just one GP victory in Belgium. And it was no coincidence that win happened on a circuit where there was little aerodynamic load to favour speed on the straight – where KERS is exploited.

Because of his accident at the Grand Prix of Hungary, Massa's place was taken by Luca Badoer, who in turn was replaced by Giancarlo Fisichella towards the end of the season: above is the F60 being driven at Monza by Fisichella, where Kimi Raikkonen came third (left). Opposite page: Giorgio Piola's illustrations show details of the F60, the first F1 Ferrari with a single piece bottom rather than separate units. The bulk of the KERS system (top) forced a slight lengthening of the wheelbase, which was shorter in the car raced at Silverstone and shown on page 299.

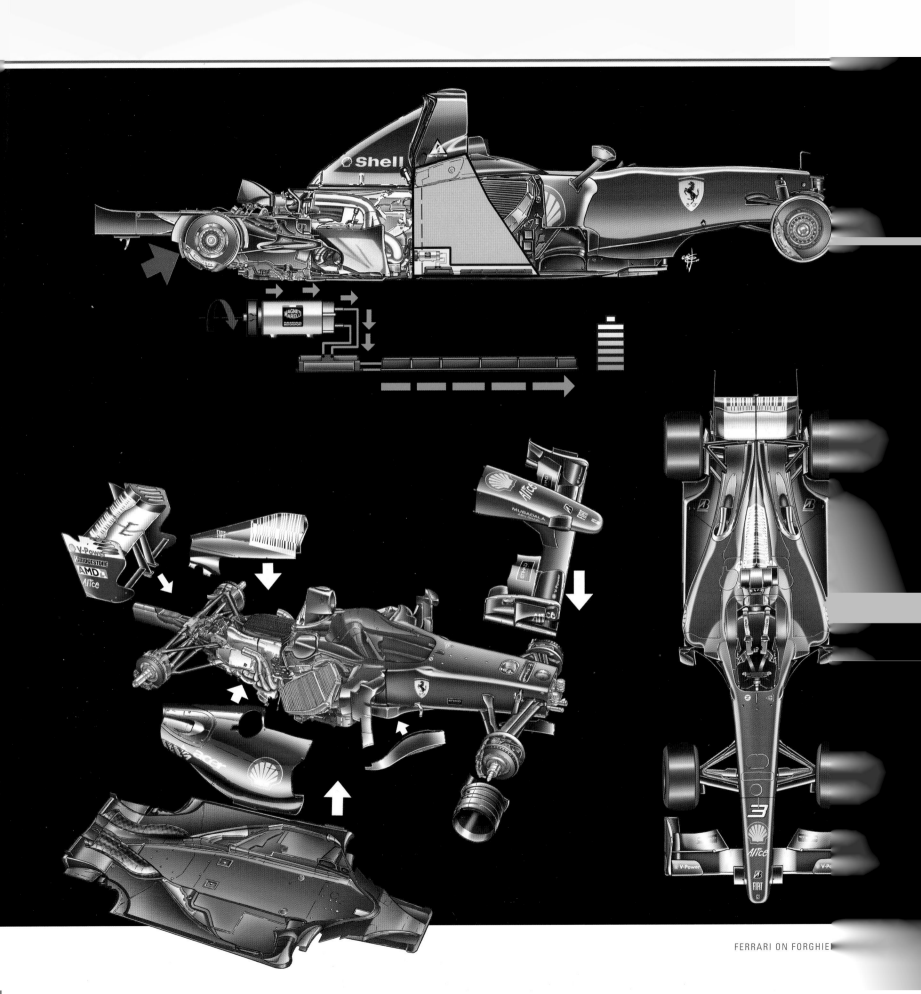

With the abolition of refuelling during a race, a bigger fuel tank than in recent years was adopted increasing from the previous season's 140 litres to 220 litres. The new Ferrari's wheelbase was lengthened once again, it having already exceeded 3 metres by a few centimetres with the 2009 car. The F10's came close to 3250 mm and was not justified by the larger fuel tank alone. It was necessary to find rear space – the length had little influence up front – for a new carbon fibre gearbox, which was narrower and extended. Together with the revised location of the suspension components, the slimmer 'box helped lower the centre of gravity and especially the effectiveness of the aerodynamic diffuser. To further improve air flow, the engine was raised by 4 cm and inclined by a few degrees, the result of systematic research into the load (particularly in the rear, due to the regulation small winglets) and a greater weight distribution, the two major problems of 2009. The whole front of the monocoque was raised and made concave low down along the body to the height of the sidepods, which had a smaller intake developed in relation to the longer water and oil radiators. Research for maximum tapering was clear to see and was confirmed by the upside down position of the V8's exhausts. With Alonso making his Ferrari debut, the F60 won the first race of the season in Bahrain. Subsequent development didn't seem to be at the level of Maranello's main opposition, but Ferrari still did better from the end of the summer. The season's final GP at the new Abu Dhabi circuit became part of F1 folklore, as it would have been enough for Alonso to take sixth place to become world champion driver. But due to an error of strategy in the pits and even more so because of a regulation that had flattened the performance of engines – as well as an excessively tortuous track – the Spaniard was unable to make a simple overtaking manoeuvre and so his world title dream just slipped away.

Grand Prix of Abu Dhabi, the last of the season: conditioned by a new, excessively tortuous circuit, Fernando Alonso was unable to take that 6th place with which he would have won the 2010 Formula 1 World Championship for drivers. Apart from its numerous new regulations, the 2010 season was dominated by the F-Duct introduced by McLaren. It was a duct in the left sidepod that exited in the cockpit (white arrow in the illustration below) that could be closed by the back of the driver's hand. That way, the jet of air continued towards the rear wing (red arrow) "stalling" part of the load to increase straight line speed. Opposite page: the F10 (above) compared to the previous F60 (below). The longer nose (1) is almost imperceptible as the wheelbase was about 20 cm longer, which was exploited in the rear. The front suspension mounts were also unchanged. (2) Regulations demanded that the front tyre's footprint decreased from 275 mm to 245 mm. (3) The radiators were curved to create a belly with a smaller and higher opening. (4) The engine cover was longer. (5) The exhaust exit area was substantially changed. (6) The different position of the rear axle highlights the zone of greater length. The illustration in the centre shows the exhausts (1) installed upside down as on the F2005 and are more advanced towards the fuel tank (shown in grey) the capacity of which went from 130 litres to about 230 litres. The slightly inclined engine meant an increase in the exit angle of the rear diffuser (2).

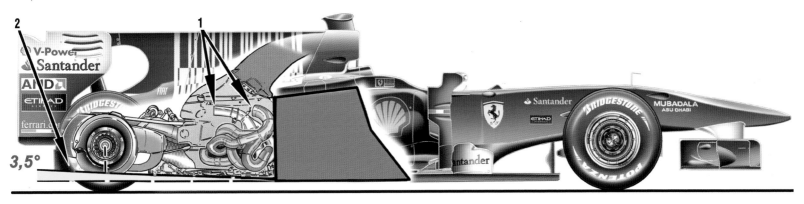

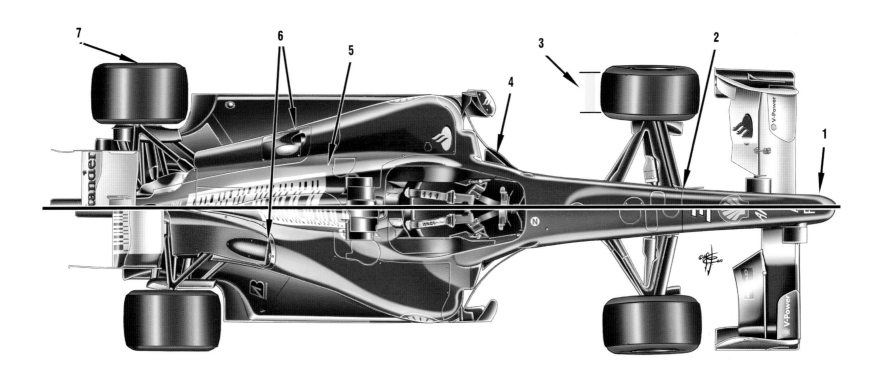

The Ferrari 150th Italia was labelled too conservative in relation to the less conventional Red Bulls and McLarens and Fernando Alonso's grit and determination were not enough to allow him to fight it out with the front runners, even though he won in Britain. In a season feeling the effects of Pirelli being selected as the sole tyre supplier with covers of a limited lifespan – a technically debatable idea – Ferrari often used soft tread compounds, because the hards didn't reach optimum operating temperatures due to a lack of aerodynamic load. An eternal problem that saw Adrian Newey emerge as the most ingenious of the modern designers. His Red Bulls stood out for their balance despite their 170 kg of fuel at the start and their empty tanks at race's end. This even with the extreme effect of lowering the centre of gravity, together with a reduction in the unsuspended mass; current F1 cars don't vary more than ¾ of a millimetre, because the dampers have been almost replaced by the tyres and suspension travel is less than one inch. With minimum suspension travel, the calculation of roll centres is fundamental: they condition the modest movement of the car and provide understanding of how the car presents the tyres' surface to the ground. Until a few years ago, front suspension arms were parallel to the track's surface, or at the most had a slight downwards inclination towards the monocoque, with external rotation and roll centres more or less on the asphalt. Now, the arms are inclined towards the exterior from high on the monocoque, at least on some cars: the rotation centres end up down low and the roll centres extremely high up and above those which are real. The suspension has a totally different secondary movement compared to the past, and the teams are beginning to apply the same techniques to the rears, again to benefit aerodynamics. It is important that there should be cohesion between the front and rear suspension, the basic concept for a racing car, especially one with a long wheelbase. Equally essential is the ratio of height from the ground between the two axles to control aerodynamic load between the front and rear, which is among the fundamental concepts that have enabled technicians to overcome regulation restrictions on aerodynamics. If a 120 mm height from the ground were obligatory, most of the downforce would simply disappear.

In 2011, Ferrari scored just one victory in the GP of Great Britain at Silverstone. It was a highly successful GP in which Vettel and Webber, stars of the season in their Red Bull RB7-Renaults and on the podium with Alonso, had to surrender in the face of the Ferrari 150th Italia's constant rhythm. It seemed like a resurrection after a troubled start to the season due to insufficient aerodynamic load compared to teams whose cars used the system of exhaust gas blowing into the diffusers. The subsequent evolution of the 150th enabled Ferrari to aim for more podium places, but without being able to battle it out for the win. During that British GP weekend, Alonso gave an exhibition drive of a Ferrari 375 F1 (above), owned by Bernie Ecclestone, to mark the José Froilán Gonzalez victory in such a car at the same track 60 years earlier.

F150 **F150 EVO**

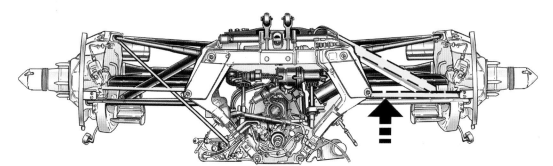

Above: the Ferrari 150th Italia also had an extremely high nose, with the entire front area concave down low to favour air flow. KERS made its Ferrari comeback, this time a miniaturised version of about 20 kg housed in a niche next to the fuel tank. Left: the rear end layout of the 150th with push rod suspension, the mounts of which were modified on the EVO version that made its debut at the Grand Prix of Spain.

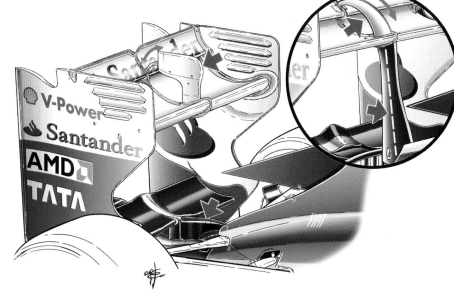

Above: the rear wing flap control system of the Ferrari 150th was changed from the GP of Great Britain: it no longer had a hydraulic jack in the central pillar (see small illustration) but a more precise electro-hydraulic drive with its actuator above the gearbox (see red arrow). Left: the steering wheel "computer" of the Ferrari, with its various paddles: the small illustrations are of the underside of the 150th Italia's wheel, for which four levers (illustration left) were originally envisaged, but they became six after tests to facilitate the management of KERS and the mobile rear wing.

Printed by
Giunti Industrie Grafiche (PO)
February 2013